Do I Belong?

Do I Belong?

Reflections from Europe

Edited by Antony Lerman

PlutoPress
www.plutobooks.com

First published 2017 by Pluto Press
345 Archway Road, London N6 5AA

www.plutobooks.com

Copyright © Antony Lerman 2017

The right of the individual contributors to be identified as the authors
of this work has been asserted by them in accordance with the Copyright,
Designs and Patents Act 1988.

British Library Cataloguing in Publication Data
A catalogue record for this book is available from the British Library

ISBN 978 0 7453 9995 9   Hardback
ISBN 978 0 7453 9994 2   Paperback
ISBN 978 1 7868 0099 2   PDF eBook
ISBN 978 1 7868 0101 2   Kindle eBook
ISBN 978 1 7868 0100 5   EPUB eBook

This book is printed on paper suitable for recycling and made from fully
managed and sustained forest sources. Logging, pulping and manufacturing
processes are expected to conform to the environmental standards of the
country of origin.

Typeset by Stanford DTP Services, Northampton, England

Simultaneously printed in the United Kingdom and United States of America

Contents

Foreword

In June 2012 the Bruno Kreisky Forum for International Dialogue in Vienna hosted the first of a series of seminars on the missing sense of togetherness and belonging in Europe, which we named the Vienna Conversations. As a think tank specializing in bringing together intellectuals, politicians, academics and civil society activists for confidential discussions on difficult social and political problems, focusing particularly on the European arena, this seemed like an obvious matter for the Kreisky Forum to take up.

The proposal for these open-ended conversations, which had no predetermined agenda, emerged from discussions I had with fellow partners. The problematic was set out in a paper, 'In search of the missing other', written by Dr Diana Pinto, and sent to a diverse range of people, from across the continent, who we thought would have something vital to contribute.

Over three years, meeting in the former home of the late Austrian chancellor, Bruno Kreisky, in Vienna, we covered the issue from many angles in lively, informed, challenging, collegiate, as well as sometimes contentious debates. There was much we agreed upon, but significant differences also surfaced. In the letter of invitation to participate in the discussions we wrote that we thought of this 'all-Europe debate as a book', but in a metaphorical sense. There was no pre-planned scheme to produce one. However, the phrase has proved prescient: when the discussions seemed to reach some kind of natural end in early 2015, thoughts turned to producing something that would be a permanent reflection of what turned out to be the key theme. And so a proposal was made to produce a book of original, personal essays on belonging in Europe, which found favour with everyone. We asked one of our participants, an experienced editor, Antony Lerman, to commission the essays and edit the volume. Eighteen months later, with Pluto Press as our publishers, the project came to fruition.

Without the personal involvement and support of Patricia Kahane neither the Vienna Conversations nor this book of essays would have seen the light of day. Thanks are also due to our institutional sponsors.

The Forum is also indebted to all those who participated in the Conversations. Most came from across Europe and brought their diverse range of professional expertise and personal experience to bear on the subjects discussed. A few came from beyond Europe, and their external perspective proved valuable in ensuring that the discussions took into account the relevance of the continent's internal wrestling with issues of belonging and difference for the wider world.

While the publication of this rich, diverse and absorbing collection of essays marks the formal end to the Vienna Conversations, it is also the opening of a new conversation with a wider public about how people can live together in difference in Europe. At the time of writing, the challenges to the future viability of the European project seem to become more severe by the day. It is the Kreisky Forum's hope that a more realistic and sensitive understanding of the multifaceted nature of belonging, which these essays provide, will contribute to discussions across the continent as to how to meet these challenges.

Gertraud Borea d'Olmo
Secretary General
Bruno Kreisky Forum for International Dialogue

Introduction

Antony Lerman

No single reason can explain why, in June 2016, British voters decided in favour of leaving the European Union, just as there was no sole motive driving Americans to elect Donald J. Trump to the presidency of the United States in November. But one factor looms very large in both cases: the appeal of promises (or rather threats) made to exclude millions of 'undesirables' from belonging to the national community.

First in line would be those characterized as 'intruders': immigrants, migrants, asylum seekers, refugees – call them what you will – who allegedly take the jobs that should be preserved for 'native' workers and 'dilute' national identity and culture. Feared, hated, demonized and dehumanized, these seekers after home can no longer be allowed entry in such 'destabilizing' numbers; some insist that there simply should be no more 'foreign' additions to the population. Next come Muslims and possibly other 'suspect' religious, ethnic or cultural groups who must be placed under radically increased surveillance, and therefore ever more decisively alienated from society, out of fears that they support terrorism and are disloyal to the state. Then diverse groups would be turned into internal enemies or outsiders by severe limitations placed on some fundamental human rights such as freedom of expression, a woman's right to choose, speaking truth to power and choice of personal sexual orientation. Even if such measures were not always fully articulated by the principal figures in the Trump and Brexit campaigns, the subtext was always clear: You are not welcome. You do not belong here.

The impulse to reject inclusivity may well begin with the natural propensity of human beings to see society/human relations in terms of 'us' and 'them'. But while the exclusivist urge was once held in check in liberal democratic societies embracing multicultural-ism, times have changed, radically. Trump's victory and the Brexit vote were decisively influenced by the politics of exclusion, even if it was not necessarily the formal leaderships who spelled out the full implications of the exclusionary rhetoric. But in Europe, there is no shortage of other leaders of today's far right, anti-Muslim, anti-immigrant and extreme nationalist parties who are on the same page as Trump and his agitators and the hardline Brexiters, and are not shy about spelling out what exclusion means, what rigidly defined belonging, or the denial of belonging altogether, actually entails. It's frightening to have to admit it, but we are surely now living in an age when the demand to satiate the appetite of nation-first politicians and electorates for excluding 'them' is not only something practically no major political leader can ignore, but is also enthusiastically espoused by some of the most powerful of their ilk.

Those who have become used to multiple, complex belongings, to successfully melding cultural difference with a strong sense of national citizenship, must be feeling pressure to conform to the narrower, one-dimensional sense of belonging being increasingly favoured by the authoritarian nationalists of the populist right and more centrist politicians who feel the need to appease such forces. And for those for whom a cosmopolitan Europeanness has become central to their sense of belonging, the Eurosceptic climate increasingly places them under suspicion. As the then newly appointed British prime minister, Theresa May, charged with overseeing Britain's exit from the EU, so chillingly put it on 5 October 2016: 'If you believe you are a citizen of the world, you are a citizen of nowhere.'

* * *

Europe's mainstream leaders are undoubtedly struggling to cope with formidable financial, economic, environmental and geopolitical challenges. And the difficulty of their task is aggravated by increasing support for right-wing populist demagogues and parties whose nativist and racist discourse has led to a spike in racist crimes almost everywhere. But at the same time as they condemn such trends, they too seek to dictate belonging and do very little to counter the trend of so many governments which are not pursuing ways of encouraging Europe's diverse populations and groups to live together in harmony. As Pope Francis warned, in his 'thank you' speech on the occasion of receiving the European Charlemagne prize in May 2016, the opposite is happening: 'new walls are rising in Europe'.

Belonging is certainly not a new concept. Fostering a sense of belonging was a core aspiration of the European project from the very beginning. Freedom of movement for workers was enshrined in Article 39 of the 1957 Treaty of Rome and it was understood as aimed at achieving the 'integration of people', their having a sense of belonging to the same 'community'. Since then, Europe has become far more diverse, especially so within what is now the EU, making achievement of this aspiration even more challenging. But the extent of Euroscepticism and the increasing undermining of the principle of open borders by some European leaders is a clear sign of their explicit disaffection with a closer union that implies any kind of deliberate policy to promote multiculturalism. They, and large swathes of their populations, believe that European societies are simply becoming too diverse and must take action to prevent further dilution of national identity. The pace of social and economic change, on both the national and local levels, fails to respect traditional bonds of belonging and is one of the factors driving some to support groups advocating a more defensive, even aggressive, national identity and to regard Brussels – the shorthand for the EU – as remote, dictatorial, anti-democratic and elitist. Others say that Europe must redefine itself according to the reality of its diversity and that it is uniquely placed to develop ways of living with the 'other'. Either way, there is no doubt that the question, formulated by the late Jamaican-born cultural theorist Stuart Hall, who lived and worked in the UK from 1951 – 'How can people live together in difference?' – is at the heart of the problem facing the continent. And what is key to difference is a sense of belonging.

While there is growing acknowledgement of the significance of belonging, there is an urgent need to rescue the concept from politicians' glib references to it as if it were motherhood and apple pie and from some academics whose understanding of it as something so inchoate makes it difficult to grasp. After all, we are talking about both a fundamental human emotion of many dimensions and a political project that affects millions. There is nothing intrinsically progressive about someone's sense of belonging, whether to Europe or anything else, or about how it is politically determined, managed and policed. One of the strong left-wing arguments about unacceptable aspects of the EU is that there are systemized policies of exclusion and bordering aimed at the disadvantaged, refugees and Black, Asian and minority ethnic groups seeking entry to the EU; that there is a prejudicial and discriminatory, institutionally supported political consensus to turn people away who are deemed not to belong in Europe. It's easy to forget this in the flow of warm words about the joys of belonging.

Feelings of belonging or non-belonging can be very complex. For example, individuals may experience different and sometimes contradictory senses of belonging within themselves. EU bureaucrats may see national belonging as antithetical to a sense of European identity, but this may well be a myth. A sense of belonging in Europe may be engendered in many indirect ways, such as feeling safe within one's faith or ethnic community whose participation in public life is encouraged and promoted by local leaders and national authorities, but not necessarily through grand cultural or educational projects initiated by the European Commission aimed at persuading people to feel 'European' or to lay claim to a European identity.

Moreover, there are multiple ways in which people express their sense of belonging, whether that is to the continent, their country of residence, former country, cultural group, political party, environmental cause, gender, family, gang or secret society, or to a combination of two or more of these. And some choose not to belong – to anything. Is there good reason to think that the former are somehow 'better' for society than the latter? That is usually the assumption. But the path of belonging is not necessarily linear. Belonging is fluid, imagined, created and recreated. So the idea that there is one sense of 'good' belonging in Europe that should apply to all is unreasonable and rather dangerous since it is so easy to abuse it in order to make nefarious judgements about who to exclude.

So what might be a good way of exploring this significant, very real, but somewhat elusive state of being that politicians tend to envisage as formally defined and rooted in tradition, and want more of and more control over, and yet actual experience suggests is always a dynamic process and never immutable?

*   *   *

This is the question that faced the participants in the Vienna Conversations, a series of seminars organized by the Kreisky Forum for International Dialogue, after three years (2012–15) of wide-ranging, and at times somewhat diffuse bi-annual discussions on the barriers preventing people in Europe living together in difference and how to overcome them. Out of those discussions had come an understanding that the issue of belonging was a key, insufficiently explored and acknowledged factor influencing the patterns of behaviour that have given rise to some of the most acute tensions within Europe today. The unanimous answer was a decision to ask a diverse group of contributors – some members of the discussion group and some additional thoughtful writers – to reflect, in the form of an essay, on their own personal sense or senses of belonging, set against the background of the crises and challenges facing Europe we had already spent so much time discussing.

We asked contributors to avoid writing academic articles or policy papers, although they could draw on their academic expertise, experience and knowledge of policy ideas to inform their essays. The only premises all were asked to share were that: belonging is irreducibly complex; broadly speaking, the institutions of the EU should not be prescribing precise, homogenous parameters of belonging for individuals within its member states; there are many ways of being European; and multiple belongings and the choice not to belong are all acceptable.

There are 51 countries in Europe by its broadest definition, and 27 currently in the EU, so ensuring any fully satisfying mathematical national diversity – or any other kind – of contributors was impossible. Nevertheless, among the 18 writers, bearing in mind that each one has a range of competences, there are novelists, philosophers, social scientists, a former judge, journalists, serving and former policy think tank heads, diversity experts, a theologian, arts professionals, political scientists, a museum director, historians and two academic experts on belonging (and this is not an exhaustive survey).

You might expect that the Introduction to a collection of essays of this kind would provide brief summaries of their contents, explain how they relate to each other, cluster and categorize the various kinds of conclusions and generally give a broad outline of the contents. I decided not to do this because we want readers to come to the essays with the minimum of prior knowledge or preconceptions of what they are about to read; to discover, enjoy, be surprised by, fume about, learn from what our writers have to say and tell with as little mediation as is necessary. And then, if they wish, draw their own conclusions about the messages that each essayist conveys. There seemed little point in commissioning original essays, most of which rely on timing or at least the steady absorption of a prior narrative before reaching conclusions or uncovering personal details, only for the editor of the book then to reveal all the best bits in the Introduction.

However, I don't think I'll be giving anything away by highlighting a few broad points about the volume as a whole.

While there are significant differences in the contributors' personal experience of belonging and their views on just how diverse societies can be, and no one was invited to write an essay on the basis of any interrogation of their politics, the overall thrust of the essays is towards a very radical critique of the top-down imposition of what the EU and national governments regard as acceptable forms of belonging for citizens and residents of European countries. Some of those for whom the terrorist attacks in France loom large in their narratives and analyses strongly emphasize the need to defend those values of free speech and personal liberty that the attackers deliberately set out to undermine, but any temptation to suggest more extreme administration of borders or measures of exclusion directed at Muslims are strenuously resisted. Sharpening distinctions between those who are 'allowed' to belong and those who should be 'denied' belonging do not figure in any of the essays. The fortress Europe reality is roundly condemned. The thrust is to single out methods of exclusion, restrictions on the expression of Muslim identity and so on as some of the very things that contribute to the alienation that is one of the causes of radicalization and the turn to violence. When politicians are lamenting the lack of belonging in Europe it is often a way of saying that they would prefer everyone to be more alike for immigration control purposes, social cohesion (for which read 'control') and economic and social management, making a mockery of claims to value and welcome diversity.

Judging by the biographies of the contributors and the status they have in society by virtue of their professions it would be tempting to assume that problematic belonging is not something they have to face in their lives. Even that the irreducible complexity of belonging that all acknowledge is not something that applies particularly to them. But such an assumption would be entirely wrong. One of the standout features of almost all the essays is not only complex personal belonging narratives about the essayists' pasts, almost always originating in childhood and arising out of sometimes voluntary and sometimes forced movement from place to place, country to country, but also present feelings of dysfunctional belonging due to discrimination, racial prejudice, assumed religious affiliation or unresolved ethnic conflict. 'The unfinished business of our own belongings' could easily have been the subtitle of this book, not only for those whose diasporic status remains central and still dynamic with respect to their identity, but also for those whose sense of Europeanness is very strong and who are therefore more affected by the instability confronting the EU.

This leads me to conclude that if people for whom European belonging should come easily and naturally have such complex belongings, with which many are still grappling, how much more prepared we should be to understand the problems facing refugees who probably hail from places where settled belonging is strong and commonplace, but who are wrenched, or who are forced to wrench themselves, from those moorings and find themselves confronting situations in which they and their assumed senses of belonging are seen as a threat. Some might say they are at an advantage because their sense of belonging to their former homes, regions and countries is more straightforward, more one-dimensional – something which anyway may be far from the truth – and therefore they have less to worry about. But the opposite is of course the case. While the cosmopolitan European who can write an essay for this book has other resources to draw on, with which they can manage the complexity of their belonging, this is a luxury the refugee does not have.

Writers stress that it is equally important to understand the belonging concerns of the very large numbers of people across Europe who are drawn to the politics of exclusion and restriction. These disaffected, disadvantaged, mostly working and lower middle class sectors of our societies feel globalization has left them impoverished and uprooted, immigration has changed the face of their formerly stable communities and the consensus across Europe that there is no alternative to the austerity agenda for returning to financial stability has fatally damaged the employment and career prospects for their children. Politicians who have notoriously failed to listen to the belonging fears and complaints of the population are pushing such people, who are not by any means necessarily racist, into the arms of the populists and the far right. Listening to the refugee's story does not preclude listening to the story of the underclass youth living in social housing in any major European city.

Finally, the element of racism in the politics of belonging, discriminating between 'us' and 'them' on the basis of colour, ethnicity, religious identity and so on, remains strong, although the existence of the EU and its role in promoting and maintaining human rights standards and anti-discrimination measures have had a positive impact on reducing this. But what emerges from a number of the essays that focus on the rise of populist parties peddling extreme nationalism, the parties devoted to combating the 'takeover of Europe by Islam', to restoring sovereignty to national parliaments, to defending Western civilization, is the existence of a rationale, a discourse that seeks to present the far right's politics of belonging in terms of the defence of human rights and freedom of speech. It aims to portray indigenous populations as the real victims of racism because of the influx of 'others', these days largely people like the Poles in the UK, who look no different and are allegedly favoured with already hard-pressed and scarce local resources and services, while local people suffer and end up being discriminated against. Communities cannot cope with this change, parties like UKIP say; their sense of belonging is under attack. But of course in the UK, since the Brexit vote, it is precisely the Poles and other East Europeans, who are increasingly subject to vilification and demonization, legitimized by this 'reverse' racism argument. This way of determining belonging is equally a form of racism and needs to be called out as such.

* * *

These rich and diverse essays are not without ideas for ways to enable us all to live together in difference. But there are no dogmatic policy diktats, no magic bullets. While some of the essays lean more to the analytical, the philosophical and the interpretive, and others tend to be more narrative-based, telling stories and exposing myths, the personal is a thread running through all of them. And the personal perspective humanizes and individualizes the belonging experience. I hope it also helps to stimulate discussion of an issue too often confined to the seminar room or left to politicians to manipulate to suit their own agendas. If these essays succeed in helping to open up a subject that is central to the future of Europe and, through further exploration, can pave the way to new thinking

1

Europe's Problem with Otherness

Zia Haider Rahman

In an interview in early 2016, the American critic and public intellectual Leon Wieseltier argued that America ought to take in more Syrian refugees. When his interviewer countered that the US might share the same anxieties as Europe, Wieseltier's response was that Europe's problem was that its tradition of national identity had no natural understanding of a multiethnic society. 'According to traditional European nationalism,' Wieseltier said, 'the political boundaries and the cultural boundaries should ideally coincide. In a nation state, the state should personify a nation and a nation should be incarnated in a state, so that you have a series of happy homogeneous societies living side by side. Europe has a cultural problem with otherness.'

In New York in the 1990s, when New Yorkers asked me where I was from, all I'd say is that I grew up in Britain. Mentioning that I was born in Bangladesh only drew more questions: New Yorkers quite evidently just wanted confirmation of what was to them the distinctive cultural marker, my British accent.

That accent was learned from imitating BBC newsreaders on a cassette recorder. At a young age, in the days when children on council estates and in subsidized housing could rely on decent public libraries, I learned about the Holocaust, the destruction of millions of Jews at the hands of Europeans. The fear that gripped a child was that if they – the Whites – could do that to people who looked like them, imagine what they could do to us, to me. There was nothing I could do about my skin colour but there were certain things that I could mould to make myself less alien to these

Europeans who seemed so ill at ease with difference. I grew up in a Britain that, only the other day, spat at non-Whites, beat us, and daubed swastikas in public spaces.

Britain constantly exhorts its immigrants to integrate better, constantly frightens its natives with the spectre of the fifth column, and in a million subtle ways tells anyone with a touch of dark skin that they should do more to become British and adopt British values. Do it and you'll earn your stripes. But the promise is hollow, for Britain and the rest of Europe fail to keep their side of the bargain, and never had any intention to do so.

In January 2016, the hugely popular *Daily Mail* ran the kind of front page that makes it the laughing stock of thoughtful people, or at least those with a taste for irony. On the right was a picture of Johanna Konta, the Australian-born tennis player who moved to Britain at the age of 14 and was the subject of some controversy concerning the legitimacy of her playing under the British flag. 'Hands off our tennis golden girl, Aussies!' proclaimed the *Mail*. Meanwhile, the main headline on that same front page, referring to the British prime minister, declared in vast bold caps 'PM: WHY WE MUST NOT TAKE 3,000 MIGRANT CHILDREN'. Later in the year, another front page in the same paper trumpeted demands that child migrants should be subject to dental tests to verify age, while at the same time the page sported an image of model 'Cindy Crawford, 50, and her daughter Kaia, 15 ...' and posed the question: 'Spot the difference'.

But progressive Britain, readers of the *Guardian* and listeners to BBC Radio 4, rely on the likes of the *Daily Mail* and the *Telegraph* as an alibi, taking comfort in the thought that bigotry and blindness are confined to the pages of such papers. Yet if you want to grasp the deeper underlying assumptions that dominate White British thinking (or European thinking, for that matter), it is to the writings of the progressive elites, the presumed standard bearers of openness and enlightenment and the self-proclaimed allies of the oppressed, that you must go, writings rich in parapraxes.

Early in 2016, I was invited to join the judging panel for the PEN Pinter Prize, English PEN's award for an author of a significant body of plays, poetry or fiction of outstanding literary merit; a writer who, according to English PEN's terms, 'casts an unflinching, unswerving gaze upon the world, and shows a fierce intellectual determination ... to define the real truth of our lives and our societies'. Previous winners include Carol Ann Duffy, Salman Rushdie and Tom Stoppard. Unusually, the winner shares the prize 'with an international writer of courage selected by English PEN's Writers at Risk Committee in association with the winner'. This makes it a rather special prize, in my view.

When my agents learned that English PEN intended to issue a press release about the composition of the judging panel, they sent them the text of my preferred bio: 'Zia Haider Rahman is the author of *In the Light of What We Know*, a novel (Farrar, Straus and Giroux/Picador 2014), for which he was awarded the James Tait Black Memorial Prize, Britain's oldest literary prize.' PEN replied that they wanted – entirely understandably – to issue something that would give a sense of why they'd ask me to judge an important prize with a human rights dimension. We agreed to their suggested text and the press release included the words: 'Born in rural Bangladesh, Zia Haider Rahman was educated at Balliol College, Oxford, and at Cambridge, Munich, and Yale Universities. He has worked as an investment banker on Wall Street and as an international human rights lawyer. *In the Light of What We Know*, his first novel (2014, Farrar, Straus and Giroux/Picador), won the James Tait Black Memorial Prize, Britain's oldest literary prize.'

A few days later the Man Booker Prize's administration issued a message congratulating Peter Stothard, a former Man Booker judge, for his appointment to the PEN Pinter committee. It's a long message in which they mention the other two appointments, 'Vicky Featherstone, Artistic Director of the Royal Court Theatre, and Zia Haider Rahman, a Bangladeshi banker turned novelist.'

I have no idea what citizenships Peter Stothard and Vicky Featherstone hold; rather unhelpfully, Man Booker evidently did not feel compelled to supply that information. It does, however, come as a surprise to learn that I'm Bangladeshi. I don't hold a Bangladeshi passport; I do however hold a British one. In fact, until one of them expired in 2015, I held two valid British passports (to enable me to travel to so-called incompatible countries: two countries that each won't permit entry if your passport shows a stamp from the other). Clearly, holding two British passports doesn't make me doubly British, but surely we can agree that in order for something like the Man Booker Prize administration, a bastion of the British establishment, to call me Bangladeshi they ought to have sufficient reason to believe that I am precisely that. Shall we just put the error down to carelessness, a slip born of ignorance of the fact that millions of British citizens are descendants of people born in the post-colonies? Of course, keeping me Bangladeshi does have the advantage of enabling some people to tell me to go back to my own country.

Had the Man Booker's message been drafted by an educated New Yorker for an American audience, it might have described me as Bangladeshi-American. Arguably, much more likely, ethnicity and nationality would have been deemed irrelevant to the context; drawing attention to such things would have been embarrassing (though they might instead have mentioned my human rights background for its obvious relevance, and not banking). Educated New Yorkers might pause to consider. It is worth noting that a few weeks after the *New York Times* published an op-ed I authored discussing this matter and including a hyperlink to the Man Booker post, the post was taken down.

The issue is not what I choose to call myself but what the supposedly educated Briton chooses to call non-White British citizens.

In 1999, William Macpherson delivered a report following the public inquiry into the murder of Stephen Lawrence, a young Black man, and the subsequent failures of the British police. Macpherson, a former High Court judge, overcame his establishment pedigree and delivered a stunning report that ought to have roused Britain to begin a process of ongoing introspection. Too many natives still take any criticism of racial bias as a charge of bare, outright racism. In your defensive pose, you cannot listen. Macpherson brought 'institutional racism' into mainstream vocabulary.

But what Britain and other European states, particularly the post-colonialist ones, have failed to undertake, including their liberal elites that believe themselves exempt, is a sustained enquiry into their own assumptions. Only with hard work, only when it is uncomfortable, will such an inquiry then begin to yield its rewards. Macpherson's report highlighted how an institution's processes can deliver outcomes that are racist. The intractable matter, however – the one that pervades every issue to do with Johnny Foreigner, including immigration or asylum seekers or membership of the EU or wearing the hijab – is that Britain has a cultural problem with otherness.

Perhaps it was too much to hope of a legal document. After all, the problem is *cultural*, and culture moves slowly or in unpredictable ways. The image of a dead boy lying on a beach, his head turned away, thereby allowing us all to project on to him our own beloved son, nephew or godson, arguably did more to move the debate on refugees than all the earnest roundtable discussions in Brussels. Cultural change is so slow that, aside from the occasional shock, all that is available to us is to engage in introspection as a society on a level that is necessarily deeply uncomfortable. Unless I am wrong, this is a project that will find no political champion. What must come under scrutiny are the assumptions embedded in the psyche; assumptions borne of hundreds of years of looting and oppression, of colonial presumption and racism. Those pictures of Tony Blair standing shoulder to shoulder with George Bush, the leader of the last remaining superpower in the world, both males readying for war – those images of sublime hubris only make sense against a history of violence.

You're talking about the empire, you say. All that was so long ago. Time to move on. But do we ever hear the same said of the Second World War that came to an end long before the sun set on the British Empire? Your finest hour is well remembered but the colonies' darkest days are best forgotten, old chum.

Instead, the BBC turns out documentaries about India with the same tired content and format – 2015 was a bumper season. The *Guardian* published a hilarious and serious piece by the

novelist Amit Chaudhuri ridiculing these shows, in which White
talking heads opine on Britain's legacy of democracy and clueless
White hosts take you on those railways – those bloody railways.
Meanwhile, the Indian account is rather different and scarcely gets
a look in. No doubt the British media machinery will continue
to ill-serve the British people, not to mention history, and churn
out the same nonsense in the next cycle. At the Oxford Union last
year, in one of the finest defences of historical accuracy (including
some solid facts about those fucking railways), the super-articulate
Indian MP and former UN under-secretary-general Shashi
Tharoor successfully argued that reparations be paid to India. The
video went epidemically viral. Intelligently, he said that for him
even one pound every year for the next 200 years would be enough,
thereby moving the focus away from quantifying harm and on to
admitting guilt and embracing history. A phalanx of gout-addled,
White, establishment fogies opposing him looked on bemused.
Meanwhile, according to a recent YouGov poll, 59 per cent of
Britons think that the British Empire is more something of which
to be proud rather than ashamed.

In February 2016, Prince William, who is British, gave a
speech at the Foreign Office. 'For centuries, Britain has been an
outward-looking nation. Hemmed in by sea, we have always sought
to explore what is beyond the horizon ... wherever we go, we have
a long and proud tradition of seeking out allies and partners.'
Not to mention colonies and plunder, of course. Referring to his
and his wife's forthcoming trip to India, he added that their visit
'will reflect the best of the modern, forward-looking relationship
between India and Britain'.

Let's set aside the optics of this, the inherent comedy of a
British heir to the throne in the twenty-first century speaking of
'forward-looking relationships'.

But what that speech exemplifies by its conspicuous omission
is the fundamental denial of a nation of its colonial history; the
denial, that is, of a country otherwise obsessed with its history,
if daytime television is anything to go by, or the popularity of
historical fiction, or period dramas. The psychic rupture involved

in denying its colonialist guilt and all the horrors and the energy required to maintain that rupture exacts a penalty.

There will be no new reckoning of its changed and changing place in the world – a vastly diminished place – until that history is interrogated at home. The dissonance was evident in the contortions of the former British prime minister, David Cameron, when he and an entourage of business people visited India. British newspapers obliged by refraining from showing their home audiences the PM as supplicant. But how could he manage to persuade Indian businesses to invest in Britain; how could he urge Indian students to come to the UK and pay hugely over the local odds for a British education? The number of Indian students coming to the UK had already fallen off sharply. Those shockingly bright graduates of the Indian Institutes of Technology now go to MIT and Stanford for their graduate degrees, after which many *stay on* – horror of horrors – and already dominate Silicon Valley. How could the PM represent Britain as open for business when it isn't even open culturally?

In November 2015, I received an invitation to Christmas drinks at the London Library. The invitation card, relayed by my agents, gave no clue as to how I came to their attention. The London Library, by way of background, is a 175-year-old institution; its patron is the Queen, who is British. Membership costs about £500 a year. It is not a public library.

When I looked it up on the internet and discovered that its president was Tom Stoppard – who is British, by the way – I recalled that in an interview for *Vanity Fair*, the playwright mentioned that he was reading my novel. That's why I was invited, I supposed. But it was something else on the London Library's website that caught my attention.

I wrote to Howard Davies, former British director of the London School of Economics, former head of the UK's financial regulator and chair of the trustees of the London Library, copying each of the trustees and the president. The first substantive paragraph of that letter reads: 'London is routinely trumpeted by British politicians and commentators as the most diverse city in the world, a melting pot. According to the Greater London Authority, ethnic minorities constitute 44 per cent of the city's population. On the library's website, the faces of 16 trustees and 13 staff are proudly displayed, every one of which is White.'

I pointed out to Davies, the former financial regulator, whose grasp of elementary probability could surely be assumed, that even with an absurdly low assumption of 2.5 per cent of filling any given slot – trustee or employee – with a non-White (in a city with 44 per cent from ethnic minorities), it was less likely than not that all 29 would be filled by Whites. And yet that was precisely the case.

His reply was familiar enough: the governance and staffing did not reflect the diversity that he and his colleagues aspire to and they recognize that there's work to be done.

When I shared Davies's response with a very close friend, White, British, someone who acknowledges her decidedly conservative disposition, her reaction typifies the White British attitude to change on matters of race. She thought his reply was an excellent outcome, a good ending, and she was pleased to see that Davies acknowledged the problem and he was doing something about it. I pointed out that far from describing what they were doing, the letter did not even say that they were doing anything at all; it merely acknowledged a duty: 'we have to find ways ...' The fact is that no great change ever came about by simply writing a letter to the powers that be and thanking someone for his attention – and it is, too often, *his* attention.

What came to trouble me most, however, about Davies's letter was a small remark he made, a correction he sought to make to something I said. In my own letter, I had stated that '[i]t would hardly be surprising if some people, browsing the library's website, formed the view that adequate efforts were not being made to draw trustees and staff from all sections of the London that the library presumably aims to serve'. Davies, in his response, wrote that he 'would like to correct the suggestion that the London Library serves the community of London only. Our membership is a national, and to some extent international one, and while we are physically situated in London, our members are much more geographically dispersed.'

At the drinks, I met one of the library's senior staff, who was aware that I'd written to Davies. I asked her what proportion of the members resided outside London. 'A half?' I asked. 'No. Much less', she replied.

The reason it came to trouble me is that it makes no difference at all to the mathematical reasoning. The only thing that it alters is the relevant comparison percentage. In my letter to Davies, I'd pointed out that according to official figures, 44 per cent of Londoners came from ethnic minorities. This 44 per cent would have to be adjusted and, using the most recent census figures and further assuming, generously, that the London Library's membership outside the capital is 33 per cent, the relevant comparison figure turns out still to be more than 25 per cent.

Why, then, did Davies point this out? If it doesn't undermine the force of the argument I made by one iota, why would he raise it? Does it simply muddy the waters, so that anyone reading the exchange of letters who doesn't have a strong grasp of probability or mathematics might think that an important counter-argument has been made? Or is Davies simply unaware that not enough of the library's members reside outside London to make the arithmetic work differently? Or has Davies, the former financial regulator, simply not grasped the mathematical implications, which are that my argument is untouched?

For many months the reply I drafted has been sitting in my computer in a heavy folder called 'Hope'. There's the mental and emotional energy of taking up a fight to think about. We have to pick our battles. Davies wrote in his letter that he looked forward to meeting me at the drinks. My reply, still unsent, begins with the regret that we did not meet, 'especially since it would have been very easy to spot me in the assembly'.

But the problem with otherness is not just a British one. A nasty undercurrent in the Brexit campaign, ahead of the referendum that determined that Britain should exit from the EU, was hostility towards European immigrants. Overnight, there was a huge spike in reported incidents of racist attacks. And, with the election of Donald Trump, the right wing of the Tory government has gained further traction in Britain.

Yet, like it or not, the British do share something with the mainland. I recently appeared on *Buitenhof*, a Dutch politics show, arguing that Europe's colonial history has left a stain on its psyche, an animus towards foreigners. Afterwards, aside from the usual racist mail, there were messages from non-White Dutch people, most taking issue with one thing. Apparently, I needn't have qualified my remarks by suggesting things were worse in Britain. I shouldn't have let the Netherlands off the hook. Things were just as bad here.

I was cosseted in Amsterdam, where I was writer in residence at the university and my novel was a national best-seller. In March 2016, I attended the annual *Boekenbal*, a gala celebrating Dutch publishing, the main purpose of which, as was explained to me, is to generate gossip about who had been deemed worthy of tickets. In other words, its function is to establish an inside group.

My publisher invited me to a pre-ball dinner at a restaurant. Midway, I remembered my coat: on arrival, I'd left it on a seat somewhere and forgot about it. When eventually a staff member and I found it, valuables still present, I thanked him.

'It is a pleasure to have you here', he replied.

Slightly odd formulation, I thought, putting it down to translation.

'No, sir,' he added, lowering his voice, 'I mean it is an honour to have you here.'

I looked at the man again.

'I saw you on *Buitenhof* last week, and everything you said was right. But the Dutch won't understand it because they just can't see it.'

'What's your name?' I asked.

'Emile', he said, shaking my hand. 'It's the name I use at work. My parents are Egyptian but I was born in the Netherlands. I'm the sommelier here and I know everything there is to know about wine. I speak Dutch fluently,' he told me, in English, 'I know more about Dutch culture than most Dutch people. I *am* Dutch but I am never really accepted as Dutch.'

The encounter moved me, and I stepped out into the cold Amsterdam night to recover my composure.

Life for immigrant Europeans is a daily confrontation with micro-aggressions and gestures of alienation. Not long ago, I ran into a well-known British actor and author who lives next door to the house I stay in when I'm in London. Without even greeting me, he exclaimed in thunderous Shakespearean tones, as if remembering something he believed I would obviously want to hear, 'I was just in India, as a matter of fact.' (He might have rounded it off with 'Old boy'.) Should I have pointed out to him that India was not my provenance, that South Asia contains nearly a quarter of the world's population and that there are over 3 million people of varied South Asian descent in Britain, and 300,000 of Bangladeshi descent in London alone? America never held as a colony the lands that comprise China, Korea and Japan but Britain owned India for 200 years. Yet an educated New Yorker understands not to make assumptions about origins on meeting an East Asian. Why is it that an educated White Londoner cannot do the same with South Asians? The answer must owe something to the history of empire: the South Asia engrained in the White British psyche is a subjugated greater India.

To the White Briton, each instance of alienation might seem small; after all, they will be aware of only the odd one. But what the non-White experiences is the accumulation, the steady barrage of incidents. Professional women know this. In legal practice, I saw more than one female lawyer – never a man – mistaken for a secretary. The embarrassment of the clients or the opposing side's lawyers is apparently dissipated, one imagines, when they reassure themselves that they had not made the mistake often. But the female lawyer might have experienced micro-aggressions on many occasions, being mistaken for a secretary or being ignored in meetings or being engaged in cases where the other side was represented by a lawyer of junior status to hers.

These days, when a New Yorker asks me where I'm from, sometimes I still might say, just for the hell of it, 'I was born in Bangladesh'. Unfailingly, it's not enough. Sometimes, bless 'em, he or she says 'Yeah, but you're British, right?' It seems I have to cross the Atlantic to hear this.

I can cope: sheer luck conferred on me a great deal of resilience. But when I think of the children in the projects where I grew up and in the underprivileged school in London's East End where I sat on the board of governors, I know that taking refuge in the novelist's seclusion would be an abrogation.

Every battle of ideas is fought on the terrain of language. George Orwell, who was British, reminded us of that. In the north-eastern US (and certain other parts of the country), the hyphenated identity does not make you any less American. (By the way, no comparison of a European state with the US as a whole makes sense: have you seen how big America is, how many time zones it straddles? It is a federation of culturally very different states, in some ways even more so than the EU project, with the avowed mission 'to form a more perfect union' – a fact that must be borne in mind in any assessment of how Donald Trump ascended to the presidency.) All of New York turns out for the St Patrick's Day parade to celebrate America's Irish-American heritage. Educated Americans feel no unease in identifying someone else, let alone themselves, as Italian-American or Indian-American. An American might even describe herself as Italian-American and Indian-American. It is merely a marker of heritage.

To the native Brit, the hyphenated identity – Bangladeshi-British, Pakistani-British – only highlights otherness, each side regarding it as a concession to the other, rather than both rejoicing in a new stripe in a rainbow nation. It does not come easily, face to face, for White Britons to speak of a non-White Briton's nationality. The shuffling feet, the throat-clearing, the unmet eye give it away. Hyphenation sounded clunky, felt awkward; even calling someone just British was less pointed, less charged. The British have history; the British-Bangladeshis have punctuation.

The conversation about banal identity (as opposed to the richer concepts that scholars deal with) was always going nowhere because it was never a conversation to begin with. It was the confrontation of two monologues with wildly different premises. The natives brought to the table their fears, their hysterical terror. The outsiders, newcomers, Johnny Foreigner, Pakis, Wogs, call her what you like (Bangladeshi, for example) – the immigrants came to the table with their dashed hopes and dreams. This was a case study in talking at cross purposes.

It is Britain's inherent cultural problem with otherness that makes it difficult for the native to call me British, difficult even for those who, one might naively have thought, should know better. If you're not going to call me British when I grew up in Britain; when I hold a British passport and don't hold a Bangladeshi one; when I don't even speak Bengali; when, good citizen or mensch that I try to be, I help the elderly neighbour put his flat-pack bed together and dig out the old ceanothus that another neighbour cannot uproot; when I was educated in Britain, worked in Britain, 'A body of England's, breathing English air, | Washed by the rivers, blest by suns of home'; when I wash the dishes at the church's fundraiser for its mission to the homeless (because whatever faiths we might declare, surely we can all believe in the importance of community?); and, again – it bears repetition – when I hold a British passport 'without let or hindrance' – if you still won't call me British, then you can't be surprised if, doubting your good faith, I want to grab my bags and get the hell out. After all, how much more can I integrate, what more is it you want from us? To be White? To be you?

Part of this essay was published as an op-ed in the *New York Times* in April 2016.

Bibliography

Brooke, Rupert, 'The Soldier', www.poets.org/poetsorg/poem/soldier.

Chaudhuri, Amit, '"Did the empire do any good?" British TV is revising India's history. Again', *Guardian*, 13 October 2015, www.theguardian.com/commentisfree/2015/oct/13/empire-british-tv-india-dan-snow-jeremy-paxman.

Coates, Ta-Nehisi, *Between the World and Me*, New York, Spiegel and Grau, 2015.

Dahlgreen, Will, 'The British Empire is something to be proud of', report of yougov.co.uk survey, 26 July 2014, https://yougov.co.uk/news/2014/07/26/britain-proud-its-empire/.

Fanon, Frantz, *Black Skin, White Masks*, London, Pluto Press, 2008 (first published in France in 1952).

Goldberg, Jeffrey, 'Is it time for the Jews to leave Europe?', 15 March 2015, video of *Atlantic* editor in chief James Bennet moderating a discussion between Goldberg and contributing editor Leon Wieseltier, www.theatlantic.com/video/index/387793/should-the-jews-leave-europe/.

Hiro, Dilip, *Black British, White British*, London, Paladin, 1992.

Tharoor, Shashi, 'Britain does owe reparations', speech given at the Oxford Union, published on YouTube, 14 July 2015, www.youtube.com/watch?v=f7CW7So zxv4.

Wieseltier, Leon, quoted in Cody M. Poplin, 'The Lawfare Podcast: Leon Wieseltier on the moral dimensions of the Syrian refugee crisis', 20 February 2016, www.lawfareblog.com/lawfare-podcast-leon-wieseltier-moral-dimensions-syrian-refugee-crisis.

2

When Do You Eat Lunch?

Isolde Charim

Then

We are two kinds of citizen: *bourgeois* and *citoyen*. Private individuals pursuing private interests and relationships, and public persons participating in public life. And just as we are two kinds of citizen, so our sense of belonging is of two kinds: private and public. Yet the relationship between them in one and the same life is not always without friction.

When I was a child, a Jewish girl growing up in post-war Austria, I could sum up this relationship in one sentence: Austrians eat lunch at noon. This was a constant refrain for us at home. And it was really all one needed to say. But what did it mean? First and foremost: *we* do not eat at noon. We are not Austrians. This tacitly implied a degree of contempt for a culture in which the norm was always to eat at noon. We ate at 1 pm, or 2, or even later.

Those who ate at 12 had no problem with their sense of belonging: to them, public and private belonging were one and the same. For us, by contrast, they were not merely *not* one thing, they were in conflict with each other. Public and private images, ideas and cultures did not correspond. They could not be made to coexist harmoniously. I would never have eaten at noon. Society then was still strongly characterized by the traditional notion of a division between friend and foe: 'we' against 'you', 'us' against 'them'. And our relationship with 'the Austrians' seemed to represent a form of this 'us' and 'them' distinction, as indicated by the refrain: Austrians eat lunch at noon. And yet it was something else entirely.

For it matters whether making such a distinction is aimed at rallying the majority, and is therefore hegemonic, or whether a minority expresses itself in this way. By distinguishing ourselves from 'the Austrians', we grasped the lifeline that was thrown to us: we accepted the difference assigned to us and fulfilled the role we were required to play. This is a typical strategy diaspora communities adopt to protect their own identity. But remarkably it was not aimed at our separation.

Having exposed this difference, what did it contain? Something substantive of an ethnic, religious or cultural character? In fact the basis of this difference was something else: namely a different *experience*. Jews who live in Austria may be no different from Austrians. But they constructed a different experience, which did not even have to be their own. It could also be that of their parents. A characteristic of diasporas is to de-individualize experiences, to establish them as spanning the generations, in order to aid identity formation. This process is indeed nourished to a considerable extent by familiar narratives and is transmitted far less through formal means.

All this – the difference that stems from another experience, other origins, another language, culture – Jews share with all other migrants. So too the experience of being a stranger when your parents' language is not that of the society in which you live. Or when the rituals at home are not those of your school friends. In short, the otherness that results when you do not eat at noon is the fate of every diasporic group in Austria. And naturally many of these also have histories of suffering caused by persecution and repression that deviate from the experience of the majority. But nevertheless, the Jewish situation is a special case.

By that I am not referring to the uniqueness of the Holocaust – at least not its quantitative dimension – but rather to its 'European character'. For in Central Europe, there was no Jewish difference. Jews, in themselves, bore no signs of difference. It had to be constructed. The imposition of the yellow star proves that Jews had to be marked in order to identify them. The Nazis were paranoid about having them in their midst yet not recognizable.

It was indeed this sameness which made it necessary to introduce criteria of difference in order to track down those who were to be subsumed under the category 'Jew'. This was a very specific Jewish experience, and perhaps not one applicable to migrants more generally. It reverberated in the words my mother used about the neighbours, landladies or women grocers: 'Do you think she knows?' My mother feared, indeed dreaded, they might notice that this difference, this other experience, was indeed visible.

At the same time, however, this construction of a sense of otherness pinpoints a specific feature of Jewish identity. In a word coined by Jan Assmann, the Egyptologist and professor of cultural studies, it is essentially 'counter-presentist'. Jews understand their history as the experience of being strangers in a strange land. Their identity depends on maintaining that strangeness – what the philosopher Jacob Taubes has described as the maintenance of 'the memory of the desert' – in a counter-presentist way, that is against all lived experience. Jewry sustains its identity precisely by preserving its difference, by maintaining distance from all other peoples. Significant here is the fact that these elements of religious self-understanding continue to exist, even if secularized. Thus the counter-presentist memory of the desert can assume the form of rejecting lunch at noon.

It is perhaps not surprising that this affinity with Judaism as religious text can render all kinds of textuality accessible. But when the idea of being the chosen people is secularized, by contrast, it can surface in extraordinary ways. For example, it was clear to me as a 12-year-old that the initials 'SF' on my great grandfather's silver cutlery could only refer to one man: Sigmund Freud. It seemed self-evident that I was the great-granddaughter of Freud and that the exceptional loomed large in my life, that I had privileged access to it. When I later discovered that 'SF' stood for 'Simche Freund', my disillusionment was profound.

I experienced being thrust back into the banality of a completely 'normal' Jewish family as narcissistic injury. At the time I had no idea what was really sensational about this cutlery – namely that we still had it at all; that to this day it lies in a drawer in my home;

a heavy, monogramed silver cutlery set that made an incredible journey from Galicia and eventually to Vienna, via Palestine. These objects are signs of a different time and their presence in my kitchen creates a strange continuity: today, when my children eat with their great-great-grandfather's cutlery, they are making the break, and at the same time demonstrating continuity, with this already broken belonging.

This also applies to the pictures that my father bought in the 1950s in the Dorotheum, a Viennese auction house. They were not valuable pictures, but pictures of ladies in fur coats. Pictures of 'Mama', which middle class families used to commission. But it was not our family. For us this was a bought past. We knew nothing about the ladies in the pictures. Hanging in our home they secured and guaranteed the continuity of something quite different from the experience of our family: the bourgeois culture from which my parents came. Over time, for us children the strange ladies became members of the family. And for my children they are – rightly – rather like ancestors.

The Jewish diaspora in Austria was special because it was the carrier of a bourgeois, urbane culture which no longer existed. In the narrow post-war world, Austrian Jews bore this culture like the pain from a phantom limb. Even those from the *shtetl* became guardians of this dream of the metropolis and the wider world. But this is not a dream about a space in which differences are eliminated. It is the longing for a space where difference no longer matters. In that wider world one can easily eat lunch later than noon.

Now

What I have described above is a divided sense of belonging, the difference between private and public belonging, when the society was relatively homogenous. At that time the signifier 'Austrians' was an unambiguous symbol for an unambiguous picture.

This homogeneity may have been a fiction but it was a fiction that served a function. As Benedict Anderson taught us, the nation is a socially constructed, 'imagined political community' – imagined, and believed in, by the people who feel part of that national group. And for that reason the fiction of the nation has actually spawned national societies. This does not mean that homogeneity was ever fully achieved in reality. But the nation became *the* political form capable of integrating heterogeneous masses by means of stories and practices. Anderson even includes among these practices the weather reports on television, which are broadcast in front of a map of the particular country and thus subtly reinforce its boundaries. This is one of the many ways in which the nation emerged as the hegemonic and predominant narrative.

According to Anderson, the members of a nation live under the illusion that they know everyone else in this 'imagined community'. However, this illusion only works because, through the form of imagining the nation described above, the nation is able to provide positive identity traits, a national type with clearly defined characteristics.

An awareness of some historical context is important here. In the nineteenth century, two movements coincided: the democratization of European societies and the rise of nationalism. They were connected because the growth of democratic politics was coupled with the creation of a national majority culture. Now, however, these two processes run counter to each other with respect to the politics of identity. So what is now actually happening with regard to the formation of an individual's identity?

Democratization, as we have understood it up to now, means the creation of what Pierre Rosanvallon, the French historian, has called 'the universal individual', that is the constitution of man as political subject – the citizen of the state 'sharing in sovereignty through exercise of the right to vote' – and as legal subject – 'the bearer of rights guaranteeing freedom of thought and action, property, and autonomy'. It is important to recognize that individualism is not a movement which arose in our time but, rather, one that developed from about 1800. In any case – and this is the important point – it was a new kind of individualism, the creation of a different type of individual.

The legal subject, the voter, the state citizen – all arise in the abstract; privately, people are separate individuals, each taking concrete shape and being quite different. As public persons individuals only become equal by abstracting them from what distinguishes them. That is to say, only by disregarding their specific difference(s) do they become equal parts of the whole, equal parts of the sovereign body. In this respect what links the individuals is their abstraction from their specific features. We can only become equal parts of the whole if we ignore what divides us. The abstract and general nature of the universal individual is particularly striking with respect to voters who are – disregarding specific differences – arithmetical equals: each has one vote. Historically, we know that it was a long and sometimes bloody process to achieve this abstraction (as in achieving women's suffrage for example). But what is decisive for this essay is that the individual can only become an equal part of the whole by being abstracted from his or her specific circumstances – emphasizing how we are the same means disregarding what distinguishes us.

This abstract equality was thus created by the thoroughly progressive and emancipatory process of democratization. The formation of the nation, by contrast, was a counter-movement with respect to the politics of identity. For what does the national narrative create? It offers the democratic subject, the abstract *citoyen*, or the abstract legal person a gestalt that provides the individual with positive identity traits as a public person. While the democratic, political or legal subject is an abstract equal with regard to the sovereign body, the national subject is publicly specific and has concrete characteristics (which of course ignore individual particularities). We all know the national stereotypes. The Austrian is charming but underhanded. The German is pedantic and a slave to authority. The Italian loves life but is unreliable. Recently, during the Greek crisis in 2015, these stereotypes received a new lease of life.

The jokes about such national differences are legion. They serve to delineate and reinforce the national character. The narrative of the nation therefore bracketed the specific individual and the abstract public individual together, offering them a specific gestalt for their public identity. This individual became a figure who could be integrated into the whole, not merely as something abstract or numerical, but also as a concrete entity with positive identity traits. In short, the national narrative offered the democratic individual a gestalt through which they could recognize themselves again as a public person.

The homogenization of a society, however fictional it may be, thus works by creating specific identities and specific forms of belonging. A society is not homogenous when there are no differences. A society is homogenous when one belongs to it directly and completely. And that is precisely what has fundamentally changed.

The Man with the Traditional Hat

From late March 2015, in Vienna you could repeatedly come across the same turquoise-coloured poster on public transport, on billboards and in newspapers. Beneath the slogan, 'Listen to your gut feelings: respect is in your head', there are the backs of four heads: a Jewish man with a *kippa*, a Black man, a Muslim woman with a headscarf and a man wearing a traditional Austrian hat. The title of this poster campaign was: 'Together we are stronger' and it aimed to be 'a statement against racism and for cohesion and diversity'. But what kind of a statement was it?

The text of the poster says: the differences are visible – our heads display them. Let's use our heads to combat prejudice. The head thus becomes a metaphor for reason which should be brought to bear against feelings – which we characterize as originating in the gut. This appeal therefore says to us: emotions are triggered by external factors, by what we see. And these feelings require reason, rational understanding, to be transformed into respect. Respect is thus a feeling purified by reason. Quite apart from whether reason can actually master negative emotions, the question also arises: is what results from this really 'respect'?

It is the great picture underneath the slogan that answers this question. By showing the backs of four heads it is not about the individuals themselves. Rather, they are bearers of ethnic, religious or class signs and characteristics, which distinguish them. Interestingly, there is no representative of the group that would define itself as having no such characteristics, because its normality is society's standard: modern White men. Modern simply because they would not be marked out in terms of ethnicity or religion. However, it is even more interesting that the wearer of the traditional hat is included.

It is wonderful that here, this type is only one among others. That indeed corresponds to reality today. But you must bear in mind what it actually means. When I was a child, the hegemonic type was the man in the loden coat wearing the traditional hat decorated with a tuft of chamois hair. He and the woman in the dirndl skirt were dominant culturally and with respect to the politics of identity. They set the tone. They were the ones who determined 'normality'. Today, he may still eat at noon, but this rhythm no longer determines the life of the country. He is not merely lined up on the poster now, one type among others. He has also lost his hegemony in real life. The picture shows that very clearly, and very memorably.

For the wearer of the traditional hat the loss of his primacy has been a painful process. The juxtaposition of the people on the poster is not the result of growing respect of difference. It is the consequence of a social dispute. At its root is a conflict, a struggle for power in society. Only when the traditional hat is lined up, one among others, and no longer dominant, will diversity become a lived reality. We should have no illusions. Diversity is not cosy togetherness. Is it cohesion, or respect? Even the fair juxtaposition on the poster is image and prayer all in one. Put differently: it is a hope.

Understanding this pluralism entails recognizing that it means change on the level of belonging and on the level of identity, the identity of us all. For pluralism is not simply an *external* relationship. It is also not mere coexistence that leaves the constituent parts untouched. Rather, pluralization or diversification means a process in which diversity affects everyone, indigenous people and migrants, and in which difference changes the whole of society.

The specific characteristic of a plural society is not simply that it is morally and religiously diverse. Rather, it lies in the fact that such societies no longer have any kind of world view – to use the philosopher Charles Taylor's term – that is shared by all. We thus have no world view that unites us all. However, that also means that we have no world view from which we might deviate – by, for example, eating lunch later. Such a world is indeed completely different from the one in which I grew up. A society that is radically new.

My Festivals, Your Festivals

My friend at the supermarket checkout told me that he was celebrating Christmas, even though it is not his tradition (he comes from Afghanistan). Likewise New Year's Eve, and then he was celebrating his New Year and another two festivals. Isn't that the old multicultural dream – my festivals, your festivals, everything is celebrated?

However, what is the difference between observing festivals from one's own tradition and celebrating festivals that are not one's own? A simple question, and an acute one in a pluralist society. The answer, however, is highly paradoxical.

One's own festivals are those of one's own religion. (And Christmas, for all its consumerism and secularization, despite being turned into kitsch to the point of general mawkishness, is still a religious festival.) However, religion embeds the believer in a total social universe. It assigns the individual their place in this world. And that place is determined by tradition. Tradition comes from our ancestors, passes through the generations, who add nothing to it, and is transmitted to our children. Religion is thus not only a vertical relationship (with heaven, with God). It is also a horizontal connection through time, linking the individual with his ancestors and with his descendants. In this sense religion is de-subjectivating.

It does not promote individuality. Rather, it places the individual in a chain, in a sequence of generations.

In pluralist societies, however, things look quite different. In ineluctably pluralist societies faith requires a decision. But that means that an essentially secular element has found its way into faith. Such a decision is a secular element because the individual who is taking the decision, the individual who is making up their mind, requires a subjectivity which is not the subjectivity of the believer but rather its opposite. They are deciding on a religion as a responsible, autonomous individual. However, rational decision-making is not the way in which most religions regulate who joins them. From a religious perspective the believer is not a responsible citizen who freely chooses his religion; there is no choice of faith. That would presuppose that the latter-day believer had been someone else previously. But from a religious perspective, religious identity is the fundamental, definitive, obvious identity from which all actions follow. Belonging to a religion is not the same as being a member of a club. To a certain extent it is the opposite.

The new form of religious faith in plural societies now consists of precisely this: one chooses a faith. One selects a personal identity. This is a total change. For instead of being slotted into a tradition, one now adopts traditions – your own or an alien one. It makes no difference.

For this reason exactly, the paradigmatic figure of the believer today is the convert. The shift in the form of faith means all who believe are converts – even within their own religion. It is not only the migrant who can decide to celebrate Christmas. In a secular, pluralized world, even the native Catholic can, indeed must, decide whether to celebrate Christmas – or indeed not to celebrate it (which can create problems within the family if it is the last remnant of their religious practice). In a pluralist society even the Catholic must convert to Catholicism, or the Jew to Judaism. For the basis of faith, the way in which we inhabit our faith, is that of the convert: it is a decision.

So we choose a faith. Or several. It doesn't matter. The vital point is: the new tradition of choosing for yourself – what a paradox

34

– has the opposite effect of religiosity as previously acquired. Instead of being de-individualized by being incorporated into the generational chain, the ego is strengthened by the act of choosing. Instead of being allocated a place in a religion, it has become a question of subjectively adopting one. Faith today therefore serves ego formation. If my friend celebrates Christmas in Vienna, it is in this sense more *his* than the festival of his own tradition: the latter was prescribed for him. But he chose Christmas as an autonomous individual, thereby exemplifying the fact that religion today can promote responsible citizenship.

But if traditions now stem from our personal decisions, such decisions can also always be revoked. We have turned faith into something different, indeed almost to its opposite: to an identity. That also changes our sense of belonging to it.

Clash of Civilizations?

In the film *Ninotchka*, three Soviet comrades are living a life of luxury in Paris in 1939 and consequently forget their mission to bring about world revolution. A female commissar is sent after them – Greta Garbo as the epitome of revolutionary asceticism. She is immune to material pleasure. What she cannot resist, however, and where her revolutionary virtue fails her, is the pursuit of 'higher' pleasure: true love. It is love that 'converts' her and conquers her asceticism.

Ninotchka is a story about the superiority of the West's way of life, a way of life that can cater to every need. In fact the West was for years a place of longing, the promise of happiness and pleasure – for those who did not live there. Hence the West was not so much a geographical location, but rather came to mean a way of life and an ideal political system. That was the case for people in the Eastern bloc as well as for those in the Middle East. 'Once the West was chic', the German-Iraqi writer Sherko Fatah observed. Baghdad and even Kabul were in this sense once 'Western' cities.

The 'sleepers' of 9/11 mounted a sustained challenge to this myth of the West, the myth of the good life as panacea – simply by resisting it. In doing so, they represent a decisive break in the domination of this way of life. They lived in the West for years without having been 'infected' by Western civilization, without the Western way of life 'corrupting' them and nullifying their 'mission'. Today we are experiencing a twofold movement: on the one hand there are the jihadis who – immune to Western ideas of happiness – sally forth from their childhood bedrooms to make holy war. For them *Ninotchka* has had its day. The seductive power of the West is spent. That goes deeper than the failure of integration in the socio-technical sense. It is the rejection of what was central to the supremacy of the West, the rejection of its dream. Its superiority was not simply economic or military. It was essentially a mental superiority: the seductive power of an idea of happiness.

At the same time, however, we are experiencing a mass movement of refugees. For these refugees, Europe – or certain parts of Europe – is very much their place of longing. What characterizes this place of longing has yet to be studied. It is clear that they have definite ideas; so definite that they leave Hungary, Serbia, Croatia and even Austria behind them – and head only for Germany, Sweden or Great Britain, which seem to them to be the 'promised' lands. Even if this were the result of an economic attraction, an idea of a secure life in prosperity, the receiving countries hasten to make emphatically clear to the new arrivals that they have arrived in the West, not simply a society with a different economic order.

As a result of these upheavals a new demarcation line is in the process of being drawn: a 'clash' of civilizations which has nothing to do with Samuel Huntington's prognosis of a 'clash of civilizations' as the new paradigm of world history after the end of the Cold War. The question is no longer the one posed by Huntington, 'Which side are you on?', but rather, 'Who are you?' When fanaticized men crying '*Allahu-Akbar!*' murdered the editors of the satirical magazine *Charlie Hebdo* in January 2015; when murderers slaughtered Jewish customers in a Paris supermarket in the name of Islam at the same time; when throughout the world young people want to give up their lives to make jihad – that is not a 'clash of civilizations', at least not in the sense of a collision between the West and Islam.

It is especially important to bear this in mind today precisely because we are living with such an acute refugee situation. That situation makes it essential for us to establish where the line that divides our societies internally is located, and where might it divide them even more in the future. The new front – for such it is – does not run between the West and Islam. It does not run between civilizations or cultures, or between religions. Indeed, it does not even run between secularists and believers. It does not divide the Occident from the Orient – only followers of Pegida, the German Islamophobic political movement, believe that. It does not even run between Islamophobic racists and Islamists. This is what makes the present situation so confused: the division in our societies follows no declared line of demarcation. The declared opponent is not the real opponent. The horrific attack on *Charlie Hebdo* made that absolutely clear. As did the horrific attack on the Labour Party youth gathering on the island of Utøya by the Norwegian Anders Breivik in 2011. The Islamists did not shoot at racists and Breivik did not shoot at Muslims – quite the opposite in both cases. Racists and Islamists are not enemies who want to fight each other, but rivals. The victims, however, were cartoonists and Jews and young social democrats – because the real enemy for both sides is the pluralist, open and liberal society, which finds itself caught in a pincer movement, attacked from two sides.

It is an urgent political imperative to mark exactly the course of the social divide. Today, defining that as the 'clash of civilizations' is not an analysis, but itself a partisan position. For 'clash of civilizations' implies that the acute fault line runs between different religions and ethnicities. In fact, it runs through all cultures, civilizations and religions. It is not cultures or civilizations that are competing against each other here with such hatred and murderous intent. What divides us far more is how we live within them, how we inhabit our identities, how we determine our senses of belonging and practice our religions. The demarcation is defined by the question: pluralism or no pluralism? *That* is the key question of our age.

Pluralism does not mean a mere collection of different cultures and religions. It is not simply an addition, something new that is added to what already exists – whether in Austria that means Turks, Yugoslavs or Muslims more generally. For pluralism is not an external relationship. Whether it is wanted or not, it changes everyone – the old indigenous population and the newcomers.

But, as I mentioned above, if pluralism means that there is no longer a common world view that unites us all, then pluralism also means that our only commonality is a minus, a deduction, a diminished identity, less of a sense of belonging, a weakened faith.

Today, every identity exists alongside other identities. Every sense of belonging exists alongside other senses of belonging. Every religion exists alongside other religions, or alongside atheism. Everyone now knows that what determines who they are is not fixed; it is only one option among many. That accounts for our diminished commonality. At the same time, this diminution poses a different, but decisive question: in the knowledge that our religion is only one of a variety of options, do we or do we not practice it in a pluralist way? Do we inhabit our identity openly, as one choice among others, or do we inhabit it as a closed identity, cut off from others? Therefore the decisive question is not: Who are you? but rather How do you see yourself? What do you think or feel about being an Austrian, Turk or Chechen? How do you practice your Christianity, your Judaism? How do you live as a Muslim or an atheist?

Or to put it differently: When do you eat lunch?

Bibliography

Anderson, Benedict, *Imagined Communities: Reflections on the Origin and Spread of Nationalism*, London, Verso, 1983.

Assmann, Jan, *Das kulturelle Gedächtnis. Erinnerung und politische Identität in frühen Hochkulturen*, München, Beck, 2013.

Fatah, Sherko, Interview, *Die Zeit*, no. 36, 11 September 2014.

Huntington, Samuel Phillips, *Kampf der Kulturen. Die Neugestaltung der Weltpolitik im 21. Jahrhundert*. München, Siedler/Goldmann, 1998.

Rosanvallon, Pierre, *Die Gesellschaft der Gleichen*, Hamburg, Hamburger Edition, 2013.

Taubes, Jakob, *Abendländische Eschatologie*, Bern, Francke, 1947.

Taylor, Charles, *Ein säkulares Zeitalter*, Frankfurt am Main, Suhrkamp Verlag, 2009.

3

The Missing Link? Building Solidarity among Black Europeans

Rob Berkeley

I grew up in London. The city had fewer Black people in the 1980s than now, but was still a more visibly multicultural place than many other British or European cities. I spent the Saturdays of my formative years working at my father's 'Afro-Caribbean' grocers, so was surrounded by Black people. Imagine my sense of dislocation when I moved to study in an Oxford college at the start of the 1990s with only two Black students. It was then that I noticed the phenomenon of the Black head nod. When I saw another Black man in Oxford I would acknowledge them with a slight incline of the head that would usually be reciprocated. That head nod was an act of unspoken ethnic solidarity. In that simple, ergonomically efficient movement was recognition that in a space potentially rife with racism, someone had your back. In that small muscle flex was the acknowledgement of a shared relationship to history, a suggestion that the counterparts have a connection that needs to be recognized and an affirmation of the other's success as a Black person in a White space. While the head nod lacks the drama of the black-gloved, raised fist of John Carlos and Tommie Smith at the Mexico City Olympics in 1968, the nods of strangers in 1992 helped get me through the alienation of my first months living outside of multicultural, multiethnic London.

I noted the head nod phenomenon again when I was lucky enough to start travelling further afield. In West Africa, the Caribbean and North America: the head nod. In European cities with smaller Black populations, again the head nod. For me it began to be a simple way of reaching out, offering support and respect, acknowledging the struggle, and acknowledging a connection. The nod has been the start of many conversations and more enduring connections over time, but has also been a driver in shaping my sense of belonging – at home and abroad.

I grew up in London. A more visibly multicultural place than many, it voted, unlike the nation of which it is the capital, to stay in the European Union when given the opportunity to express a view on 23 June 2016. I live in an area where four out of five people voted 'remain' (second only to Gibraltar in its lack of enthusiasm for Brexit). We were outvoted, and while we are learning to live with the consequences, I have since been reminded that I don't know the people around me as well as I had thought. In the 42 per cent upsurge of racist incidents that followed the vote, it became clear how thin the layer of civility and cosmopolitanism and how prone to eruption the potential for hate is even in my supposedly progressive, outward-looking city. Again, I felt dislocated in a place I call home and reached out – this time not for a nod of the head (30 per cent of the people in my neighbourhood are Black), but for the comfort of my overwhelmingly London-based Twitter silo and Facebook bunker, where I could sneer at the Brexiters of Thurrock and Hartlepool without retort, and fume at the xenophobic short-sightedness of Bostonians. They are not my kind of people, after all. I don't know them and they were not part of the society I imagined that I lived in. That is until a rather rude awakening on the morning of 24 June. I had drawn boundaries between my fellow citizens on more than phenotypical grounds, simply not seeing those with whom I disagreed on such a fundamental level. Perhaps this is why Brexit took me by surprise. The referendum result brought home to me that there are dangers in assuming knowledge of my fellow citizens based on imperfect information. Information made even more imprecise because I find myself operating increasingly within an echo chamber of the like-minded.

The nod. This simple understanding of such a small interaction has informed my thinking about the potential benefits of ethnic solidarity. It creates an echo chamber where I don't have to explain myself from first principles; where I can nurture and be nurtured; where I am an insider. The nod has helped me shape my resilience in being able to resist ethnic nationalism. Yet, it catches me in a dilemma. I want to be able to defend the building of solidarity along ethnic lines because I appreciate the benefits of shared recognition that I have felt in societies where 'race-thinking' still constrains opportunities and acts of violence and exclusion based on racism are a real threat. I know, however, that in this simple understanding of a simple act, there is an implicit challenge to the liberal social model, which has led in the UK to the supposed 'end of multicultur-alism' and the rush to a 'post-racial' world view. Exhortations from 'mainstream' (for which I assume we are supposed to read 'White') politicians and social commentators have increasingly called for us to 'focus on our commonalities rather than our differences'. It is argued, as part of this logic, that the practice of nation-building is better pursued through establishing stronger borders between in- and out-groups, but also through discouraging minority ethnic groups from taking social action solely with others who share their ethnic identity. According to this logic, the reminder that 'Black Lives Matter' can only be rejected in favour of the truism that 'All Lives Matter'. In one fell swoop, denying the agency of the victims of racism while asserting a post-racial myth that maintains the unequal status quo. The head nod, already loaded with cultural significance, becomes a subversive act. In this neoliberal space it would seem to be fine to create an echo chamber based on values (remain or leave, progressive or conservative, red or blue), but not one based on a shared set of experiences of racism.

Working in a large, 'hideously white' organization like the BBC I have again noticed the importance of the head nod as a route to building solidarity. It acts as an emotional response to both institutional racism and racist economic superstructures, and an acknowledgement of the struggle, successes and challenges of 'people like me' within it. Far more meaningful for me than the anodyne, wine-quaffing and canapé-scoffing of the corporate ethnic diversity network, the simple nod again provides a grounding and sense of belonging that situates me in relationship to others, and enables me to start to make sense of my marginalization. A rather expensive education in a liberal rationalist tradition should make that head nod and my need for it obsolete and archaic, but in that nod lies the heart of a key challenge at this moment in late modern society: the persistence of the benefits of ethnic solidarity within the nominally post-ethnic nation state. This challenge is more often posed as a concern about the persistence of racism in the post-racial state, but this raises the question whether, if racist superstructures were to be magically dismantled tomorrow, there would be any place in that brave new world for ethnic solidarity? Is racism all we have?

* * *

I grew up in London. Tip O'Neill's now famous dictum that 'all politics is local' could well be extended to the claim that 'all racisms are local'. Structural and interpersonal patterns of racism and racist behaviours are all grounded in the local. English experiences of racism are bound in and shaped by the post-imperial melancholia that the philosopher and social theorist Professor Paul Gilroy succinctly describes. An English narrative of 'race relations' that is shaped around, among other things, slavery, self-congratulation about emancipation, imperial ambition, colonialism, Raj, post-empire, post-war reconstruction, the SS *Windrush*, multiculturalism, post-multiculturalism, samosas, steel bands, saris and Sir Lenny Henry seems like such a specific context that the building of connections and a sense of belonging across national boundaries feels like a stretch.

Indeed, building a shared narrative among those racialized as Black within national boundaries is a difficult task. When I speak to Black people from Liverpool, for example, I'm reminded of the very different narratives of race relations that shape their identities. Toxteth and uprisings there in the 1980s do not hold the same resonance for me as those of Brixton or Tottenham (and I'm even slightly uncomfortable to suggest that racism as experienced in North London is the same as that in the south of the capital).

When I connect with people whose families migrated to South London from East Africa, South East Asia or Brazil I recognize that their relationship to the racist superstructure is different to mine and their histories, like mine, shape their understandings of their spaces in society and senses of belonging. When I have spoken with millennial racial justice activists I have often been struck by their confidence in organizing around and beyond identity markers that they have explained to me is a function of being 'digital natives'. Similarly some older activists have noted a decline in the salience of the workplace and trade unionism in organizing against racism. So it would seem that not only are all racisms bound by histories and geographies, they are also time bound.

Does this mean that we are stuck on a solipsistic merry-go-round for one when seeking to consider solidarities between ethnically minoritized people within a space as contested and ephemeral as Europe? Given the necessarily very different relationships with racism across space and time, it would seem sensible to conclude that 'having experience of racism' is a very tenuous starting point around which to build solidarities. However tenuous, there does appear to be a phenomenon worth exploring. It is a phenomenon that will increase in importance over coming months as we in Britain begin to reframe what it means to be European outside of the EU. It seems sensible to begin to consider what it might mean to be a Black European.

*   *   *

When Beyonce marched in full Black Panther pastiche across the Super Bowl half-time field of play and right onto front pages internationally in February 2016, I felt like she was talking for me (and I don't even carry hot sauce, in my bag or otherwise). Black Lives Matter beyond US boundaries and the roll call of America's shame – Dontre Hamilton, John Crawford III, Michael Brown, Ezell Ford, Dante Parker, Tanisha Anderson, Akai Gurley, Sandra Bland, Tamir Rice, Eric Garner, Freddie Gray – feels like a call to action for me as well. I want to add Mark Duggan, Rocky Bennett, Christopher

Alder, Sean Rigg, Sarah Reed and Sheku Bayoh as British victims of the same disease: institutional racism and disregard for Black lives.

I look across the Atlantic at our American cousins and realize that so much of the debate about race and racism in the UK is coloured by their experience. Perhaps this is simply about numbers or critical mass. While only 12 per cent of American citizens describe themselves as African-American that is still nearly 40 million people, compared to the just under 2 million British citizens who describe themselves as Black British. However, both these numbers pale into insignificance when set against the near billion Black people in Africa and the Caribbean.

Perhaps then the US dominance is a function of US cultural imperialism and an increasingly globalized media. British debates closely mirror those in the States. #OscarsSoWhite becomes #MOBOSoWhite, activists for racial justice in the UK adopt African-American turns of phrase as descriptors of their struggle from 'stay woke' to 'white tears' or 'unapologetically Black'; so much for Bernard Shaw's 'two nations separated by a common language'. Was it ever thus? After all, Runnymede, the UK's leading racial justice think tank, was founded in 1968 in the wake of a brief visit to the UK of Martin Luther King. Core reading for racial justice activists includes a litany of American writers from Booker T. Washington to Ta-Nehisi-Coates, via Skip Gates, Cornel West, Alex Haley, Zora Neale Hurston, Eldridge Cleaver, Stokely Carmichael, James Baldwin and Angela Davis. The exploits of the US Civil Rights Movement inspired mass action in the UK, for example in the Bristol bus boycott of 1963 which presaged the development of comprehensive race relations legislation in Britain in 1965. African-American superstars from Josephine Baker, Jesse Owens and Muhammad Ali to Diana Ross, Oprah Winfrey, Eddie Murphy and Prince have shaped our public conceptions of Blackness in a way that continental Europeans and Africans have not been able to do – particularly powerful when we recognize that racial categorizations are 'imagined' rather than based on any essentialist biological phenomena (step forward Rachel Dolzeal).

The American civil rights movements (in their Student Non-Violent Coordinating Committee or the Black Lives Matter-led forms) are exactly that: American. They derive from a particular experience of history and play out in a particular present experience. The tragedies of extra-judicial police killings are bound up with US gun laws and culture, and fuelled by a prison-industrial complex that plays out a delayed backlash that has been named 'The New Jim Crow'. Yet despite (or maybe because of) this essential Americanness, the civil rights movements remain powerfully relevant in constructing a racial consciousness among people racialized as Black beyond US borders, including in the UK. However, while powerfully relevant for the formation of British racial consciousness, understandings of racial dynamics in the US are hardly, if at all, influenced by the experiences of the British. For Black Americans, the local racisms of the UK are barely relevant to their struggle for justice.

In May of 2016, the British rapper and anti-racism activist, Akala, was interviewed by African-American author and popular talk show host Tavis Smiley. Smiley asked: 'For a guy born and raised in the UK, how does Malcolm X get into your conscious-ness?' Displaying both an ignorance of how significant the US Civil Rights Movement is for Black British people and reaffirming how little is generally known about the British struggle for racial justice in the US. This vignette also shows how and why the British anti-racist activist is likely to remain at best marginal and often invisible in the definition of a struggle in which she is so clearly invested.

This makes sense in the model of distributed leadership and organizing that Black Lives Matter has adopted – rejecting the 'community leader' model in favour of chapters of activists defining the movement in a way that is relevant to their context and the responsibility that they take for their communities. It is remarkable (if not surprising) that in response to the most recent tragic violations of African-American life at the hands of the American state – Alton Sterling and Philando Castile – solidarity marches were held in London, Berlin, Paris and Amsterdam. Black people in Europe wanted to express their support both for the struggle of the activists in the US with whom they identified, but also to make clear that Black Lives Matter in Britain, France, Germany and the Netherlands as well. Black Lives Matter demonstrations have been witnessed in Ghana, South Africa, Tokyo, Canada, Australia and Kenya, creating new forms of diasporic connection: connecting local racisms to global awareness of exclusion, marginalization and unfair discrimination. This is more than a nod of the head towards ethnic solidarity.

Yet expressions of solidarity are unevenly shared. The solidarity expressed in the UK with the victims of US state-sanctioned racism is not matched by expressions of solidarity with state racism experienced by Black people geographically closer to these shores. One week after the death of Philando Castile at the hands of police in Minnesota, and hours before the shooting of Charles Kinsey, a carer who was lying prostrate with his hands raised, in Miami, Adama Traore died in police custody. His family allege that he was beaten to death in the back of a police van, while the police claim he had a heart attack. The death of Traore was marked by nights of rioting and a series of demonstrations demanding 'Justice for Adama' in the neighbourhood in which he lived. Significantly there has been considerably less attention given to Traore's death in the UK. He died in a northern suburb of Paris. One month before Adama Traore's death, Emmanuel Chidi Nnamdi, a man seeking sanctuary from Boko Haram's reign of terror in north-eastern Nigeria, was beaten to death in the street in front of his wife, allegedly by a farmer with links to neo-fascist organizations. The street was in the small town of Fermo in central Italy. The Italian prime minister, Matteo Renzi, condemned the murder. His death was reported in British newspapers but barely registered in the Black Lives Matter 'filter bubble'.

The dynamics, drivers of, and resistance to racism in the US appear to loom larger in the European-inflected version of the imagined community of a global Black diaspora than those apparent in neighbouring countries. This appears to hold despite members of the aforesaid diaspora having lived within the shared political space of the EU for a generation. It was not always this way. Commenting on the history of pan-Africanist movements, which sought to build political solidarities among people of African descent, Clarence Lusane notes that the (sometimes competing) efforts of W.E.B Du Bois and Marcus Garvey regularly focused on solidarity among people of African descent in Europe – with London, Paris, Manchester and Berlin acting as sites for international conference meetings in the early part of the twentieth century. This locus was due in part to Europe's colonial power in Africa and the Caribbean. As the post-Second World War settlement shifted power westwards, it would appear to have also pulled with it the focus of efforts to define and resist racism.

It is perhaps unsurprising that attempts at building solidarity across national boundaries should become prey to the homogenizing effects of global capitalism that have sought to make the local generic. As Paul Gilroy notes, 'there is a much greater reliance upon what I call generic racial identity. It's often created from the fantasy version of African-American culture that's been exported to the rest of the world. That Blackness derives in large measure from the dream worlds of global consumer capitalism.' If Gilroy is right in identifying a pattern in which racisms, while experienced and resisted locally, operate through the prism of a 'fantasy version' of American Blackness, this could begin to explain why the warp and weft of US movements for racial justice are more attractive and compelling in their call to action than the counter-hegemonic action of building solidarities within national or supranational polities like the EU.

*　*　*

I grew up in London, in a period when it became so much easier to be internationally mobile. The 1990s revolution in budget flights, leading to a shift in holiday habits from the annual two-week vacation abroad to several overseas weekend breaks a year, has democratized travel. The weakening of ties to the Caribbean islands of my parents' birth became inevitable as time passed, families grew and memories faded. The long-haul flight to Grenada has become less relevant as well as less regular. It has also meant that I'm more likely in coming years to visit Berlin, Lisbon, Krakow and Marseille than Hull, Dundee, Sunderland or Padstow.

I can now seek out 'people like me' across continents and distance myself further from those I don't like, don't know or don't understand. With the additional benefits of new media technologies I can more easily identify and locate my ideological or cultural affinity group. Recently, Facebook has helpfully revised downwards from 6 to 3.57 the degrees of separation between me and the rest of the planet. In this brave new world, where geography matters both less and more, there has been a stirring in the building of cross-border ethnic solidarities but not a revolution on a similar scale to these changing travel patterns. Despite the traditions of Black travel writing represented in the emancipation narratives of Olaudah Equiano, the twentieth-century political writings of Zora Neale Hurston, Richard Wright, James Baldwin and Maya Angelou, or the more contemporary travel-infused fiction of Caryl Phillips, Ekow Eshun and Chimamanda Ngozi Adichie, there does not appear to be a considerable growth in writing about the African diaspora in general and in relation to Europe in particular. While there has been an increase in the sharing of travel experiences by people of African descent, indicated by the 'Travelling While Black' hashtag and the Black Travel Movement, a growing band of travel agents and social networks that celebrate and promote travel by people of colour, this is yet to translate into significantly greater cross-border connections and links being built between people from the African diaspora. This anomaly seems to be even more glaring when we consider the existence of the shared polity of an EU that had provided a rationale for people to come together in common cause – even if that cause is no more than working together against racism.

Perhaps this anomaly tells us something about the limitations and challenges of the ideal of an EU and highlights a central problem for those in the UK who were arguing to remain a part of it in the referendum campaign. The EU that Britain is in the process of leaving is a union of institutions rather than a union of people. The remainers, compelled to argue for a too-distant parliament, a pork-barrelled council of ministers and big business trade deals, struggled to present a hearts and minds argument about the benefits of cooperation between people. By comparison, the leavers were able to paint a picture of individuals back in control, decisions made closer to the people and the building of new solidarities between people beyond the seemingly arbitrary borders of Europe.

The struggle against racism in Europe for people of African descent is inspired by the US because we think we understand African-Americans as people. People of African descent in Europe negotiated the failure of European broadcast media to reflect our existence by immersing ourselves in American media and pop culture. As the Dutch writer Giselle Defares notes (on the US-based *Huffington Post* blog): 'The black experience isn't just the black American experience. But, through the consumption of black American culture, I was able to figure out what being black in Europe meant to me.'

Despite geographical proximity, shared political institutions, increasing ease of locating those we share an affinity with and greater ease of physical travel, a strong pan-European African diaspora has failed to emerge. Perhaps this is because we don't know each other. This lack of knowledge was unlikely to go unchallenged forever. In a world where there are fewer costs of entry and exit to creating our own media, there are green shoots of activity that are beginning to address this gap. Earlier this year, working with the Bruno Kreisky Forum, I had the privilege of bringing together a small group of younger activists, bloggers and artists who are working on building new forms of belonging and connection among people of African descent across Europe. Activists who have sought cross-European support to raise the profile of local struggles against racism and in favour of the development of European-African identities. Our discussions were incredibly rich and enlightening, encompassing responses to the Zwarte Piet (Black Peter) debates that have been part of the challenge to the racialized undercurrents of Dutch identities, or the French boycott of the iconic Guerlain perfume brand in response to racist comments by their CEO and the emergence of the Afro-Swedes as a strong political voice in Swedish politics. Typical of political movements among millennial generations, these activists were developing narratives about the relationship between the personal and political and were highly focused on the use of new media technologies and the arts as a space to organize: from Afropean.com organizing a festival of 'Afropean Narratives 1600–2066' at London's Victoria and Albert Museum, to Ezibota creating a media platform for diasporan Africans led by an editorial team based in Norway, the UK, Canada and Ghana, or the Strolling Series, using film as a means of 'Connecting the scattered and untold stories of the Black/African diaspora'.

The European Network Against Racism has worked over the past five years to explore the particular ways in which racisms impact on the lives, rights and well-being of people of African descent in Europe. This process of documenting racisms is a necessary one, but the work of the activists who are seeking to build belonging among people of African descent in Europe has highlighted the limitations of this approach and the potential for complementary activity beyond the lens of racism. The experience of Brexit should remind us that we can operate in silos, speaking only to those we agree with, leading us to believe we have built a consensus which turns out to be a mirage. Finding ways of connecting beyond these silos has become a more urgent task for those who want to engage in creating political change. As the British 'in' campaign discovered, too late, facts and figures can be easily trumped (used advisedly) by emotion. The approach of activists who are using the arts and understanding the potential of media technologies to engage our imaginations in the formation of 'imagined communities' seems to be a crucial step in the right direction. Understanding that it has been a key failure of the European project to move beyond institutions to people, then extending our activism to address racism beyond an institutional focus towards the trickier, more emotional and less predictable realm of movement-building would seem to follow. For a movement to be effective, at minimum, its members have to know each other.

＊　＊　＊

I grew up in London. I grew up in a city where I am a visible minority, but a city that has been shaped by the influence of mass migration of people of colour for 75 years. It was an experience of marginalization informed by a belief in the possibility of influencing change. In that context the instinct to reach out to others, to offer support and solidarity, was manifested in a simple nod of the head. That head nod is, however, just a first step in seeking to disrupt an imposed ideal of colour-blind liberalism in favour of a pluralist, collective challenge to an unequal status quo. In seeking to continue and to grow that disruption new opportunities presented by travel and media technology have created routes for me to get to know other Europeans of African descent. To nod towards them in a way that offers reciprocal support and solidarity. The decision of my compatriots that the UK will leave the EU has perversely made me even more determined to explore my Europeanness as a relationship between people rather than institutions. I choose Europe because despite its many detractors in the UK, there is a greater chance of being able to shape, influence and be influenced by the discussion among fellow Black Europeans than to intervene in the exceptional American story. An initial step in a journey towards creating a sense of belonging in Europe among people of African descent is to get to know each other, to tell each other our stories, hopes and dreams, so that we can build an authentic movement that leads to uplift for us all. It starts with a nearly imperceptible nod of the head, but has the potential to create the kind of solidarity that can move mountains.

Bibliography

Alexander, Michelle, *The New Jim Crow: Mass Incarceration in the Age of Colorblindness*, New York, The New Press, 2012.

Defares, Giselle, 'I grew up in Europe, but found my Blackness in African-American culture', *Huffington Post* blog, 9 August 2016, www.huffingtonpost.com/entry/i-grew-up-in-europe-but-found-my-blackness-in-african-american-culture_us_57aa0315e4b024b403af24b7.

Gilroy, Paul, *Postcolonial Melancholia*, New York, Columbia University Press, 2006.

Khan, Omar and Elahi, Farah, *Capital for All: Ethnic Inequalities in London*, London, Runnymede Trust, 2016.

Lusane, Clarence, 'Pan Africanism and the Black European moment', in *European Network Against Racism, Invisible Visible Minority – Confronting Afrophobia and Advancing Equality for People of African Descent and Black Europeans in Europe*, 2014, www.enar-eu.org.

Okwonga, Musa, 'The ungrateful country', in Nikesh Shukla, ed., *The Good Immigrant*, London, Unbound, 2016.

Phillips, Caryl, *The European Tribe*, London, Faber and Faber, 1987.

www.afropean.com

www.blacklivesmatter.com

www.mediadiversified.com

www.strollingseries.com

4

From the European Puzzle to a Puzzled Europe

Marion Demossier

Over the last three decades, notions of both belonging and identity have attracted a great deal of interest and generated intense debates in the public sphere as well as in academic circles. Individuals and groups increasingly take for granted new public claims and expressions of belonging, even to the extent of committing appalling acts in their name, while the new social media have witnessed a rise in hate speech, sometimes disguised as exercising free speech. Such actions have taken place against the background of the proliferation of new forms of media, which have permitted the banalization of the violence we see from the comfort of our living rooms. As illustrated by the tragic attack on the French satirical magazine *Charlie Hebdo* on 7 January 2015, or more recently the terrorist massacre in Paris on 13 November 2015, claims of belonging and not belonging, inclusion and exclusion, have assumed a new transnational dimension. In France itself, these terrorist outrages have obscured broader issues of inequality, power and rights in the context of a country where seemingly perennial ideas of *liberté, égalité, fraternité* are both deeply entrenched and divisive, but have never been fully translated into the social and political realm. Moreover, the global nature of the *mise en scène* of these extreme forms of belonging has heightened our sense that ever more violent and disturbing crises are constantly flickering across our screens. To understand this current situation, the anthropologist Thomas Eriksen uses the term schimogenesis developed by another anthropologist Gregory Bateson: today's intercultural encounters, he writes, are 'self-reinforcing, spiralling conflicts'. The recent Brexit debate in the UK is another form of this phenomenon.

These global events have taken place against the current state of crisis facing the European Union and the rise of neo-nationalism in different configurations. An increasingly polarized world seems to have emerged, shaped by a new geopolitics of borders and a discourse of humanitarian versus xenophobic values. The EU occupies centre stage between these ideological poles and has to face a growing period of uncertainty. The recent Greek economic and financial crisis has fuelled some of the debates at the heart of the process of European integration, questioning the *raison d'être* of the project as well as the values for which member states stand in a collective endeavour to propose a pan-European vision of the world. The latest ingredient in this reconfiguration of our world is the incapacity to manage the Syrian refugee crisis and the abandonment of both human rights and collective thinking in the face of vast movements of people, against the background of extremism and terrorism.

Perhaps more than ever, a more cultural and historical perspective is needed. In a recent radio programme on BBC Radio 4, the historian Sir Ian Kershaw, best known for his work on twentieth-century Germany, was asked to compare the displacements of the first half of the twentieth century to our contemporary 'refugee' crisis. He argued that the current situation is nothing compared to the major upheavals of the First and Second World Wars and that one of the major historical differences is due to the role of the EU which, despite its flaws and limitations, remains a major actor in the ongoing management of the crisis beyond the nation state.

Our contemporary world is punctuated by these sudden crises with the terrible image of Alan Kurdi, the young Syrian boy washed up dead on a beach in Turkey, provoking global outrage. Such images of humanity and the accompanying words and discourses present different facets of our new virtual, violent and banal modernity and illustrate how belonging regains part of its salience. It is in this new context that I would like to reflect on the idea of European identity as something changing, negotiated and fundamentally political, which is currently buffeted by a phase of crisis and possibly renewal, but seems at the same time to be trapped in a neoliberal, bureaucratic and remote view of the world. European integration was inspired, in part, by an alternative vision of the role of the nation state, its borders, sovereignty and underlying definitions of belonging. But this vision is now threatened by the refugee crisis and terrorism. As a reality, it has become messy, paradoxical and limited by the nature of its political and deterritorialized form. Yet the history of the nation state in the first half of the twentieth century convinces us that it is better to live in a world *with* the EU rather than in one *without* it. This is my own understanding of the tragic legacy of the last century.

In this essay I aim to question the meanings attached to 'belonging' today for European citizens in the twenty-first century. By using my own journey, from Burgundy to the UK, through adulthood and maturity, I seek to unpack more clearly what belonging entails and how belonging needs to be conceptualized and refined further in the light of people's experience. Anthropologists Thomas Wilson and Irène Bellier have argued, in *An Anthropology of the European Union*, that one of the problems facing the continent is that the building of institutional Europe and top-down efforts to get Europeans to imagine their common identity have not resulted in political and cultural unity. Belonging to Europe in this context presents other challenges as the EU remains a strange political object and is now the target of growing criticism and hostility.

There is no doubt that the idea of belonging is central to these questions. Following the social anthropologist Joanna Pfaff-Czarnecka when she differentiates 'belonging with' from 'belonging to', I define belonging as created by individuals in their negotiating of constellations – distinct forms of social, political, cultural, religious, friendship, interest etc. groups to which people are variously attached or are obliged to encounter – and how they navigate through the diverse constellations of belonging encountered in their lifetime. By constellation of belongings I mean the ways in which empirical descriptions of attachments facilitate the unfolding of the underlying structure behind the formation of groups in the public, social or political spheres. Moreover, belongings cover different forms of expression from political or collective actions to feelings and emotions, discursive narrations and boundary drawing. I will argue that European integration has created a multi-layered and complex space of differentiated narratives which have triggered new lines of division around the question of who does or does not belong, at both national and supranational levels. There is, on the one hand, the reification of national boundaries which takes different forms and is context-bound, while, on the other hand, there is a dilution of those national contrasts in the face of globalization. To some extent, globalization has offered the possibility of not belonging, but also that of expressing a strong sense of being part of something else. This essay asks if the nature of our political democracies, the crisis of politics and the rise of global capitalism have widened the gap between citizens and their political systems. Moreover, it discusses new forms of political engagement and resistance as possible platforms for fostering a new interpretation of what it means to belong in contemporary Europe. A new post-democratic order is yet to emerge as new forms of communication and encountering have emerged.

Anthropologists and Belonging

My sense of identity has always been shaped by my refusal to belong and the ease with which anthropology has enabled me constantly to question boundaries, belongings and identification. I must confess that the question of belonging characterized my personal quest for what we could define as 'feeling at home', or in other words, 'being happy'. Throughout my life I have felt uneasy about my own social positioning as anthropologists prefer to be in between, becoming rather than being. I have always loved sitting on the other side of the fence and making sense of people. Yet I have also been fascinated by extreme and less extreme forms of belonging and, partly because of my upbringing, have always been attracted and interested by those who feel part of a collective, expressed their strong attachment to a group and performed their allegiance to the community to which they belong. As an anthropologist, it is no accident that I have devoted three decades to the study of identity and to the concept of *terroir*, which I define in my 2012 essay 'The Europeanization of *terroir*' as the European idea of a connection between locality and quality, in an era that is often described as intensively globalized.

Yet belonging and identity are often used interchangeably, leading to vagueness, confusion, lack of analytical acuity and hasty statements. Over the last three decades, I have been involved in the teaching of two concepts – identity and culture – to students of European politics, language and society, constantly questioning their sense of belonging and their identification with specific values and ideologies. Yet my students often had difficulties in explaining what identity means as a practice and as a discourse. These students – mostly international, but also British ones – have often shed light on my questions and have, in turn, started the process of questioning what those claims of belonging entail and signify in a context of globalization and the rise of individualism. Potentially polemical and often ideologically charged, the terms belonging and identity, despite their limitations, offer a platform to question further the meanings attached to 'belonging' for European citizens in the twenty-first century.

The idea that culture and consequently people are naturally rooted in particular places has long been questioned in theoretical anthropology. Recent debates have focused both on the theories of what it means to be human in a particular location as well as the methodological underpinning of the study of 'cultures' seen as increasingly separated from space. While most of the anthropological literature has focused on exacerbating the production of local differences or representing space as a place of break, rupture and disjunction, emphasis has been placed upon the isomorphism of space, place and culture, or on the role of specific individuals in guaranteeing the permanence of the fit. The erosion of the 'natural' connection between place and culture has undeniably taken centre stage in most analyses, leading us to think of a globalized world as a culture without space. Yet rather than being mutually exclusive, the local and the global feed upon and reinforce each other, and the production of locality relies on imagination mediated by local agency, but articulated differently by individuals depending on their social positioning at local and global levels. Issues of belonging and identity have therefore acquired a new salience in the context in which they are formulated, which has radically altered our theoretical approaches to both concepts. Jean-Luc Nancy argues that we need to move beyond the failure of identity politics and consider how we can still speak about 'we' without transforming it into a substantial and exclusive identity.

For anthropologists, belonging refers both to notions of being and self in a specific context or location, but also to the active process of becoming part of, or engaging with, the world we live in and people we share life with. In this context, they are interested in understanding how these notions can be studied empirically rather than asking, like the sociologists, if identity politics is the best way forward. Like other difficult-to-capture analytical categories, it is worth defining it through an ethnographic window, which, as Matei Candea has convincingly argued, provides an 'arbitrary location' or methodological instrument for deferring closure and challenging totality: a window into complexity. As part of our contemporary expressions of forms of being human, belonging has come to encapsulate paradoxically both the self and its negotiation with the social environment in which it is defined, expressed or acted upon, and more broadly the political structures in which those forms take shape or are creatively and subversively expressed. Pfaff-Czarnecka speaks of the quest to 'uncover the multiple, subtle and shifting modalities of forging and thinking the collective dimensions of the social life and the dynamic nature of social boundary-making'. Using the framework proposed by Rogers Brubaker and Frederick Cooper when writing their 2000 paper 'Beyond "identity"', Pfaff-Czarnecka goes further by suggesting that belonging offers a greater analytical refinement, which can be defined as an emotionally charged social location combining perceptions and performances of commonality, a sense of mutuality and more or less formalized modalities of collective allegiance, and material and immaterial attachments that often result in a sense of entitlement. If this framework facilitates our analysis of belonging, it does not however question the postmodern character of the self, which characterizes our forms of social being, nor the new spaces in which they are expressed. What has become highly problematic in my eyes is the decline of traditional forms of togetherness, or *communitas* and *Gemeinschaft*, and the evanescent expressions of our modernity. Belonging today entails an ongoing process of locating ourselves somewhere comfortably between different, unstable, ever-changing and disjointed worlds. Time, space and the quest for self are the essence of this process of constant relocation.

Ambiguities of Belonging

For me, this process has been very real. I wrote above about my ambiguous attitude to belonging. Some additional personal history might further clarify the matter.

I was born in the 1960s in Burgundy, but until recently never experienced or witnessed salient forms of French belonging. I moved to the UK in the 1990s as a PhD student ready for a new adventure and embraced a language for which I did not have particular talent as German was my first love. I am an anthropologist by passion and academic training and I have now lived as long in the UK as I have in France, my birthplace. Yet I remain 'French' for the British, mainly due to my strong accent, and 'in exile' for the French. What characterized my journey as an individual is my lack of a sense of belonging and my curiosity for observing others in their individual and collective engagement with commonality, mutuality, allegiance and attachments. This is not new to me and it could be explained by the fact that both of my parents came from different social groups and had radically different origins. On my father's side we have been rooted in the Auvergne, belonging to a noble lineage of both Protestants and Catholics with a number of intermarriages between the same families that can be traced back to the sixteenth century, both before and after we lost our fiefs. I recently discovered that we had a tradition of service as king's musketeers on my father's side, a discovery which has helped me to understand better my political being. On my mother's side an alliance between a lineage of small entrepreneurs and a successful jewellery maker who migrated to Burgundy from Switzerland in 1922 makes the quest for family origins less romantic. Both genealogies came together in Burgundy, the land of history, tradition, heritage and *terroir* where belonging is defined by 'having three graves in the cemetery'. Three generations later my family is still not locally rooted and a strange feeling of 'not being part of' characterizes my relationship to this locality that later became the object of my ethnographic gaze for three decades.

In the light of this background I would like to return to specific events I mentioned in my opening paragraph, which have been relentlessly replayed and performed in the media. From an anthropological perspective, the analysis of belonging can be conducted through a wide range of ethnographic windows focusing on what could be defined as 'crises of our times', condensing clashes and frictions between different views of the world that are likely to become historicized or narrated for future generations. Discussing the *Charlie Hebdo* attack, the Greek Eurozone crisis, the Paris massacre of 13 November and the Brexit crisis provide windows on to the construction, expression and negotiation of new forms of belonging of all kinds, which I would like to interrogate from an anthropological perspective. Moreover, their deployment in the public sphere and on television have had a direct impact on how my own sense of belonging has been questioned and purposively directed towards a form of auto-ethnography as discussed in this essay.

On 7 January 2015, while working from home on a new book on *terroir*, I stopped to listen to the radio announcing the Paris attack and found myself obsessed by the unfolding of what was being described by BBC Radio 4 as a terrorist attack on *Charlie Hebdo*. As a French person, I had long been accustomed to seeing cartoons and covers of *Charlie Hebdo* and I also regularly read the *Canard Enchaîné* to which the murdered cartoonists also contributed.

My first memory of *Charlie Hebdo* as a violently satirical magazine, and not necessarily a pleasant one, goes back to a horrific bus crash on the motorway near my home town of Beaune in which more than 50 schoolchildren perished when the vehicle caught fire. The accident was caricatured on the front cover of *Charlie Hebdo* by a giant barbecue. This recollection immediately came back to me while I listened to the events unfold and later came to encapsulate my uneasiness and paradoxical discomfort as the story and the debates provoked by the killing developed. And when the attack then became the object of constant analysis both in France and in the UK, I came to realize how distant, and at the same time emotionally engaged I was in relation to France and its republican ideology.

The diverse comments on the attack posted on Facebook left me perplexed in the face of a rise of what I would regard as inappropriate, sometimes violent nationalistic sentiments and emotional outbursts. Freedom of speech was presented by some of my Facebook friends as a way of 'defending France against the enemy', but I remained unconvinced about my attachment or belonging to such an ideological posture, especially because of the ways in which freedom of speech was defined in their eyes. I had lived long enough in the UK to appreciate the benefits of respect and of not being gratuitously offensive. These values are central to the well-being of a society, especially at a time of major upheavals and transition.

Throughout the attack and the subsequent intellectual, political and public debates, Frenchness became vividly articulated on the global stage through the use of the flag or strong political statements. In his March 2015 *Anthropology Today* article 'In the name of the Republic', Didier Fassin refers to this political mobilization as shedding new light on the debate. What was striking in the aftermath of these tragic crimes was both the process of ethnic categorization, essentialism and reification which portrayed the protagonists in different locations and on different sides of the spectrum according to the republican grid of analysis – that of republicanism and *laïcité* – while ignoring the global historical and geopolitical context. The underlying political structure of inequality, which has characterized French post-war society and more generally the global world in which we live today, became less visible to commentators. Abdelmajid Hannoum engaged critically with Fassin's analysis in October in the same journal, arguing that the lack of equality and fraternity he observes is not due to religious, political or historical reasons, but to the permanence of the Christian legacy in the supposedly secular state, which has constructed Muslims in France as the 'other'. This internal other, Hannoum argues, constitutes itself as an inaudible, yet expressive, counter-public, which he calls a 'sub-public', 'composed of those who know that they cannot afford to express what they think out loud lest they be reproved, rejected or even punished'. Hannoum's analysis demonstrates how notions of belonging form part of a politics of identity in which political and institutional structures, the public space, but also the media, converge in creating spaces in which expressions of marginalization, violence and extreme despair are usually silenced. In the context of France, Hannoum speaks of a sub-public as a space of discourse for those who whisper their disagreements and endure verbal violence from the majority. For the anthropologist, the sub-public 'is located in the zone of "no rights" of expression in a society that had defined itself as a society of those rights exercised often against the zone of sub-public'. The terrorists belong to these marginalized groups who have always been relegated to a 'no rights' zone. Power is thus always constitutive of expression, and power and the sub-public together form the backdrop of any forms of identity discourse, but also more deeply of any forms of mobilization, be they extremist or not.

For a French citizen, French republicanism and the values it encapsulates is the framework through which belonging is framed and, I would even argue, coercively imposed. Claiming that you do not feel French is an insult to Frenchness and the same applies to a lesser extent to being a republican. Most of the debates which have surrounded Muslims in France have been constructed in such a fashion that they leave little space for a more creative and modern understanding of what it means to live together. As Hannoum argued, the republic is rarely questioned, nor is *laïcité* in the context of an increasingly globalized world. Yet it is a matter of ongoing debate. In France, the republican model has its detractors and its supporters, and both camps are furnished, as such camps often are, with a mix of arguments: the reasonable, the well informed and the crudely simplistic. One of my fellow French anthropologists recently argued in favour of the ban on the veil introduced by President Sarkozy in 2010 on the grounds that it was necessary for Muslims to become French. When I consider my own belief in those values of Frenchness I have a long list of questions about their validity. What does being French mean in today's world? Belonging is about negotiating where you feel more at home and on which values your social and political being relies. Yet these questions take different forms depending on where you were born and what you have experienced in your life, and in which context you articulate them. Post-war Western societies had the luxury of debating such questions, while most of the rest of the world suffered from war, hunger, disease and economic upheaval. In the wake of the refugee crisis, belonging has acquired a new resonance and has become, for some, a matter of economic and human survival, which would be best served by a transnational approach. Yet the EU seems almost largely overwhelmed and overtaken by events.

Europe: Identification and Engagement

Another key event has also recently played an important part in the ways in which public debate about the European story of belonging has become increasingly ambiguous and full of paradoxes. The Greek Eurozone crisis has heightened our sense of belonging to different national and often obsolete political structures and ideologies while imposing a new economic understanding of the world we live in. Austerity is the backdrop against which European economies have been functioning, but it has also become a common feature of how European citizens experience the twenty-first century and navigate through economic crises, pension reforms and fast capitalism. So far the story of European integration has been perceived as an economic enterprise that was supposed to convince European citizens of the *bien fondé* of the common taxation system imposed on EU members. To begin with, the European social project was associated with the project of European integration, but the Eurozone has paradoxically transformed the rules of the game by imposing a new restrictive economic framework on community members that was particularly challenging for the Southern European economies, which were encouraged to join the euro despite doubts about its compatibility with their economic and political structures. Economic integration through the adoption of a common currency was fast, short-sighted and divisive, and its longer term impact is still unclear. If the European integration project was imbued with specific collective values at its inception, it has also created strongly differentiated pathways to prosperity and growth. The anthropologist Cris Shore describes the euro as the symbol of cleavages and tensions that most divide Europeans.

The Greek euro crisis which started in 2009 and unfolded with the government debt crisis and the series of negotiations between the European Central Bank, the International Monetary Fund and the Eurogroup, and led to the political turmoil of the Greek referendum of 5 July 2015, exemplifies how polarizing the European project has become. Starting as a story of unity in diversity, European integration rapidly became a story of economic rationality, planning and compliance with Eurogroup rules. This was first and foremost a way for the Eurogroup to impose a certain reading of the debt crisis and create by the same token the category of the 'bad student' of European economic integration. As the crisis was played out day after day through the media and social networks it rapidly became global. The charismatic and unusual role played by the former Greek finance minister, Yanis Varoufakis, added a new dimension to the drama as it became a political game in which the Greeks lost the battle even before making their first move. The game was characterized by distrust, political upheaval and economic arm-twisting. Yet despite the measures Greece implemented and the deep recession affecting its economy, the system survived and the Greeks demonstrated both a strong reliance on old forms of collectivism and a desire to remain in the euro.

The crisis illustrated the strong political nature of the commitment towards the European project especially among the founding member states, but also the lack of a real 'Europolitics' which would facilitate a common endeavour to confront globalization. Yet as several commentators have pointed out, the Greek saga, as reflected in and partly orchestrated by the old and new media, has created a new platform of contestation for European citizens. Greece has been presented both as the 'bad student' of European integration, saddled with a corrupt and archaic political system still based upon clientelism and elitism, and led by a wealthy oligarchy, but also as demonstrating a strong, resilient societal model based upon collective values, solidarity and *communitas*, which has left the rest of Europe intrigued. As a result, it has opened the door to a less monolithic and capitalistic view of the European project, which permits more differentiated readings of and engagements in its future direction.

Belonging to Europe has therefore become increasingly problematic for the proponents of the original European project. As Europeans, whether we embrace the term positively or not, we occupy centre stage of an increasing polarization, which is economic, political and social and questions the nature and vision of what the European project encapsulates. The *Trente Glorieuses* of French social and economic progress (1945–75), which were the background to my childhood, are distant memories for my children who experience economic uncertainties, terrorism and the expression of difference as the ingredients of their modernity. The economic condition of this modernity has been the development of a wider gap between the world's wealthy and the rest of humanity, with some social groups living on the fringes of society as they struggle to come to terms with post-colonial legacies and the construction of their otherness in public debates. We know that the gap is about the nature of our political economies and the commitment to a fair society, but it demands much deeper investigation.

A reformulated European political project that addresses the interconnected issues discussed above can only emerge if true transnational cooperation and governance are at its heart. Such a movement needs to offer greater equality and more opportunities to young people across the member states. It needs to reach a consensus on the principles on which its model of economic integration should be based, be able to recognize its mistakes and undo them, but also propose a differentiated reading of the European project that provides its proponents with a more diverse range of engagements and a more democratic political platform. And it's no accident that the issues of inequality and economic solidarity link the many thousands of refugees and the social classes who are left behind in the new economic order.

We Must Refashion Our Thinking

One of the paradoxes of our time is the upsurge of strong preoccupations with belonging, particularly in Europe, in a world that is said to be globalizing. More than ever, a new anthropological project is needed to contribute to the debate on belonging. The task is to refashion our thinking in order to adapt to a deterritorialized, decentralized and deregulated universe where social, religious, cultural and political life construct and deconstruct themselves and the borders between them in novel ways that perhaps lie beyond the grasp of the anthropological tradition. Reflecting on the Paris massacre and the Syrian refugee crisis, the anthropologist Thomas Erikson argued that the world has evolved into a multi-layered set of divisions and points of tension, from the regional asymmetries between the northern and southern coasts of the Mediterranean, the varying value of human lives depending on where you live and who you are, and orchestrated through the global hierarchy of values, and the double polarization in Western Europe: 'The first is the symbolic competition between Islamists and nativists, the second the conflict between identity politics and secular politics.' This has occurred against a backdrop of deterritorialization and globalization: 'In the present age, nothing can be contained geographically.' Yet our tools of analysis remain sketchy and ineffective in solving the crises and in embracing the analytical challenge of transnationalism. To state the obvious, the more globalized we become, the less likely we are to understand our differences. Yet those differences are articulated more violently when the economic, political and social reality fractures and inequality becomes glaringly obvious. The Bataclan attacks illustrate the blurring of traditional identity markers and the growing gap between young people in today's world: homegrown jihadists target educated, liberal and open-minded youth, who have demonstrated their resilience by singing the *Marsellaise* and waving the flag. As William Connelly has stated: 'There is more in my life than any official definition of identity can express. I am not exhausted by my identity.' This more or less sums up my feelings about belonging.

Bibliography

Appadurai, Arjun, *Modernity at Large: Cultural Dimensions of Globalization*, Minneapolis, University of Minnesota Press, 1996.

Bateson, Gregory, *Steps to an Ecology of Mind*, Chicago, University of Chicago Press, 1972.

Brubaker, Rogers and Cooper, Frederick, 'Beyond "identity"', *Theory and Society*, vol. 29, 2000.

Candea, Matei, 'Anthropology of cross-channel debates: a response to Fassin (AT22[1]) and Bazin et al (AT22[2])', *Anthropology Today*, vol. 22, no. 4, 2006.

Connelly, William, *Identity/Difference: Democratic Negotiations of Political Paradox*, Minnesota, University of Minnesota Press, 2002.

Demossier, Marion, 'The Europeanization of *terroir*: consuming place, tradition and authenticity', in Rebecca Friedman and Markus Thiel, eds, *European Identity and Culture: Narratives of Transnational Belonging*, Farnham, Ashgate, 2012.

Eriksen, Thomas, 'The Paris massacre and the Syrian refugee crisis', http://thomashyllanderiksen.net/2015/11/14/the-paris-massacre-and-the-syrian-refugee-crisis/.

Fassin, Diddier, 'In the name of the Republic: untimely meditations on the aftermath of the *Charlie Hebdo* attack', *Anthropology Today*, vol. 31, no. 2, 2015.

Geschiere, Peter, 'Autochthony, citizenship and exclusion: paradoxes in the politics of belonging in Africa and Europe', *Indiana Journal of Global Legal Studies*, vol. 18, no. 1, 2011.

Gupta, Akhil and Ferguson, James, *Culture, Power, Place: Explorations in Critical Anthropology*, Durham, NC, Duke University Press, 2002.

Hannoum, Abdelmajid, 'Cartoons, secularism, and inequality', *Anthropology Today*, vol. 31, no. 5, 2015.

Mukherjee, S. Romi, 'Fragments and fissures: towards a political anthropology of the global', *International Social Science Journal*, vol. 61, no. 202, 2010.

Nancy, Jean-Luc, *Being Singular Plural*, Stanford, Stanford University Press, 2000.

Olwig, Karen Fog, and Hastrup, Kirsten, eds, *Siting Culture: The Shifting Anthropological Object*, London, Routledge, 1997.

Pfaff-Czarnecka, Joanna, 'From "identity" to "belonging" in social research: plurality, social boundaries, and the politics of the self', *Working Paper* no. 368, Bielefeld, www.uni-bielefeld.de/(de)/tdrc/ag_sozanth/publications/working_papers/WP368.pdf.

Shore, Cris, 'The euro crisis and European citizenship: the euro 2001–2012 – celebration or commemoration?', *Anthropology Today*, vol. 28, no. 2, 2012.

Wilson, Thomas M. and Bellier, Irène, *An Anthropology of the European Union: Building, Imagining and Experiencing the New Europe*, Oxford, Berg, 2000.

5

The Bird's Religion

Şeyda Emek

November was always a sad month, cold and grey. She had never liked it. She halted her brisk walk at the horseshoe-shaped, three-storey housing block. It was a typical 1930s workers' housing complex with a wide lawn in the inner courtyard and iron frames for hanging washing out to dry, grey and arranged symmetrically next to tall, old trees. Everything was carefully designed to be functional. It was in one of those districts where elderly war widows still bolted to the cellar with their bank documents whenever there was thunder. A district where the smell of boiled potatoes being cooked for lunch drifted down the hallways at 11.30, and rules were fastidiously observed. In short, where proper German orderliness still held sway.

As she crossed the courtyard, the frozen grass crunched under her feet. She walked purposefully up to the tall, slender tree with the black trunk growing in the middle of the courtyard, and looked around searchingly until they appeared in the distance.

*   *   *

They were buzzing about like bees on the grass between the old trees. The two girls, aged ten and eleven, were using broken branches to sweep out the houses they had made from thick, crooked tree roots covered with shrubbery. The singing of the younger girl, high and clear as a bell, was carried away in the sunshine that was reflected like highlights in her chestnut hair.

The boy, by contrast, wandered aimlessly, sometimes lingering by a tree trunk, sometimes looking at the buds on a branch. He was four years old, slight and finely drawn. Suddenly, he cried out, pointing to the ground beneath a black-trunked tree. Alarmed, the girls ran to him. As they neared, they saw a bird with crushed black feathers lying motionless on the ground. It must have fallen from the tree. As the bird lay face down, its beak and eyes could not be seen. Nimbly, the smaller one took a small stick and turned the bird over while the boy whimpered fearfully. Now its eyes were visible. They stared motionless, fixedly. The bird was dead. The boy's whimpers became sobs. The little one's crying joined his.

Until then, she had simply stood there, watching. Now she bestirred herself. She spoke calmly and firmly to the two younger ones. The bird was dead. There was nothing they could do.

'But we can't simply leave it lying here! We have to bury it!', the smaller one cried reproachfully.

Nodding slowly, she agreed: 'All right. We'll bury it.'

Once again they buzzed about. The two girls searched for small sticks they could use to dig up the ground. The boy produced a small, white shoe-box in which he kept his toy cars. Then they began to dig. After only a few minutes, it was clear that they could not possibly dig a hole big enough to bury the bird in the shoe-box. The earth was too hard. They were forced to abandon the idea of a coffin, even though the younger girl vehemently objected: 'The bird has to be buried properly!' In the end they dug a hole big enough to partly hold the bird. They carefully lowered it into the grave and covered it with earth.

As they stared silently at the grave, the boy made two sticks into a cross and placed it on the earth. Instantly, loudly, the smaller girl protested. Quick as lightning she knocked the cross off the grave: 'Are you mad? What's that for? Crosses are for Christians!'

It was clear from his startled look that he did not understand. He went to a kindergarten next to a Lutheran Church. On the graves in the church cemetery were crosses. They did not know of any other graves. And they had never been to a funeral.

Now the words tumbled even faster from the younger girl's mouth. 'Auntie said we should never forget we're Muslims! Crosses are for heathens!' She did not know there was a difference between Christians and heathens. The little one was simply repeating what she had heard from her aunt, who did not distinguish between the two.

Not that anyone else was careful about such affiliations either. On the first day of school, for example, when the new teacher asked her how to pronounce her name, and tell her date of birth so it could be entered in the register, there was always that knowing nod, followed by 'And your religion, Islam'. To the teachers, it was self-evident. She didn't have to say anything herself. Only for the others did the teachers pause when entering their religion, waiting to hear whether the response was 'Lutheran', 'Roman Catholic' or 'none'.

The smaller girl eyed her reproachfully for so far being silent. Now she intervened. 'But he has no idea! He's still much too little.' Then she fell silent again. She knew why the younger one had exploded. She was no less frightened herself, even if she did not show it. They had angered Him once before. And His punishment had been dreadful.

They did not know then how they had so enraged Him. Was their banishment a punishment for being naughty on numerous occasions, or for doing something particularly bad. The only thing she knew was that it had hurt a lot. They could not anger Allah yet again. Next time He would surely show no mercy.

* * *

It had been the most brutal thing she experienced in her young life. The pain of her homesickness was like an unhealed wound that continuously reopened, causing severe internal bleeding. Night after night, while the others were sleeping, the pulsating lesion kept her awake. The longing coursed through her body, like thick, oozing blood. It always began with the soft sound of her mother's voice in her ear. First gently, then more urgently, her mother called her name, with a tenderness only she could express. The more often her mother called, the stronger the longing coursed. Hot, robbing her of breath, it rose up, forming a hard lump in her throat. At some point it became so unbearable, so constricted her breathing, that she could no longer hold back tears. The more she cried, the more fervid her longing became. She missed her home intensely, her mother, her father, everything.

She cried herself to sleep under the bedcovers, exhausted from the tears. She cried softly because she knew that crying of homesickness showed gross ingratitude. Her grandmother made this absolutely clear to her the first few times it happened.

'*What* a punishment of Allah!', grandmother exclaimed. 'Day after day I do my best for these crazy brats and then this. As if I had chosen this fate for my twilight years. Allah will teach you how to behave towards your grandmother!'

After that she kept quiet. Since they had arrived in the tiny village, with its flat-roofed mud houses, she was silent most of the time. The burbling child in kindergarten with sparkling, chocolate-coloured eyes, whose dark curls the adults playfully liked to pull, now bore the weight of serious responsibility. At five years old she became responsible for the younger one. Their grandmother was too old. The little one was a tomboy, a bundle of energy.

They had scarcely known their grandmother before this, their cousin even less. He had started his first job as a teacher in the village and grandmother kept house for him, her oldest grandson. They lived with grandmother, their cousin and the other teachers, in the teachers' house. Small and square, with a red tiled roof. It was the only house not made of mud, Together with their grandmother and their cousin, they lived in the biggest room. The communal kitchen was always cold; only the bedrooms had stoves. They did not dare go to the toilet alone. Mice often darted through the cold corridor.

How it happened that the two of them no longer lived at home, she did not quite know. They must have argued again, she thought to herself after the initial shock. What else could explain it? Her parents must have had another row. But it was not in her presence, that was clear. She was always on guard against these rows, anxious that one of them might actually carry out the threat of leaving. Despite her vigilance, her ability to recognize any resentment in their tone or behaviour, this time she hadn't noticed it. Her father had simply taken them to his mother and returned home alone.

So there they were, with their grandmother, in this strange country, this strange place. Grandmother had taken them with her to the village, where everything was different from home. There weren't any playgrounds, or their favourite dolls. The cartoon characters on television spoke in shrill, high voices in the new language and often used words they did not understand. The other children frequently laughed at them and didn't believe what they told them about their home – for example, the matter of the other language.

The first time she told them that a different language was spoken in the place they came from, a big boy stood menacingly in front of her and ordered her to speak it. But what can one say on command? Nervously, she forced out 'Hello' and 'How are you?' Not convinced by her language skills, he drew close to her. Afraid, and because she truly was unable to think of anything to say, she failed to utter another word. Furiously, he seized her by the shoulders and hurled her to the ground. She found herself lying on the earth, the back of her head throbbing with pain. From then on she avoided the places where the big boys were. However, if she ran into them, her fate was sealed. 'Hey *Almancı*-girl! Lie to us again about how you can speak this heathen language!' This tormenting continued for so long that eventually she didn't say anything at all. In response to her silence they often ended by throwing her forcefully to the ground.

They knew nothing about this new way of life, neither the children's games nor their code of behaviour, nor the strict moral expectations of the adults. So they often played alone, in their own world, where, in their imagination, everything was the same as at home. To the other children they seemed very strange, scarcely mastering the language and even then only speaking it in an unpractised, adult way.

When the others let them play with them, often there was trouble. Once, the other children allowed them to come along to steal apricots. They all climbed a tree and even helped the two of them to clamber up. While the children were filling their pockets with fruit, the neighbour appeared. The other children all jumped down and ran away. Only the two remained crying in the tree because they did not know that they were doing anything wrong and had to make themselves scarce. The woman picked up their shoes, put them in the pockets of her long baggy trousers, fetched them down from the tree and complained to the adults about them.

Another time, when playing tag one evening on the flat roofs of the mud houses, she fell through a hole in the roof. Suddenly she was sitting on a haystack in a dark, dank stable, surrounded by the bright white eyes of animals. Rigid with terror, she screamed her head off, unsettling the animals further. The noisier the animals, the more they shifted uneasily to and fro, the more piercing her cries for help became. The women cooking on one of the roofs heard her. In panic, her grandmother, who was among them, reached down through the hole with a wooden cooking spoon. She gripped the spoon, and her grandmother and the other women pulled her out.

At some point grandmother conceded defeat. They were not her only grandchildren. But she had never before encountered children like them.

So they returned to their mother, who was now living with their other grandmother in the small town, in a small mud house. Here, at least, they were in a town. It had a small town centre with shops, horse-drawn carts, cars and cobbled and tarmacked streets. As in the village, girls in the town were forbidden to do many things. Boys could simply jump into the fire brigade's water tanks in the yard of the power station when they wanted to cool off. If someone caught them at it, they were merely reprimanded because swimming was not permitted. For girls, on the other hand, it was forbidden to show any uncovered flesh. It was a sin. If they did it, Allah would turn them to stone. Girls in the neighbourhood told them that.

Inevitably they were reminded of their favourite activity at home: in kindergarten in summer they were like mermaids, and it was impossible to get them out of the paddling pool, or the swimming pool. Just like their mother and the other women, they wore two-piece swimsuits – and they had never seen any of them turned to stone. But the other girls didn't believe this.

Because there was no swimming pool in the town, their mother placated them by filling a plastic canister with water and placing it on the flat mud roof of the outside toilet. It heated quickly in the scorching sun. And their mother would bring it down to the inner courtyard, pour it into a big tub, so that they could play while she was washing the dirty laundry in a bucket nearby.

Then came winter, with ice and snow. One icy day they set off, excited and proud, to travel to the capital city with their mother. The long bus trip was interrupted several times by soldiers with machine guns carrying out identity checks.

Covered with snow, the capital was cold and grey, making the old doctor in his white coat seem even warmer and friendlier. He sat with her for a long time at a child's white table in a bright, pleasant room full of toys. Encouraged by his kindly voice, she played numerous games with him and now and then they chatted.

Back in the small town, her cousin, a year older, who had just started school, looked down at her triumphantly. 'You're developing a childhood trauma', she said condescendingly. 'What's that?' she asked, alarmed. 'A trauma is when you talk loudly in your sleep at night and call to your father that you would like to go home, like you do. Hah! It wasn't just a trip. You went to the doctor. And he said that they have to be careful. You're developing a childhood trauma. But you are not falling behind, he tested you.'

How could it be that she spoke in her sleep and didn't know it? And the doctor? They hadn't even talked about that. Hadn't he just played with her? It was true that when they chatted, he asked her about her father and whether she missed him. She had told him about home and that everything was much nicer there, and how very much she missed it. But they had not talked about traumas. This was the first she had heard of it.

Her cousin seemed to have learned this from the adults who would occasionally talk when they thought they were unobserved. She heard her uncle talking loudly to her mother, saying that her parents should finally stop their stubbornness. The children were already quite ill and would eventually go insane, he had shouted, and then left the room with an angry red face. Her uncle. The most gentle soul imaginable.

How it came to be that her father indeed fetched them back, this too she did not know. It had been a beautiful summer's day. They had played with spent machine gun bullets that glittered in the sunshine. To impose the nightly curfew, the soldiers used to fire at the street corner when darkness fell. A bright green diesel-engined Ford roared up to the house. Hearing the familiar sound, she looked up and her heart almost stopped. It was him! He had come to take them home! And just as unexpectedly as they had come, all four of them got into the car and drove off. Home.

But home was no longer the home that she had known. They did not drive over the green iron bridge spanning the two rivers that kissed each other below. There was no still unworn pale green duffle coat, none of her dolls, no spacious apartment. The car stopped outside a strange house in an unfamiliar town. Their new two-room home contained nothing from her old home, not even the tiniest speck of dust. But much worse was to come. When their neighbour (an old pensioner in a white shirt, with thick, long legs enveloped in white shorts, seeming huge, with a face as red as a crab) looked down on her in the garden the first time and blared something in a friendly baritone voice, the inconceivable happened. Although he beamed kindly when he spoke, all she heard was a succession of unfamiliar sounds, mere gibberish that made no sense. It was as if he were speaking backwards. She was dumbfounded. Then she realized that he did not understand her either.

They said she had repressed the language. The words, the syllables, everything had been swallowed up by the trauma. To accelerate her recovery of the language, in addition to preschool, she began to go to an afterschool centre. And there she started exactly where the big boys in the small town with the mud house had left her: on her back on the floor. On the very first day, after the teacher introduced her, she was approached by a few of the children. But she could only look at them mutely. After a while one of the boys grabbed her. He flung her to the floor. From then on, being shoved aside or, when the adults weren't looking, sat upon and pummelled, again became routine. So, for her protection, she was often taken to the headmistress's office. There she would look at the most wonderful picture books, and time flew by. Often, the headmistress sat with her and taught her vocabulary. So she learned the language again in no time at all and conquered her silence.

*   *   *

All this went through her head as she stood by the bird's grave. 'If anything,' she said, 'the bird will be Christian, probably Lutheran. There are no Catholics here. It might be that he flew here from far away and that where he comes from, people are Catholic. But we don't know that.'

She knew from experience that she could only calm the younger girl and convince her if she could think about the problem logically and carefully, and offer her a plausible explanation. The younger one promptly snapped back: 'But we are Muslims! We can't simply bury the bird like Christians do!'

'Yes, we are Muslims. But how do we know that the bird is too? What if it is Lutheran or Catholic and we bury it like a Muslim? What if God doesn't accept him in heaven because of that? Because of us? Then perhaps He will punish us again. And who knows how it will end this time?'

Now the little one looked dejected. 'But auntie said that Allah punishes us when we Muslims behave like Christians. We aren't Christians.'

It was a moral dilemma. They could not bring disaster upon the poor bird or upon themselves.

She raised her voice. 'I suggest we do what we always do – we do both. I know that in most cases up to now that has not achieved anything, especially not in maths. But if we do both, then we will at least have done our best. God won't punish us or the bird, for one of the two will be right.'

The younger girl remained silent. She understood they had no alternative: 'Well, all right. But we'll just pray in both languages. We certainly won't make a cross and place it on the grave.'

So, in the end, they prayed that the bird might be received in heaven. In one language they spoke to 'Allah' and opened their hands in prayer towards the sky, as they had seen their aunts and grandmothers do. In the other language they spoke to 'God' and clasped their hands together, as they had seen in films.

* * *

She had in mind this hotchpotch ceremony as she looked at the dark tree trunk, enveloped by the grey November chill. The sudden and brutal uprooting, the childhood grief she experienced over the loss of the unworn duffle coat, her dolls and the enjoyable nursery, had marked her. To what extent she only appreciated years later. She had come to understand that most things in life did not last. They were simply objects that surrounded you. In most cases, if they did not fit into a suitcase, you could simply shut the front door, leave them behind and go away. The uprooting had also taught her that realities could diverge vastly. What was acknowledged to be the truth here and now might not apply elsewhere, with others.

But the issue of religion was more difficult, much more complicated.

How she envied the others back then, when she gazed after the green coffin. The bell-like singing was no more. Her chestnut hair was wrapped in a white burial shroud. The elders had decided to bury her in the small town. So here they were again, after all the time that had passed, back in the small mud house with the flat roof and inner courtyard where they had so joyfully played in the tub. As she watched, the men carefully placed the swaddled body in the green wooden coffin provided by the local mosque for the short transport from the mud house's hallway to the mosque for the funeral prayer. They did not permit her to accompany it. Women were not allowed at funerals, they said. It was yet another of their inexplicable rules and she went along with it.

Powerless, she did not object or resist. From the upstairs window, she merely watched the coffin with the bridal veil someone had put on it, a note of grief for the death of a young unmarried woman who was overtaken by death before her life could blossom. The veil was swaying back and forth. Slowly, the community of men advanced, taking turns carrying the coffin. And she stood rigidly at the window above them, following the movements of the coffin with her eyes until it turned the corner.

In those days of mourning she watched them very closely, especially the ever-present women who embraced her gently and firmly and spoke to her tenderly. She observed and envied them. They really seemed to believe that He had called her to Him. That it was Allah's will and they could not question it, regardless of how much it hurt. She watched them out of the corner of her eye in those moments when they thought themselves unobserved. They looked contorted with pain, yet at the same time resigned to their fate. During the seven days and seven nights they came together, chanting their prayers collectively, their heads wrapped in white scarves, she watched them, silently and surreptitiously, from her corner. They cried together, prayed and grieved for her with an almost contented certainty that Allah had taken her in. Their faith seemed to give them strength, succour, consolation.

Despite her best efforts she could not muster this certainty in herself.

She did everything necessary in the beginning, dutifully and quietly. The elders had been rendered powerless. Despite her young age, it was her task to bring them the worst possible news and catch them when they collapsed. The others did not dare to. None had found the right tone or the words for the unspeakable. She too could not find them. How could she? What words could she use to say that she was no more? How did one say that all the energy, devotion, warmth and love given to her were destroyed from one moment to the next? Irrevocably. Forever.

But she did not have to. Her untimely appearance, her demeanour and the stammering of the name were enough to make them break down. One after the other, they collapsed. With wide, fearful eyes, they watched her approach. The closer she came, the better they understood the name she was stammering, the more their eyes widened. Helpless, like hunted, wounded deer, they collapsed in front of her; thereafter completely shattered, overcome by rivers of tears.

She, on the other hand, had functioned: inwardly limp and empty, outwardly steady and calm. Sinking into her rocking chair and staring out of the window, after everything had been done.

Nothing made sense anymore. If everything could be destroyed from one moment to the next, why did anything exist? Why get up, wash, leave the house in the morning and go to bed in the evening? Why work? Why study? Everything that existed previously seemed senseless.

So she sat there and reflected, while outside the window the seasons turned.

At the same time the total apocalypse broke out. The dreadful pain reoccurred, again and again. It struck suddenly. Unexpected, brutal and loud, during the light of the day as well as in the dark of the night it ripped through her. Thunderous, crashing and choking her with both hands, it hurled her from wall to wall, back and forth, without letting go. Tearing at her relentlessly, it paid no heed to her streaming tears, ignored her cries, until it had almost robbed her of her last breath.

When the raging became so frantic that she could scarcely breathe, the pain drove her out of the house, swept her along the streets, far from everyone and everything, into the forest that swallowed up the thunder. She ran through it, racked with pain, like an injured, helpless animal with its intestines hanging out – an animal that cannot understand what has happened; overcome with pain, staggering, out of its mind, in despair, trying to escape the unbearable torment, wandering about aimlessly until its vitality succumbs to agony.

At those moments when she surrendered to the pain and sacrificed herself to it completely, when she crawled under the bedcovers, alone and weary with tears streaming down her face, she often longed for an anchor. Then, she envied them their faith;

their rock which seemed to give them strength, their trust in God that whatever came to pass was how it had to be; their trust that it could not be otherwise because it was preordained. That He steered everything and that everything was part of the divine order. That she was fine because He took her home.

But she was unable to accept that anchor. She was unable to believe in predestination and transcendence.

Yet the excruciating pain taught her the meaning of religion. Before, religion seemed to be only incomprehensible rules, about which she could only wonder. Now, it seemed also to give support and strength in times when everything was in danger of being swept away, in times of utter loneliness.

By contrast, she was alone with her despair, her search for meaning and the penetrating pain. She *had* to cope on her own. And she did. When the worried whispering about her state of mind and stasis increased, she roused herself. Words were still unbearable. Words and explanations felt like empty phrases. She still remained silent. But sitting around made no sense. So she started out again, a little bit more every day.

*   *   *

Smiling ironically, at the black earth, at the small bird's grave that was no longer there, a report in that morning's newspaper came to her mind. The Pope had consoled a boy who was mourning his dead dog by saying that it was fine; God had received it in heaven, like all creatures. A spokesman for the Vatican immediately denied the story. The Pope had indeed met with a boy who was grieving for his dead pet. But the Pope had certainly never pronounced that, as God's creatures, animals would also go to heaven.

How much this had annoyed her. If religion was indeed really there to help people and give them support, why must its guardians be so dogmatic as to deny people the reassurance that they seek? Why could they not simply let a grieving child believe that his favourite animal was fine?

The ironic smile gave way to an amused grin. What would they have done with the shoe-box if they had known more about the differing funeral rites of Muslims and Christians back then? Pulling up her coat collar, she turned and trudged on into the cold November darkness. The difficulties of belonging to a religious community were really too complicated for her.

6

The Constructed European

Catherine Fieschi

Let's start with misplaced hopes: I wrote this essay in the run-up to the UK referendum on membership of the European Union thinking it would need only a few tweaks after the vote. Tweaks, of course, had to be turned into tugs and slashes. Rereading the first few paragraphs after the events of late June 2016 felt a bit like rereading letters from a lover after a break-up. Was the relationship ever what you thought it was? Were you, simply, leading parallel lives? (Apparently so.) How could you not have known?

What first surfaces in the wake of the vote to leave the EU is a much more accurate and poignant sense of the essential vantage point Britain has provided as a place from which to write and think about Europe. A deeply tragic irony then, that this home that has allowed me to conjugate my Europeanness in a way no other has, is now demanding an exclusivity that is at odds with both my past and its own. Not to mention at odds with its future. As a result, it may be that it is from here – both geographically and temporally – that the real questions about European identity will finally be answered, or at least addressed, because they seem to have been asked and answered so brutally in Britain.

Aftermath

Let's face it, the past few years have been a relentless struggle for those of us arguing for the good of Europe; a hailstorm of body-blows crystallizing around a set of crises so severe that the conversation had shifted from the once benign, and rather wistful,

'How do we build a European demos?' of the Maastricht era, to the desperate: 'Can Europe survive?'

Europe has done itself no favours – apparently incapable of protecting the vulnerable (both its own and those of neighbouring countries that look to it for succour), or of delivering the living standards it blithely promised, or of knowing itself sufficiently well to put forward a shared blueprint for the future. It had become, in recent times, increasingly difficult – in fact near impossible – for men and women of good European will to make the case for Europe. In the UK that paralysis felt all the more tragic as we hurtled towards the existential question of the UK's place in Europe – in or out?

There is no doubt that, for many of us who have called Britain our home for decades, there is a barely articulable sadness in this moment. Stunned disbelief despite the warnings and a sense that, as many have expressed since late June, we were 'waking up in a different country'. Even in my case, as someone who long lived outside London, and whose work led to probing into those parts of Britain that have been ruthlessly marginalized by mismanaged deindustrialization, then by years of mismanaged development into gaudy high-streets of vodka bars and pseudo-restaurants, and then, finally, by years of austerity – even for those of us who, in other words, should have known better, the shock was tremendous.

The result forces me to re-evaluate three things that bring the contours of my European identity into sharp relief.

The first, as alluded to before, is that Britain (be it London, or central Birmingham, or a lovely village in Hereford and Worcester) has afforded me the huge luxury of being a British European and provided me with an ideal place from which to continue to develop, question, configure, my relationship to Europe.

The second is that the results are a reminder that, as a European, you must be prepared for shifting borders, rules and allegiances. Central and Eastern Europeans have not forgotten this, but I fear that many of us more directly connected to Western Europe had forgotten that the nature of this continent is to undergo a form of geographical meiosis quite regularly. The fact that a majority of British voters have chosen this (and potentially set in motion the fragmentation of their own country) is perhaps proof that they are far more European than they think. Not as EU citizens, but as Europeans – by behaviour and imagination. This is what Europeans do: they divide cities, then abolish borders, create new ones and then reunite in order to divide again along new, or sometimes older, lines. Try and explain this to an American and you will likely be met with a blank stare.

Finally, what has become painfully clear is that – in the UK, as well as in other European countries where Euroscepticism is rife (the Netherlands, France, Italy) – being a European, feeling European, seems increasingly dependent on class: the divide between support for, and refusal of, the EU is one that mirrors the divide between the 'winners' and 'losers' of the last 20 or 30 years. The 'winners' are those armed with high levels of education and the kind of confidence in the future that comes from the excitement of good professional prospects, the possibility of good housing (be it bought or rented), a choice of where to live, the promise of leisure, interesting pursuits and rich social and professional circles. The 'losers' are those whose jobs are in the process of being annihilated (or have already been), whose skills and training do not satisfy the demands of a 'knowledge' (and, increasingly, robotized) economy, and for whom the last three decades have seen rising debt and declining promise for themselves and their children.

It wasn't always thus: the purpose of the European project was precisely to make a kind of social and economic cosmopolitanism (a combination of solidarity, culture, imagination) accessible to as many people as possible as a means towards prosperous peace. This is the work that Europe began to do in the 1960s and 1970s: it began its journey as a modern polity, coming to terms with those divisions (cultural and political, but also socio-economic), and attempted to set up a system that would gradually address them, diminish their relevance. And this is the work that must recommence now, in light of new pressures, new disappointments but also new opportunities and aspirations.

So we do need to ask ourselves how a project built on such a vision has become one of privilege, exclusion and disconnection.

Part of the answer lies in fundamentally changed circumstances. By this I mean that in the immediate aftermath of the Second World War, the European project was the dream of those who had lost so much, in a world characterized by shared loss. Today, it is the wish of those who have gained immeasurably, in a world characterized by selective loss. Losses from which many of us pro-Europeans seem to have been, in part, spared. Factoring in this shift is crucial: it explains why the defence of Europe, when it ends up in the hands of people like me – people who are such obvious beneficiaries of its ideals and institution – is taken as little more than the battle cry of the privileged.

As long as those who 'make' Europe do not understand the work – the emotional and psychological effort entailed in the very notion of embracing Europe (in other words, of embracing others, embracing difference, embracing 'the new') – the difficulties faced by those who feel on the periphery of Europe's cultural space, unprotected by its borders, locked out by its complexity and excluded by its easy, surface cosmopolitanism, will forever undermine it.

Being aware of this, in turn, is the first step towards recognizing that curiosity will only replace fear, and our sense of adventure will only trump our longing for predictability, once certain needs are met and certain frameworks are in place. All of current psychological and sociological research points to this.

So unless Europe addresses how to deliver a sense of security in changed circumstances, no European project can survive. Zygmunt Bauman puts it best: 'The ability to live with differences, let alone to enjoy such living and to benefit from it, does not come easily and certainly not under its own impetus. This ability is an art, which like all arts, requires study and exercise.' The necessary confidence for encounters is inconceivable without the reassurance of economic and affective security. Both of which can create the space for the ability to which Bauman refers.

The reason I bring this up is because what follows could easily be construed, and even dismissed, as nothing but the result of the kinds of privileges outlined above. What has often stopped me writing about my attachment to Europe, my 'European identity', is the embarrassed conviction that the only thing that would float to the surface of any narrative would be a privileged brat. 'Eurotrash' as the 1990s put it. A product of minor and long-declined European nobility, the vagaries of the diplomatic service, and chance encounters. This is not an ideal vantage point from which to extoll the virtues of Europe in a mass-democratic age; particularly as the latter seems to be yielding diminishing returns. But I trust that the angled light of the personal might also allow something else to surface in the pages to come: the fact that while there is much luck and privilege at play, there is also, crucially, the role of various institutions – schools, family, languages, rituals – and their importance in delivering both the necessary patterns of reassuring regularity as well as the necessary spaces for the work of belonging across cultures and borders to take place. This is a reflection shaped by family history, personal choice, but also the ideological suppleness and institutional generosity of my various homes.

Constellations

Jasbir K. Puar, the Rutgers identity scholar, suggests that identities are like the night-sky: we can identify shapes because we decide to focus on some stars – the brightest – and leave out others. Depending on the stars we focus on, in other words depending on where we stand, on our perspective, on the seasons of our lives, the shapes, the pictures change. They appear and disappear.

The metaphor is not only beautiful, but precious – it can serve as a means of reimagining what makes a European at different points in time. It can help us think of the intersections of our personal patterns with those of the collective, with the European sky.

The emphasis here is on patterns (those we choose or, simply, are able, to see and find relevant), rather than on categories. In European terms, the metaphor is an argument in favour of going beyond the categories drawn by current European institutions, and towards a reimagining of Europe based on the constellations that are visible and relevant to us now. These constellations will be a mix of the personal, the collective and the institutionalized. But one thing is for sure, they will only appear if we hold other perspectives as legitimate and real; and if we are willing to connect to new stars in order to discover new patterns.

I grew up in Italy and in the United States, then lived and studied in Canada. But my first steps were taken in Africa. I hold a French passport and, proudly too, a Canadian one. I've dithered over applying for British citizenship. But, much like those people who buy insurance the day after they get burgled, I will now. It was a measure of my comfort that I never really felt the need to do so. I feel profoundly French, culturally and unremittingly American, and nostalgically Italian. But my political and social imagination is the product of my years in Canada and Britain. Both are homes that I have chosen; vantage points from which to negotiate a quintessentially hybrid European identity. Both countries trigger a kind of institutional tenderness (yes, there is such a thing). Despite recent events in the UK, I refuse to renege on a deep and true affection that, I choose to believe, runs both ways.

War Stars

Belonging to Europe has been first and foremost the experience of a European family stretched across the globe from Europe to South Africa, Canada and the US. On my mother's side, I grew up with grandparents who met at a Franco-Swiss border town. My grandfather was a French customs officer, originally from the Toulouse area. They met in my grandmother's native Verrières, a Swiss village that provided the crossing point from one set of French-speaking foothills into another set of French-speaking foothills.

The crossing didn't make much sense to me at the time. I'd close my eyes and blink hard when we drove across just to see if I could enhance the experience. Conjure up some sort of change. Blink ... Nope. Bliiiink ... Nope. And yet that border is a crucial part of family history. My grandparents met there in 1936. Yvonne, my Swiss, prim, Calvinist grandmother was always depicted as having somewhat stumbled into Europeanness out of love. A Europeanness that would soon cost her. In 1939 my grandfather Marcel was drafted. Yvonne left the French town of Pontarlier with her nine-month-old baby girl and headed to her in-laws' family farm near Toulouse ('because, as I would hear all my life, there would always be food on a farm'). And there she remained until the end of the war: an elegant and grateful figure in photographs that document a boisterous (and terribly un-Swiss) existence in the French *sud-ouest* during the war.

The recounted memories of that time criss-cross my 1970s childhood like secret trails. We would spend a couple of months in the summers with my grandparents in that village, on that farm. The endless Sunday 'lunches' (from immediately after morning mass until early evening) were punctuated by indecent amounts of homemade foie gras, roast chickens, tapioca soup and wild stories of revenge, betrayal and disinheritance. Mauriac met Pagnol in these stories in which families endlessly composed and recomposed as women died in childbirth, boundaries were redrawn, grudges were buried through marriage and resurfaced in death. They trickled like underground streams as territories were composed, consolidated and recomposed over generations. Over the murky intimacy of family histories floated stories about characters such as the apparently, er, 'compliant', Mimi-Pattes-en-l'Air (roughly, 'Mimi-legs-ahoy'), or the boastful and despised Claquebretelle ('Snap-a-brace'). The names had us kids in peals of laughter long before we actually picked up on some of the torrid double entendres.

Towards dessert we tended to circle back to the one story I really wanted to hear. It was where Hollywood lighting met the war; a duet in which my grandmother provided the steady melody of narrative and my mother the harmonies of her own childhood experience. My grandfather only chimed in at the end, when his character burst forth again at the close of the war. It was like a mini-musical, and in my head the scene was always lit just so.

The décor was Montjoire (the very place in which we were), 1940. Population: roughly 516, give or take a few Mimis. Sitting in the very same spots 35 years later, the story captured a hot mid-morning. In it a heavy-set postwoman in one of those flowery smocks came whizzing down the hill from the village on her bicycle. I'd spotted her from afar, my grandmother would say, 'and I could tell that she had a telegram in her right hand'. In my version, the postwoman had a touch of the 1970s Jody Foster about her, and she came to a stylish, gravel-spraying halt. She delivered the news staring into my camera: my grandfather had been taken prisoner in Germany.

After a pause for breath the story moved to Pontarlier, 1945. My daring grandmother had gone to reclaim the family apartment from the German Kommandantur. As a child I couldn't resist imagining my grandmother as a cross between Edith Cavell and my favourite crime-fighter, Fantômette, asserting her rights in the face of the Occupier and involved in acts of daring-do involving breaking into the apartment as my mother kept watch (that last bit is true). This time it was the baker, Jacquet (one of the few locals with a telephone), who had rushed over with a message – 'He's been released'. And 'his' train would be arriving in nearby Frasne in two days. This, as my grandmother always pointed out, would be the first time he really met his daughter. My mother was then going on five. So the story goes that for the next 48 hours my grandmother sewed as fast as she could to produce a new dress for my mother: a dress the exact colour of my mother's eyes. Cornflower blue, with honeycomb stitching across the front and a large matching bow for her hair.

In the last scene Frasne station is all Douglas Sirk colours: the blue of the dress, the dark emerald of the carriages, the lemony hue of an early morning – and all the browns and rusts of a fading war. 'When the train pulled in, I scanned the carriages, but I couldn't see him.' The suspense killed me every time. Over 30 years, as she told the story, I never failed to doubt that he would be there. Long after he was dead, I still feared that she might not spot him. 'And then I saw him and jumped aboard as soon as the train stopped.' 'I was right behind her', my mother would finally add. 'They fell into each other's arms. And they hugged for such a long time that I thought they'd forgotten about me.' A touch of rose-coloured dismay.

The image of my prim grandmother, who I had never seen so much as break into a trot (and by then well into her 70s), flinging herself into a train, pushing people aside to cross those final few yards, was one of my favourites. All was well. The story could continue. And I got to imagine her being vigorous and possibly even slightly pushy with other passengers as she brushed them aside to be my mother's mother, to become my grandmother.

I've cycled down that hill and waved my hand just like the messenger of 1940. I've sprayed the gravel, seen the blue dress with the honeycomb stitching and caught a train in Frasne. Tiny acts of private pilgrimage, held together by the fine thread of Europe's more intimate histories.

Meanwhile my father was in Aix-en-Provence working for the French resistance. He was 18, had left his native Rome and rejoined his other country (that of his father rather than his mother). As a French national he was making maps for the Americans on the thinnest of velum paper, which he would then sew into the linings of jackets to take across to whoever needed them to plan the liberation. (There is an awful lot of sewing going on in these stories: Europe clearly owes a debt to the cross-stitch.)

When my sister and I were growing up my father would show us camouflage techniques. We'd spend evenings burning corks to rub on our faces like soldiers and resisters. Then we would take to the make-believe Maquis, in our room in Chicago overlooking Lake Michigan, or spy on our parents as they watched Alistair Cooke introduce *Masterpiece Theatre*.

Star-spangled

When my sister and I stepped off the plane at Chicago's O'Hare airport in 1976, we had precisely five words of English in our pockets. We landed in America armed with nothing but the astonishingly useful first line of a limerick: 'Number one is a duck'.

As we were driven into the city, the duck disappeared and Chicago grew into the windshield. Brick, metal and steel edged out the blueness.

We turned off the lake and checked into a hotel that offered further delights: the deepest of shag carpets in which you could sink practically to your knees. If you dragged your feet across it, it made you crackle with static electricity, raised the hair on your head and filled your mouth with the metallic taste of rusty nails. Zonked from our first proper jet lag we discovered 24-hour television and Bugs Bunny. Pleasures that were almost immediately surpassed by those of the breakfast buffet and twenty-something varieties of Kellogg's cereals in mini-packets (mini-packets!). And then *Charlie's Angels*. And then the Woolworths on Michigan Avenue with its smell of plastic, popcorn and Crayola crayons.

Within roughly a week the United States had claimed me. The hugeness was inescapable. The buildings non-negotiable. The collective instructions unfussy. None of the hieroglyphic encouragement of little red men or little green men. Just 'Walk', 'Don't walk'. You knew what to do to get across and to get ahead. Despite our lack of English, or perhaps because of it, all of a sudden interpretation seemed superfluous. Chicago was, against all odds, soothing in its Midwestern straightforwardness and its beauty.

My sister and I quickly made a pact: let's never leave. The Italy we'd left behind was that of the 1970s, the so-called 'lead years'. A country in the throes of terrorism, a major smog crisis, industrial mobilization, ideological polarization and dislocation, and deep transformational turmoil. In some respects, even in the north, still a poor country. The entertainment highlights were Rafaella Carra, Topo Gigio and the daily *Carosello* at 8.50 pm. Ten minutes of adverts, puppets and short comedy films that marked the nation's official bedtime for children: you can stay up for *Carosello* and then it's off to bed.

It was also a country in which the school principal would call your parents should you happen to be two minutes late – just in case you'd been kidnapped and were about to be sent home, one little finger at a time. Compared with Chicago, Turin seemed grey, menacing, complicated. It would take a second Italian sojourn in the 1980s as a teenager to reconcile me fully with the country. It happened largely, and despite my father's illness, through the music of De Gregori and Dalla, and a northern Italian springtime.

But back in 1976 the overpowering pleasures of the US simply took over. And during the day, despite moments of puzzlement and frustration, I was aghast to catch myself 'becoming American'. Don't misunderstand: every night, I cried into my pillow, longing to go back to Italy. I wrote to my best friend every week, letters full of delight – and grief. I wrote to my grandmother in Rome to ask her to send me the fare 'home'. Her letters in return – detailed lamentations on purse-snatching, inflation, robberies, racketeering and all the ills of an emerging modern Italy as seen through the eyes of an 80-year-old – did nothing to dampen my desire to go back. All this, while pledging my allegiance to the Stars and Stripes. Daily.

Often, I really meant it. Partly because the sing-song rhythm of the words was reassuring to someone who didn't yet inhabit the language; and the swell of the fourth grade voices was comforting – an ephemeral moment of belonging, like a practiced flight of stairs. But also like the conquest of something or somewhere that, most of the time, was conquering me.

And sometimes I crossed my fingers behind my back, doubly blushing: at what felt like patriotic wantonness (in exchange for a few bowlfuls of chocolate-coated cereal, I pledged everything); and at my duplicity in the face of fourth-grade solemnity.

What ultimately created a sense of belonging though, was neither the pledge of allegiance nor Bugs Bunny. It was the super-imposition of powerful, let's call them 'attractors' (from sports to television, from school to sleepovers, via 1940s films and 1970s Motown – and, yes, the 'Star-Spangled Banner' at Cubs games) and the ease with which, most of the time, the US seemed to wear these riches. Sure, you had no choice but to recite the pledge, but it felt as though it was up to you what you made of it: the good, the bad, the stultifying, the liberating. Perhaps that is the true definition of 'soft power', the confidence to lay out a smorgasbord of goodies secure in the knowledge that your guests will come. While granting them the necessary illusion that they are composing their own meal.

What allowed me to struggle and negotiate, and, ultimately, to belong, was the convergence of a 1970s American school of great generosity of posture (a strange mix of Latino consciousness, Catholic ritual, cheerful Irish nostalgia, post-Watergate Chicago and healthy doses of PBS interspersed in the curriculum) and a family whose own expansive emotionalism and affectionate laissez-faire, was meant to compensate for the rigours and demands of having to move country every few years. The combination of both of these sets of institutions meant that we could venture quite far socially, linguistically and emotionally (as well as geographically), without feeling untethered or unmoored.

Stars from a Distance

The turn to Canada was, to begin with, an experiment with what I thought would be a 'half-way house' between Europe and the US: a first attempt to try and live out an identity from the periphery. Not wishing to return to the US after a spell in France, Canada beckoned. Quebec to be specific. McGill, to be even more specific. And being specific is worth it because this geolocation identity game yields its own map: an Anglophone enclave, within a cosmopolitan city, within a francophone province, within a multicultural country.

The point is that nothing could have served as better preparation for what turns out to be our epoch's cardinal task: perpetual identity negotiation, and the hard work to which Bauman refers. In this respect, Canadian institutions are an 'art', and they are probably those to which my understanding of what a Europe could be, are most indebted. Multiculturalism not as parallel living but as the constant practice of the art and craft of living together: unsentimental in its practices, careful in its framing, wisely supple when it comes to categories. Canadian multiculturalism, so often depicted as goody-goody, is in reality enlightened realpolitik. It is a set of incentives for participation that force the emergence of various elites that have to put in the hard work of living together, of upholding social norms for their own sake as much as for the sake of others. That transactional aspect of Canadian multiculturalism is often swept under the carpet, as though this pragmatism detracted from the doctrine's reputation of enlightenment. In fact, this pragmatism is a powerful expression of well-negotiated necessity and of the importance of relationships over categories (despite the received wisdom on multiculturalism). And a version of the management of diversity to which Europe needs to ascribe fully – beyond wishful thinking, caricature or ideological pronouncement. It means acknowledging the moral-political imperative of recognition (in a representative democracy) but also taking on board the nuts and bolts of it: the transactions, negotiations and practicalities that allow for the reasoned political expression of these identities. Rather than the wishful thinking of symbiotic nationalism and its accompanying incantatory pronouncements about the nation or European values.

> 'But the day was warm and poetic, the sky a pale blue ...'
> Greek Constellations

In 1999, fresh from my PhD, I received a scholarship to attend the Ionian Conference. Organized by the British Council, the Greek Government and London School of Economics, the aim was to bring together freshly minted docs and post-docs from Western European and Central and East European countries to discuss the shape of what would be the new, post-enlargement Europe. Though I suspect that for many of us the main attraction, at least initially, was five days in Corfu in late May. We met in Athens then flew to Corfu. We woke up to Greece and made our way up the hill to a palace built for an Empress – Elizabeth ('Sissi') of Bavaria, Empress of Austria – the Achilleion, from where we would survey the imagined landscapes of Europe for the next few days.

Of those days I carry the memory of a palpable sense of tectonic shift. As we looked over the Ionian Sea and talked and talked, the sense of discovery, and more to the point, the sense that Europe was reshaping us and that we were reshaping Europe was overwhelming. I almost felt the continent tilt on its axis. A feeling that nothing would be the same as enlargement drew near and as we drew closer to one another. On a hot, blue night we debated liberalism, equality, markets. We also agreed effortlessly that Abba's 'Dancing Queen' should be the European anthem. The distance between us was both nothing and everything. And its crossing was both exhilarating and unforced. And Greece gathered us in. Never have I felt more hopeful. As one young colleague spoke of Kieslowski's films and another of trade and democracy, this new Europe did momentarily flicker before our eyes. I return to this moment of promise regularly and wonder at how we seem to have squandered it.

July 2015; Corfu again. Having spent a week discussing the Eurozone crisis with fellow social democrats, I was the last participant left at the hotel. On this last evening, I decided to walk up the hill to the nearest taverna. I lingered long over octopus and the view, and after a couple of hours made a joke about having vowed to leave every last one of my euros in Greece. The owner and his mother proceeded to feed me desserts drizzled with honey. They sat with me and we watched the day leave us. They both spoke quietly, with a kind of resignation only slightly tinged with indignation. So much of the past few years in Europe have been about indignation of every sort that it has become an emotion we don't quite know how to serve up anymore. And Greece gathered us in. I finally walked back downhill to the hotel in the dark. The olive trees didn't make a sound. There was no breeze of relief and no moonlight. Just dark smells and the trees. I sat down on a small bit of wall, on the edge of the road. And the cliché and delight of all that is Greece for us Europeans inevitably swooped and caught me. Greece as a thread to the inevitable and uncertain idea of Europe.

What is striking is that, while middle age does provide a vantage point from which to see these constellations, the true angle is that provided by Britain – the edge of Europe.

Postcards from the Edge of the European Galaxy: Britain

Leaving Canada, I wanted to return to Europe, but not necessarily to the Europe I knew. I deliberately chose, again, a half-way house: one where I would feel pleasantly foreign, but still close to what I knew. I kept my commonwealth connection, and my accent still hovers over the mid-Atlantic, but it was very much a matter of choosing a European future. So I even took to the pancakes that were neither real in the American sense (too thin for that), nor in the French sense (and too thick for that). This was my 'European Goldilocks' moment. It helped that I discovered this not from London, but rather from a village on the outskirts of Birmingham with a tiny station, a watercolour club and rolling accents (it took me a few weeks to realize that no one actually wants to know if you are 'oroight?').

I felt myself settle into a place completely at ease with bumbling along, or trailing behind, or blazing ahead. At ease with not necessarily knowing what it stood for because it was too busy reinventing itself. In short, sentimental about its story, but entirely unsentimental about its history. It took me a good decade to understand properly the lived and crucial reality of this distinction that explains why, in the permanent hurricane of change that is Britain (that Britain has always been) and that in many respects demands that everyone devote so much energy to becoming something else, everyday life is in fact highly ritualized as people hold on to a familiarity that punctuates the landscape of the everyday.

This ease in the face of change, this comfort with hybridity, is perhaps exceptional – but is precisely what makes Britain a good home for the wanderer, as well as perfectly suited to Europe.

Eppur si muove: *A Certain Idea of Europe*

We often reflect on the emotional work required to maintain one's sense of self in an adopted place. But we also need to give thought to what is required to maintain a sense of self (collective and individual) in a place that is changing – and that can make us feel as though we need to learn it again, to readopt it. As Europeans in Britain we now experience a double sense of alienation: we need to readopt Britain (as it continues to try and adopt us). But we are also involved in trying to readopt Europe. A Europe that has, if not failed us, then certainly disappointed us; changed – or failed to change? – and been less than what it promised. So keeping the European adventure alive in Britain is also about keeping the European adventure alive within ourselves. It is no small task.

I remain convinced that Europe is just the right form of polity to deliver the 'study' and the 'art' to which Bauman refers because, despite its bureaucratic and somewhat staid political foundations, it has hesitation – of which Brexit is just the latest expression – and hybridity at its heart.

I was struck, in the aftermath of the French terror attacks (in particular after the Bataclan events in November 2015), that many of the people to whom I spoke (both French and non-French) referred to the 'threat to a certain idea of France', and 'the end of a certain idea of Europe'. These imagined certainties have not characterized European countries for a long time, if ever they did, and these fantasized certainties are disabling both Europe and individual European nations in the face of change.

We must do better than the populists of all political stripes and use our imagination not to 'fix' Europe (in the sense of immobilizing it in the past), but, rather, to invent it for the future – with all the hesitation and contingency that this involves. This is not a satisfactory answer, in the sense that it holds little of the kind of promise that we enjoy as children: knowing exactly when and where the 'good stuff' is going to happen and exactly what we need to do to ensure that it does. But it is an answer in keeping with the very nature, the historical and institutional DNA of Europe, and in particular with the way that the generation currently involved in building it for the future has experienced it.

For our European future to exist, we must put paid to this 'certain' idea (in both senses of the word) of Europe.

There is no 'certain' Europe. In this respect Europe is a quintessentially forward-looking experiment. For those of us of a generation that did not create or build Europe, but tried to 'manage' Europe, it is quite clear that Europe, while steeped in recognizable values, is also defined by uncertainty, by change and transformation.

The only certainty that Europe must offer is a commitment to the security of its citizens – security in the everyday sense. Physical security of course (and it will not come through nostalgic incantation), but perhaps above all the commitment to putting in place the kinds of redistributive mechanisms and institutional frameworks that pool risk rather than parcel it out. This must remain central to our concerns: the refusal to accept that individuals face life in our societies alone. This is what enables people to feel they can reach out to others, travel abroad, fall in love across the continent, embrace the uncertainty of twenty-first century Europe. The ability, as Bauman puts it, 'to live with difference, and to enjoy such living'.

To do this we need to recognize that moments of identity formation (and therefore the institutions that allow for them or provide for them) are built on hesitation and rebellion, on the examination and intense experience of loss, fear of loss, joy, relief – not only in quick succession but simultaneously. This is what makes human beings complex rather than just complicated: the simultaneously moving parts.

Bibliography

Bauman, Zygmunt, *Liquid Modernity*, Cambridge, Polity Press, 2000.

Cavafy, C.P., 'Alexandrian kings', in George Savidis, ed., *Collected Poems*, translated by Edmund Keeley and Philip Sherrard, revised edition, Princeton, Princeton University Press, 1992.

Fieschi, Catherine, *In the Shadow of Democracy: Fascism, Populism and the French Fifth Republic*, Manchester, Manchester University Press, 2004.

Hoffman, Eva. *Lost in Translation: Life in a New Language*, London, Vintage, 1998.

Iyer, Pico, *Imagining Canada: An Outsider's Hope for a Global Future*, Toronto, Hart House, University of Toronto, January 2001, First Hart House lecture.

Iyer, Pico, *The Global Soul: Jet Lag, Shopping Malls, and the Search for Home*, London, Vintage, 2001.

Phillips, John, 'Agencement/assemblage', *Theory, Culture and Society*, vol. 23, nos. 2–3, 2006.

Puar, Jasbir K., '"I would rather be a cyborg than a goddess": becoming intersectional in assemblage theory', *philoSOPHIA*, vol. 2, no. 1, 2012.

7

Guilty Pleasure

Lars Ebert

I grew up in Germany and went to school and university there before settling in Amsterdam for work and love. That's 15 years ago, and it didn't take me long to feel that Amsterdam had become my home. The city is colourful, vibrant and liberal, and as it is relatively small compared to other capital cities, it's still human in scale. Life is good there and the unconventional is part of the mainstream.

A place you call home does something to you. It impacts on who you are, constantly. So what did Amsterdam add to my German upbringing? A few aspects are obvious. For example, my sense of humour, my code of behaviour and my framework of cultural references have all become more and more Dutch. Humour in Amsterdam is much more ruthless and existential than I was used to. Personal behaviour is much more spontaneous and straightforward. And cultural references are fuelled by a different canon, a different historical awareness – think colonies, water and tolerance, to name just a few buzzwords that make up Dutch identity.

As I have a job in which I travel a lot, it is funny to observe how I am identified abroad: sometimes I am introduced as German, sometimes as Dutch. I don't mind either. In fact, I feel that by form I have become Dutch and by content I am still somehow German. And by content I don't mean ideas or thoughts, but rather the DNA of my thoughts, my attitude towards my very identity as a human among other humans, as one of a kind. This identification has nothing to do with pride, nor with a feeling of *Heimat*, but everything to do with a very positive form of guilt.

But how can guilt be positive? It is largely associated with wrongdoing, crime and punishment. It refers to some kind of violation of agreed ethical or legal standards. Someone who feels guilty – rightly or wrongly – believes they have crossed a red line. Obviously, this is not what I mean. I do not think that I have done anything wrong. However, I do see truth in the saying 'no pain, no gain'. Let me use a Christian image to explain what I mean by guilt: the metaphor of original sin.

*   *   *

In the second century Bishop Irenäus of Lyon described the consequences that the biblical Fall of Adam had for humanity. In his interpretation original sin is a springboard for developing mankind. When god created man he gave him free will and introduced original sin as an educational tool, so to speak, to get him to use this freedom properly. Augustine saw the guilt of breaking a divine law by eating from the Tree of Life as a fault in the human. Adam had betrayed god and all subsequent generations were also tempted to break divine law and that human morality was therefore weak, and consequently all humans were sinners. In both views the Fall is a mythical explanation of evil in the world. The religious abuse of this view of the biblical story led to suppression and moralistic intimidation by Christian denominations that deemed redemption necessary, which led, for example, to the selling of indulgences.

There are many understandings of original sin and they all relate in one way or another to the problem of free will. Are we humans free to choose? Deriving the answer from religious myth requires deduction: if you believe in god's future judgement of humanity, a person must be able to live righteously. The Catechism of the Catholic Church consequently states: 'Original sin is called "sin" only in an analogical sense: it is a sin "contracted" and not "committed" – a state and not an act. Although it is proper to each individual, original sin does not have the character of a personal fault in any of Adam's descendants.' The equivalent in Eastern Orthodoxy is similarly outspoken: 'It can be said that while we have not inherited the guilt of Adam's personal sin, because his sin is also of a generic nature, and because the entire human race is possessed of an essential, ontological unity, we participate in it by virtue of our participation in the human race.'

As a non-believer I reject any notion of sin. But I do appreciate the notion of human vulnerability and free will. This pattern of thought, the paradigm of original sin, is interesting in so far as it can help me to understand recent German and European history and especially the Holocaust: I am personally not guilty of that crime, but I inherited, as a human, the weaknesses that made it possible. I have to become aware of that. In this context I see guilt as a basic form of awareness.

I tend to see the Holocaust as the new fall of mankind, the original sin we have to relate to, although I prefer to use 'inherited guilt' rather than its synonym 'original sin', just to rid it of any religious connotations.

Sigmund Freud defined guilt as the result of a struggle between the ego and the super-ego. The source of a feeling of guilt within the unconscious was not god as nemesis but parental imprinting. Freud saw 'the obstacle of an unconscious sense of guilt ... as the most powerful of all obstacles to recovery'. So if there is some kind of fault in the way humans have been made and we want to overcome it, or at least if we want to be able to deal with it, we had better become aware of it. Consciously dealing with guilt could make us humans more humane.

In public perception Germany is understandably identified with its Nazi past, with the Holocaust and horror. In this respect my own family history is more or less unblemished – at least those parts that are talked about. Who knows what silence is hiding. My grandparents on my father's side were from Pomerania, which today is part of Poland. My grandfather was a low-ranking Wehrmacht soldier, probably a party member. I don't know where my grandmother stood. She never spoke of that time. All we know is that she was a simple woman who worked on the farm of a large landowner. The family had little land themselves. After the war, in the denazification hearings in West Germany, citizens like my grandmother would be called *Mitläufer*, fellow travellers. It was sheer opportunism that led them to offer no resistance, but they were not necessarily charged with any crimes.

Raped and abused when the Red Army forced all Germans in Pomerania to leave their homes, my grandmother walked barefoot with her eldest son and a backpack as far west and south as she was able to. Nine months later she bore a dead child. No questions were asked. Like thousands of other refugees she started a new life in the West, a hostile environment where newcomers were not appreciated.

My grandfather on my mother's side was from an old socialist family, the son of the beloved mayor of the village of Eppelheim in the south of Germany in which my parents and I grew up. My great grandfather refused to become a member of the Nazi party and consequently lost his job and income. Despite regular SA house searches he managed to avoid arrest and lived by the produce of his garden and the help of other villagers. The American army liberators restored him to his mayoralty after the war and he subsequently won re-election – a family history we were proud of.

As a child I heard the stories of this socialist great grandfather resisting Nazi membership on the one side and the traumatic history of dispersion and destruction on the other. During my eight years in the local *Gymnasium* more than half of my history lessons were about the Second World War and the Holocaust. In tenth grade the whole class travelled to Verdun to learn about the horrors of the First World War, the 'Great War', and how it and its consequences led directly to the Second World War. In eleventh grade our history teacher took us on a week-long trip to Auschwitz to see the ruins of the gas chambers and the crematoria.

We talked to survivors. One of them had worked in the part of the camp called Canada, where the belongings of the deported and cremated Jews were sorted for further use, to send them 'heim ins Reich' (back to the Reich). We went to Krakow and ate gefilte fish and drank vodka at the well-known Jewish restaurant Ariel in the old Jewish quarter of Kazimierz. And we cried a lot because we realized that *we* had brought about the unimaginable horrors of

Auschwitz; that all our families together must represent everything that made the horror possible; that contained within them there must have been victims, bystanders and perpetrators. And we were their children. Good and evil were in the goodnight kisses of our grandparents, in the stories and in the silences of our parents – in all of us. We were all potential perpetrators, victims, bystanders. That was what we realized and that was why we all cried. Being German, we were guilty.

And then I suppose that we were all, in one way or another, also very openly imbued with a feeling of superiority that came with being German. Naively, we never made a connection between this sense of superiority and what we had seen and felt in Auschwitz. When Angela Merkel was asked in an interview about Germany's best attribute she said: 'Its perfectly sealed windows', an answer that encapsulates German national pride in a nutshell. But if you delve more deeply into the answer and consider the subtext you realize that it also says: working hard, being reliable, clean, punctual, matter-of-fact, trustworthy and therefore producing windows, and many other things, of a better quality than any other country in the world – that's what comprises Germany's best attribute. Germans believe they have a monopoly on perfection.

With every new generation the proportion of guilt in Germany's collective identity diminishes and the proportion of pride increases. Hence the recent omnipresence of German flags in Germany, which was very rare in my youth. It scares me that the pride has manifestly grown larger than the guilt. I find it hard not to be worried about German success – if you want to call it that – in Europe today. It is only minor relief that Angela Merkel reinforces the notion of German guilt, when the broader sentiment among the German population seems to be that of moral superiority because of their country's self-image as a place of perfection – because of the perfectly sealed windows.

The 'never again' that was imprinted in my DNA as I grew up left me with a sixth sense that alerts me whenever I see a flag, or any other sign of nationalism, no matter which one, and has even given me a critical distance from the self-image of the Dutch, my recent fellow citizens. I say 'even' because the self-image of the Dutch consists solely of tolerant, liberal and progressive elements to which I would normally immediately subscribe. The only problem is that even these values become dangerously exclusive as soon as they are expressed as national pride, or once they define both collective and personal identity. If part of national pride is tolerance, you cease to scrutinize your own tolerance. If I grow up with the notion that I am tolerant, then I am the benchmark for tolerance, no one else. We are at home in our identity, and that is where we are vulnerable, especially when we believe that identity is something static, inherited, something to pass on, that can break or be hurt. And unfortunately, nationalism and collective identity build on just such a static notion of identity.

So if I am as alarmed by German as I am by Dutch nationalism, where then do I belong, where is the collective identity that attracts me? I am tempted to say, as many others do, that I do not belong. I am supposedly free and I belong to myself. I do not need any group to identify with. This attitude is probably triggered by the high degree of mobility that is so typical of my generation. I work in airports, hotel rooms, cafés and the premises of project partners all across Europe. I find attending a meeting with a diverse group of people a rather normal state of being. To me there is richness in cultural diversity and cultural confrontations. I experience many cultural contexts and cherry-pick the aspects that I like (food, language, fashion, literature, music and so on) and that suits my self-image as someone with a modular personality, driven by individualism and maybe a longing to be cosmopolitan. For the latter it is equally important to me to be challenged by other cultures and to look for things that take me out of my comfort zone, to places where I do not fit. Finding out whether I can deal or not with these times when I feel like a misfit is probably the most valuable ongoing learning experience of my life. Maybe that is true cosmopolitanism? The value of striking a balance between these cultural offerings is self-evident. So when I say my form is Dutch and my content is German, is such a position sustainable? Only to a certain degree.

In the last year of my studies at the Faculty of Protestant Theology of the Ruprecht-Karls-University in Heidelberg I seriously doubted not only the content of what I was studying but also the job prospects it offered. I took a break and applied for an internship in Amsterdam at the publishing house Castrum Peregrini, which means Fortress of the Pilgrim. What I found was a community in the heart of Amsterdam that came into being in the time of the Nazi occupation. Back then a group of German Jewish youngsters were given shelter from the Nazis by a Dutch painter and an exiled German poet.

Castrum Peregrini was the code name deliberately chosen, as a good omen, by the community. A crusader fortress on the seashore of the Holy Land near Haifa, it was never taken by the Arabs, but its Christian inhabitants left voluntarily. Its ruins are still extant and today are within the grounds of a military base. The community in the safe house must have thought: 'If we leave this place, we leave it voluntarily.'

In hiding, the community maintained their spiritual freedom through concentrating on studying art and literature: the German classics, Greek antiquity, art history, contemporary Dutch poetry. This was a truly modern way of looking at reality through the lenses of various cross-fertilizing disciplines. The group not only received a clandestine education, reading German poetry while hiding from the Nazis, they also learned what friendship and trust meant and how a circle of friends can constitute its own micro-culture, bubble, sense of belonging, home or whatever you want to call it. With their very existence being determined and shaped by the consequences of both German crimes (having to hide from Nazi persecution) and German pride (the humanists' enlightened ideal of education, including Goethe's *West–East Divan*), this circle of friends both belonged and was truly unique.

This spirit was still alive in the community I found in Amsterdam and I learned a lot from it. So much so, that I am still there. Maybe it is the only place where I feel a sense of belonging. But that belonging is not based on a specific heritage or a physical place. The heritage of Castrum Peregrini only teaches me one thing:

identity is dynamic, it needs to be constantly deconstructed and then constructed anew. And I constantly need to reposition myself in a changing world.

As soon as I embraced change as a core value of life, a positive opportunity for personal enhancement or development, then change was no longer a threat but a rich vista of possibilities. My belonging is now not necessarily linked to static entities like a nation, a language or a people, but rather to principles and attitudes that allow you to anticipate change, like trust, friendship and the firm belief that being human I am vulnerable and constantly need to work on self-awareness, that I have a dark side, that I am guilty. Through this awareness of my vulnerability I may become more humane and develop myself as a human in a changing world. But for this I need another person, a mirror, a critical and loving friend. Only with the other can I see myself and enter into that dynamic.

I encountered the metaphor of a pilgrim at Castrum Peregrini, and it has always been helpful to me and of strong symbolic value. The Latin name is obviously a contradiction as pilgrims are on the move, they have no possessions, let alone a home like a fortress that represents protection, security and safety. They consciously choose to have no security, but be out on the streets. A person of faith may go on a pilgrimage to reinforce his or her belief, or to embark on a spiritual journey that brings him or her closer to god and in many cases also closer to themselves.

Whoever that god may be who draws the pilgrim to the road, a pilgrimage is always the acknowledgement that belief is dynamic, not something static, not the reinforcement of a status quo. It acknowledges that life, the road we are on, is a challenge and at times a surprise, and that this challenge is in the outer and the inner world. For the pilgrim, the realities of both worlds are fundamental: it is the act of the physical being on the move that has an impact on the spiritual journey that we take with our memories, thoughts and emotions.

* * *

The famous Bach Cantata *Ein feste Burg ist unser Gott* refers to god as a fortress, the stronghold of the believer. The pilgrim acknowledges that the journey for the sake of god is more important than the goal of reaching journey's end. And that the fortress or stronghold that the pilgrimage offers does not have high, fortified, stone walls. The destination is just the trigger for being on the road, not the real goal. Pilgrims grapple with principles on their journey: how to keep moving, how to create an ever deeper understanding of god, or yourself. The pilgrimage is a method of enhancing one's awareness.

The title of Peter Sloterdijk's book, *You Must Change Your Life*, refers to the poet Rilke's experience of contemplating a statue by Rodin that formed the basis of one of his poems, 'Apollo's Archaic Torso'. That contemplation led him to change his life, to become a better person. Sloterdijk explores how, throughout history, humans have responded to what he calls 'the vertical tension' to which we are exposed. He uses Nietzsche's metaphor of the mountain top that we want to reach, the urge to become better, develop, grow towards the divine, to grasp a bit of eternity; an urge that we humans develop as a reaction to our mortality. Sloterdijk examines the opportunities humans have taken and still take to respond to this vertical tension. One of them is, of course, religion. He discusses medieval monks who turned to contemplation in the form of work and prayer as a means of trying to reach that mountain top. Sport is another such method of training to achieve change, as is art. The artwork requires that I interpret it by making a connection between my life and what I see, hear, read or experience. Through that act of empathy art gains meaning for me. But that act of making meaning requires the training of my eye or my ear, knowledge of an artistic reference system and personal vulnerability so that the artwork can reach me. In that sense making my own meaning will always be challenged by art. Whatever system we choose – religion, sport, art – we need *a* system to train ourselves in order to exploit the dynamic of the world positively for our own urge to develop as human beings. In all systems, self-awareness is the crucial factor.

In this sense I see myself as a religious person, even though I am a non-believer. I need rituals, or rather frameworks, such as art or contemplation, to feel comfortable with the vertical tension and the ever-changing world around me. For me friendship is certainly one of the central awareness mechanisms; it's one of my gods and something like a fortress. As a pilgrim I realize that this is my home, my cultural frame of reference. But I also realize that I will never be able to put my finger on anything and say 'this is it', this is me, this is us, this is the truth, because such certainty does not exist in any static or tangible form. It is the search itself that unites us and not so much what you find at the end of it. With that attitude, the attitude of a pilgrim, constantly searching for god, the truth or myself, I was able to leave many things behind and uncover a lot of acquired traits that made up my identity or rather self-image. I hope still to uncover many more. But so far, one has held fast: my guilt. Even more so, it is the driving force that keeps me moving, deconstructing and asking questions. And I must confess that it is one of the few elements, if not the only element of 'chauvinistic' pride I still cherish, because I think guilty people have a distinct advantage: guilt ensures that most of our attitudes are relative, not absolute.

Let's take the Dutch example once more. As an outsider you can get the impression that the Dutch are raised with a feeling of natural superiority; that they are a nation of tall, blond people who are convinced that they are tolerant, progressive, advanced and certainly not nationalistic. It's rather strange that it is exactly this self-image, this collective, anti-nationalist identity that actually constitutes nationalism and makes the Dutch feel superior. Or in the words of the historian James Kennedy: 'Dutch find being Dutch the "normal" state of being', probably just as 'guilt' for many Germans was the 'normal' state of being. I am not sure this is still so today.

The phenomenon of *Zwarte Piet*, Black Peter, has received international attention, but it may be worthwhile recalling it here to understand the point I want to make. It's a Netherlands tradition that on 5 December Santa Claus, with his white beard and red costume, arrives in the country on a steam boat from Spain. He then mounts his white horse and delivers presents to children. He appears in public parades, on television and in children's books.

As his task of visiting all Dutch children is huge, he is helped by a big group of Black Peters. These helpers have black painted faces, red lips and golden earrings, and they wear colourful costumes and black curly wigs.

You can see in this tradition whatever you wish, but among others a group of Black Dutch citizens with roots in the former colonies find it offensive and racist and have called for a reform of the popular children's festival. This in turn provoked a strong reaction among mainly White Dutch citizens who firmly believe that Black Peter is not racist but a harmless children's tradition that should be protected. In their interpretation the black face derives from the helpers sliding down chimneys to deliver presents to children and is not at all a reference to the slave trade. And they think the same applies to the black curls, red lips and golden earrings. The issue of Black Peter has become part of a recurring and very intense public debate in the Netherlands, almost a new, yearly tradition. In addition to the national debate, the character of Black Peter continues to draw negative attention from international commentators. Nevertheless according to yearly surveys, only 1 to 3 per cent of the Dutch public perceive Black Peter as racist or associate him with slavery, and around 90 per cent are opposed to altering the character's appearance.

In 2014, after fielding a question from a journalist, Kevin P. Roberson, the Dutch prime minister, Mark Rutte, a longstanding defender of the tradition, said: 'It is an old Dutch children's tradition ... My friends in the Antilles are very happy when it is Sinterklaas because they don't have to paint their faces. When I play *Zwarte Piet*, I am, for days, trying to get the stuff off my face.' His statements were criticized by several members of the press and people in the Antilles, as well as anti-Black Peter activists.

In early 2014, a coalition formed by the Dutch Folk Culture Centre began informal talks to discuss the future of Black Peter and whether or not the character should be modified or phased out entirely. Led by the centre's director, Ineke Strouten, several groups and individuals were consulted and presented their views, among them teachers, festival organizers, television producers, pro-Piet advocates and Quincy Gario, the co-founder of the ongoing 'Zwarte Piet is Racisme' campaign. The question of whether to maintain the tradition or alter it has become a part of a discussion about national identity: what represents 'us' and 'them', and who is to decide who is 'us' and who is 'them'? The notion that traditions and identities are socially constructed may be understood by some in this debate, but it does not suit those who fear change and seek emotional comfort in tradition. This demonstrates one of the unpleasant aspects of nationalism: if criticism of tradition emanates from those who are not 'us', such as Black fellow citizens, human rights organizations or the international media, this only enhances the blindness to prejudice based on colour. If my self-image is that I am not a racist, then no one else should tell me that I am. It is the fundamental ignorance of those who think they have a superior perspective. The idea that being White excludes me from judging the feelings of Black people, or being heterosexual (or whatever) excludes others from judging my queer perspective, or being a man excludes me from judging the female perspective, or being an insider excludes me from judging the outsider's perspective is not such a simple notion for many people. The Dutch general public would have long accepted that Black Peter is racism, or would have addressed institutionalized racism as a post-colonial heritage and many other forms of exclusion, had they grown up with inherited guilt, the notion of mistrusting yourself, the urge to be aware of your own vulnerability.

As this must certainly not become a Dutch-bashing exercise, let me be clear that I chose these examples because they are the closest to the reality of my life, and that I speak about them with empathy and the clear acknowledgement that I would obviously find similar problems in all forms of nationalism across Europe. My examples are rather a plea for all European countries to face the deep wounds inflicted by totalitarianism, colonialism, imperialism and so on, and take responsibility for them as human beings. Remember that these are visible, historical manifestations, the remembrance of which should be a universal principle. That is, they should be understood rather like the Eastern Orthodox tradition understands the biblical stories, as dramatic illustrations of a deeper truth. Eastern Orthodox churches re-enact the biblical stories to remember and to illustrate the higher divine order of the world in a visual, performative language. Just as Jesus's life was an enactment of god's universal principles.

When I began my first professional job in the Netherlands an older colleague introduced me in a meeting with the words: 'He is from Germany but he is OK.' Of course, with my 'guilt' I immediately understood and also acknowledged what she was talking about. Germans were obviously on the wrong side of history. In that period when I was new in the Netherlands I tried hard to become Dutch, to speak the language as fluently as possible, absorb Dutch habits, taste and values. It took me a few years to realize that you can't become Dutch unless you're born in the Netherlands and raised with the sense of natural superiority of that self-confident, progressive nation. So I gave up. I am now quite comfortable constantly renegotiating my belonging, and live happily in Amsterdam. My guilt makes me sensitive to exclusive thinking and nationalism. It is certainly not the only way of fostering that sensitivity, but it's one that I came to like. It constantly reminds me that all humankind is vulnerable to group fanaticism – read Elias Canetti's *The Torch in My Ear* or *Crowds and Power* – and potentially cruel to fellow human beings. It is certainly a much more comfortable starting position than growing up with a sense of moral superiority.

The question of how *we* would have behaved back then was thoroughly and seriously discussed in my youth. My classmates and I agreed that it would all have depended on the circumstances in which we found ourselves, and that privilege then would have played an important role – as it would now. And we also all agreed that Germany was guilty. Guilty to such an extent that it should never be allowed to forget what was done in the name of Germans. Today I am confident enough not to limit this moral injunction only to Germans. We must all be careful to stay human.

I still have a German passport but I would like to have a European one, or even better an international one. Then citizenship would have meaning for me again, not only protecting me with certain rights, but also acknowledging my emotions and thoughts and thus my cultural identity. Europe, as a concrete embodiment of 'never again', has made it possible for me to live my life in freedom and peace, and has taught me – both in Germany and the Netherlands – about history and myself as a human being. This is something that should unite Europe and help overcome nationalism. But the latter shouldn't just be replaced by a larger equivalent, 'Europeanism', or the search for the larger binding identity or the smallest common denominator that must hold everything together. Cultural differences and diversity are a good thing, a driver for progress and development, so we should not aim for standardization to solve the problem of the missing sense of togetherness in Europe. But there is maybe an attitude, a mindset or an ethos that we could share. We could become a band of pilgrims, exercising our search for what makes us human, what makes us vulnerable and what lets us grow and flourish. This mindset would be the binding force. So that passport of my dreams would not be linked to any national feeling but to inherited guilt and it would not display a national emblem or a circle of stars, but maybe something simple like a shell, the symbol of those on the move. A memento signalling that there is only one unifying characteristic: our vulnerability. That is our belonging and the rest is creativity. A guilty pleasure.

Bibliography

Catechism of the Catholic Church, www.vatican.va/archive/ccc_css/archive/catechism/p1s2c1p7.htm.

Freud, Sigmund, *On Metapsychology: The Theory of Psychoanalysis: 'Beyond the Pleasure Principle', 'Ego and the Id' and Other Works*, London, Penguin, 1991.

Karmiris, John, *A Synopsis of the Dogmatic Theology of the Orthodox Catholic Church*, Scranton, PA, Christian Orthodox Edition, 1973.

Kennedy, James, *De deugden van een gidsland*, Amsterdam, Bert Bakker, 2005.

GUILTY PLEASURE

Lyon, Irenäus von, *Adversus haereses = Gegen die Häresien V*, Fontes Christiane Bd. 8/5, Freiburg, 2001.

Sloterdijk, Peter, *Du must dein Leben* ändern, Frankfurt am Main, Suhrkamp, 2009.

Telegraaf.nl, 'De brief van de VN over Zwarte Piet', 22 October 2013, www.scribd.com/document/177303852/De-brief-van-de-VN-over-Zwarte-Piet.

Wekker, Gloria, *White Innocence: Paradoxes of Colonialism and Race*, Durham, NC, Duke University Press, 2016.

8

A World of Difference

Brian Klug

I am, by trade, an academic. But I do not approach this essay with the disinterestedness of the scholar. I have hung my cap and gown on the hook outside the door and I am entering upon this writing as myself. I am Jewish. I am a British citizen and I live in London, the city of my birth. I am conscious of the fact that we share an incredible shrinking world: a world in which people with different – and changing – cultural identities bump up against each other every day: a world of difference. Once upon a time it was easier to say that 'East is East and West is West'. But now the twain rub shoulders in the streets of countless European cities. Cultures can no longer be placed (if ever they could be) by the four points of the compass. This state of affairs gives rise to the question coined by the late cultural theorist Stuart Hall, who was born in Jamaica but lived in the UK all his adult life and thus was well versed in the diversity about which he wrote: 'How can people live together in difference?' I see this as the definitive political question of our times and the question at the heart of this book. It is certainly at the heart of this essay.

Not only is this a question about living, it is also, for me, a living question. It has currency in my life. It springs from my own experience and from my encounter with the experiences of others. I approach this essay as someone who is seeking to join the dots – the dots of my experience to the dots of theirs – and to see the line of thought that emerges. And, while it is useful to draw on the findings of research conducted by historians and social scientists, ultimately there is no substitute for (as it were) thinking in your own skin. This essay is an exercise in such thinking: it is an attempt to think from the inside out – and certainly not from on high.

I am wary of political thinking that takes place in a vacuum. No one lives in a vacuum. But one of the grand illusions of enlightened modernity is that it is possible to conduct political thinking from a neutral point above the human fray in a space that transcends all conditions and every way of life: a place that is no place. We are, however, creatures of planet earth, not minds floating in the ether. We can aspire to reach the plane of the universal – remote and abstract and uncontaminated by circumstances – but we dwell in the here and now, and (whether we are cognizant of this or not) our thinking is rooted in particular traditions. (This thought is both the starting point and the destination of the essay.) To think politically is to think situationally: to inhabit the moment *at* which and *about* which we think. And always this means identifying the events that burden us collectively. In our lives together, there is never a time when the sky overhead is perfectly blue. Accordingly, necessarily our political thinking is conducted under a cloud.

At the time of writing (March 2016), several dark clouds cast their long shadows over the European future. For the purposes of this essay, two loom especially large (though I shall deal with them only selectively). They are (as is often the way with clouds) not terribly well defined. Nor are they altogether separate – either from each other or from other clouds, with which they tend to merge. One is the expanding mushroom cloud that resulted from the explosive events in Paris in January 2015: the massacre on the seventh at the offices of the satirical magazine *Charlie Hebdo* (*Charlie* for short) and the murders two days later at the Jewish supermarket Hyper Cacher ('Super Kosher'). This will be my primary reference. But I begin with the other context, the other cloud: the 'refugee crisis' created by the storms of war in Syria and elsewhere. Hundreds of thousands of people – routinely referred to as migrants – fleeing to Europe, seeking a safe haven and a new future.

I begin with this context because it clarifies something about political belonging that is worth being clear about from the start. There are two levels of belonging, the second being deeper than the first. For people on the outside of Europe, peering in through frosted glass, belonging presents itself initially as a matter of legal status. What they want is a stamp from an immigration official that enables them to cross the threshold: a visa. A priceless piece of paper that lets them through the door, allowing them to resume the semblance of a normal life. Now, I have never been in their shoes. I do not know at first hand the desperation and anxiety they must feel. But I am acquainted with it second hand, via my grandparents, all of whom emigrated to Britain from Eastern Europe in the early years of the last century, three of whom were fleeing the Tsar. In the Russian Empire that straddled the nineteenth and twentieth centuries, legal restrictions (not to mention pogroms) made life intolerable for Jews. We are accustomed to making a distinction nowadays between 'economic migrant' and 'asylum seeker', but for my grandparents this was a distinction without a difference. The same is true for the preponderance of 'migrants' who are knocking on Europe's doors today. Pushed out of their countries by the grimness of war, they approach the borders of Europe and just want in. But once in, then what?

Once in, they or their children or their grandchildren are likely to aspire to a deeper sense of belonging. If this is my own family story then it is also the story of millions of immigrant families in the UK and across Europe. This second level of belonging is more substantial than the possession of a passport or even an entry on the electoral roll; these are preconditions but they are not the real thing. It is difficult to sum up the real thing – the deeper level of belonging – in a word or a phrase or even a sentence or two. Yet one word comes to mind, which I shall use to stand for this complex idea: home. Let this word in all its vagueness (but replete with benign connotations) hang in the air for now. Eventually I hope to bring it into focus.

*　*　*

I thought I was losing my grip on the word 'home' (or rather that the word was losing its grip on me) when, following the deadly attacks in Paris in January 2015, it fell from the lips of Benjamin Netanyahu. Speaking in a televised broadcast from the prime minister's office in Jerusalem, he extended the following invitation: 'To all the Jews of France, all the Jews of Europe, I would like to say that Israel is not just the place in whose direction you pray, the state of Israel is your home.' We (the Jews of Europe) would, he said, 'be welcomed here warmly and with open arms'. (He reinforced the message with a tweet sent on the same day.) Similarly, at the funeral in Jerusalem on 13 January 2015 for the four Jewish hostages murdered at Hyper Cacher, Netanyahu declared that 'Israel is our true home', where 'our' embraces the whole of Jewry, *moi aussi*. Suddenly, the word 'home' lost its lustre for me. Why was that?

While I have no wish to live elsewhere, normally I would not mind if someone were to invite me to pack my bags and move to another country. Whether I would be inclined to accept their invitation or not is another matter. But, generally speaking, it is reassuring to be told that there is a place where you would be welcomed 'warmly and with open arms' if you chose to move there. Yet, when Netanyahu issued his invitation, I backed off. More precisely, I recoiled. Why *was* that? It felt as though he were pulling the rug out from under my feet rather than offering me a roof over my head. But why? Why did it feel this way?

The answer is complex – too complex for this essay – and if I let myself pursue it for its own sake it would take me on a tangent even longer and more convoluted than the tangent taken by the ancient Israelites when they wandered in the wilderness for 40 years. Since, however, 'home' is a key word in my ruminations, and as my gut reaction to Netanyahu's intervention expresses my take on belonging, I shall try to elucidate this moment without straying from my remit.

The crux of the matter (for the purposes of this essay) lies in his use of the word 'true' in the phrase 'true home'. The word does double duty. On the one hand, it affirms the state of Israel as uniquely the home for every Jew, irrespective of where they live or the length of time they have lived there or the conditions of their lives or, indeed, anything whatsoever. Inserting 'true' before 'home' results in an *absolute* claim that Israel is the place where every Jew – me included – belongs. On the other hand (and by the same token), 'true' implies that 'false' applies necessarily to any other place which someone who is Jewish might call 'home'. Therefore it implies that I am bound to be wrong if I think of England as home, as though this were not a contingent matter but a rule written into the nature of reality. Furthermore, this is not any Tom, Dick or Harry speaking: this is the prime minister of Israel, a man widely seen (though, of course, wrongly) as representing the Jewish people as a whole. (When he went to Washington to address Congress after the attacks in Paris he said: 'I went to Paris not just as the prime minister of Israel but as a representative of the entire Jewish people.') He spoke with the authority of his office, both the authority he *does* have and the authority he *claims* to have. For all these reasons, I felt that he was pulling the rug out from under my feet vis-à-vis England, the country where I live and which, in some sense other than the purely formal, I call home.

But that is not all. Underlying Netanyahu's invitation to 'all the Jews of France, all the Jews of Europe' is a certain principle of belonging. I shall call it (for want of a better word) the *ethnic* principle of belonging. This is the principle that divides the pie of planet earth into a plethora of fatherlands and motherlands, so that Germany (for example) is the 'true home' for 'true Germans' (ethnically defined), Russia the 'true home' for 'true Russians', and so on. It is a global principle and applied to Europe it is precisely the principle that laid the basis for the political exclusion (and ultimately persecution) of my ancestors, *as Jews*, from the lands in which they lived. This principle is what drove my grandparents out. It is what led them to embark on rocky sea voyages that took them to London. It is the antithesis of the principle of belonging in which I believe and for which I argue in this essay. So, when Netanyahu invoked (if only implicitly) the ethnic principle of belonging, saying, in effect, that Israel is the 'true home' for 'true Jews', no wonder I recoiled. I would have preferred the hug of a grizzly bear to the warmth of Netanyahu's embrace.

*   *   *

Spurning his amorous advances, where does this leave me? If home is not defined by the ethnic principle of belonging, where does it leave any of us? What is the alternative at which I have hinted? Let me approach this question via a story (an old Jewish ploy that I learned at the feet of my rabbinical teachers). It is a simple story about a nice Jewish boy. Let us call him Baruch: Baruch ben Yitzchak Yehudah, to give him his full name. There is nothing special about Baruch, nor is there anything out-of-the-ordinary about his story. Set in north-west London in the 1950s and 1960s, it is an everyday story of a typical Jewish boy. Perhaps this is its strength, plus the fact that the story is true, more or less.

The north-west London world in which Baruch grew up was essentially Jewish. The family home was kosher, the two day-schools he attended (from age 5 to 18) were Orthodox, he played on the wing in a Jewish football team in a Sunday Jewish league, and the *shul* (synagogue), which was round the corner from where he lived, was a centre of social life for young Baruch and his friends. Venturing out on a Saturday evening meant congregating with other Jewish kids his age in front of Golders Green bus station, or visiting the local Odeon or Gaumont cinema with his Jewish cousins or Jewish friends. It meant, in short, remaining in a bubble. Inside the Jewish bubble Baruch had a clear sense of belonging. Outside, it was more ambiguous. The outside world was suspect; even the parts that were familiar were not to be altogether trusted. Or so it seemed to Baruch. (In a moment we shall see why.) Everywhere he went – even when he went to watch Arsenal Football Club play at Highbury stadium and cheered the team along with tens of thousands of fellow fans who included red-necked, pork-eating punters who did not know their *tallis* (prayer shawl) from their *tefillin* (phylacteries) – the Jewish bubble went with him. He was encased in it, like a ship in a bottle. Perhaps the glass was invisible to others, but to him it was palpable (though he did not consciously think of it this way at the time). In the world outside the bubble, he did not ultimately feel at home.

From his parents – plus the whole panoply of elders in his community – Baruch imbibed the idea that Jews can never trust the outside world. His parents (he learned) were lucky because they were born in London and thus escaped the fate of the vast majority of Jews in Europe, including numerous members of their own extended families: people who would never be more than ghosts whose names were spoken in whispers. But luck can run out. Baruch's father taught his children to be constantly vigilant: to be ready to pack their bags and leave – in case one day an antisemite were to seize the reins of power in Britain, just as Hitler had done in Germany. The children learned that there are Jews and non-Jews and that history showed that power is what the Jews do not possess (the opposite of the antisemitic myth). Thus, Baruch and his siblings grew up with a binary: 'us' the Jews and 'them' the Brits. In one sense, of course, they too were Brits; but not *true* Brits: not members of the group that is basically in charge. They were told that the latter, who allowed them to live in their midst, could at any time withdraw their hospitality. Baruch and his family were haunted by the sense that Britain was the host country and they were guests: guests in their own home. They did not belong the way the *true* Brits belonged; this is what made the world outside the bubble suspect. Not that his parents took a purely passive approach to life. On the contrary, they were both active and enterprising people; but primarily within the bubble.

For Baruch, the turning-point came at the age of 18. He left school and entered university. Soon he became involved, along with all and sundry, in running the students' union, formulating its policies, deciding its direction. He found himself rubbing shoulders with a mixed multitude: students from here, there and everywhere. Together, this young motley crew took charge of their own institution. Together they governed their own student lives. There were so many other 'others' in the union that the old binary – the clear-cut 'us and them' – began to fade. The union was a world of difference; and immersing himself in this world, Baruch found himself emerging from the bubble. He and his fellow students felt that they belonged to the union in a deeper sense than the formal membership bestowed upon them by their union cards (the equivalent of the entry visa or stamp in the passport). Why? Because their hands were jointly on the rudder. Together they determined the policy, the direction, the activities of the union. In short, they belonged to the union *because the union belonged to them*. And that is the point of the story.

I could say the story ends there. In a way it does, but in another sense it continues; and the telling of the story is itself a continuation of the story. For Baruch, of course, is me. His name is my Hebrew name; and, although I have never gone by that name (except in *shul*), I did not feel that in order to fully belong in the union I had to jettison the Jewish identity for which the name stands. I suppose I was lucky. If so, in telling my story I would like to spread my luck. I see the students' union as a microcosm, modelling a principle of belonging at odds with the ethnic principle that underlies Netanyahu's notion of the state of Israel as the 'true home' for the 'true Jew'. Call it the *co-ownership* principle of belonging. It is the principle that, in a world of difference, no core identity is excluded in the running of society and none is subordinate. Home is inclusion. Home is where the 'other' is. (I see this as the motto of the essay.)

This inclusiveness is what I have in mind when I speak of a deeper sense of belonging, a sense of belonging that no passport or visa by itself can give you. *This* inclusiveness: not the kind that is rooted in the ethnic principle. The latter might also generate a deeper sense of home for those who meet its criterion, but deeper is not always better. (The deepest desires of the soul can be the darkest.) Home, on the ethnic principle of belonging, is an exclusive territory; ideally, the total absence of the 'other'. Some people say (and repeat it over and again like a mantra) that 'it is only natural for people to prefer their own kind'. I am not sure what this means; it sounds like chauvinism dressed up as truism. But, in any case, natural is not necessarily good, especially as a basis for a political axiom. Some people call the idea of 'home' that is based on this (alleged) preference true. I call it toxic.

*   *   *

Home is a funny thing; at least it is when it really *is* home. As a general rule, the deeper your sense of belonging to a place, the more you can afford to parody others openly and, in turn, be parodied by them. Home is where you can laugh out loud. Which is why it is telling that, on the whole, the cartoons poking fun at the Prophet Muhammad, churned out by *Charlie Hebdo* in issue after issue, did not tickle the fancy of France's North African Arab population. Like British Jewry, French Muslims are diverse, not only in socio-economic status but also in relation to Islam. However, you do not have to be a believer (let alone devout) to fail to see the joke or appreciate the satire when the Prophet is depicted naked in pornographic poses. And even if you do not belong to a mosque, Muhammad might still stand for your collective identity. It can be enough if you (or your antecedents) are from Algeria or one of the other former French colonies in the Maghreb, especially if you live on the margins, in the *internal* colonies, as it were: *les banlieues*, the poorer suburbs around Paris and other major cities. From this vantage point, each of *Charlie*'s pointed caricatures is yet another dagger aimed directly at your heart by an establishment from which you are effectively excluded; which is hardly amusing.

It might seem counter-intuitive to refer to *Charlie* as part of the French establishment. The magazine, after all, fires salvos at every respectable target it can find. But, ironically, this is precisely the source of its status. *Charlie* is the unofficial jester of the republican court, France's freelance Shakespearean Fool, self-appointed to perform the role of lampooning the powerful and mocking the superstitious. Its origins lie in a venerable republican tradition, one that looks back to the eighteenth-century genesis of this Enlightenment state with its contempt for all things royal and clerical. Whether its relentless ridicule of Islam is true to that tradition or, on the contrary, a betrayal of its roots – a betrayal of the noble role of satire – is, however, a moot point. The magazine has its defenders and detractors. The former praise *Charlie* for its courage: for taking risks and breaking taboos despite multiple threats made against it over the years (not to mention an arson attack in November 2011). No one can dispute that the magazine has put itself at risk; it has done so by transgressing every conceivable line of good judgement, good taste and discretion. But is that courage? The question of whether it plays the part of republican hero or street bully depends on whom it chooses to pillory or taunt. The privileged or the disadvantaged? A minority on the margins or the group that is basically in charge? Those who are secure in their sense of belonging in France? Or those inside a fragile bubble, for whom the outside world, complete with its scatological *Charlie* the Clown, is more than suspect?

Into this divided France the catchphrase 'Je suis *Charlie*' fell like an axe, cutting even deeper into the very fissure in French society to which *Charlie* itself has made a modest contribution with its caricatures of Muhammad calculated to 'offend'. I put the word in scare quotes because it is problematic. In the public debate over Charlie (and over free speech in general), the word 'offend' has been stretched so thin that it covers almost any reaction that could be described as negative, regardless of the nature of the provocation or the impact it has on the person 'offended'. But there is a world of difference between, say, affronting church-goers by using an obscenity, and, say, humiliating a group that is already demeaned, accentuating their deep sense of alienation from the nation. Lumping together cases as different as these under the rubric of 'offending' muddies the waters. For one thing, it treats all negative reactions as equal when they are not. For another, it tends to reduce them all to the lowest common denominator; for 'offend' is, after all, a rather mild term. Vicars are offended in Victorian novels (especially at teatime). But they belong, securely; they *feel* they belong in the company of the people at whose words they take offence. A deep sense of alienation is the antithesis of a deep sense of belonging. The give-and-take of the game of 'offend' only makes sense among people who, deep down, know they belong on the playing field: people who feel at home. On the periphery, *le mot* is hardly *juste*. Nor is it just.

On the periphery, people know they do *not* belong, not in the full or deep sense, not in the way that the *true* French belong. Perhaps, for the latter, 'Je suis *Charlie*' worked well enough as a unifying slogan; for, although there was no consensus, the dissidents among their number were not *threatened* by it. But on the periphery, for those who not only were *not Charlie* but felt nullified by *Charlie*, the slogan was a gauntlet thrown down at their feet. It conveyed a message sent from the centre to the periphery: 'If you want to be one of us, identify with *Charlie*.' France closed ranks; and each of the 'unity marches', which were held across France in the days following the slaughter in Paris, was a *mise en abyme*, a reflection of the French self to infinity. This was *fraternité* with a vengeance. Meanwhile, at the main 'unity march' in Paris, footage appears to show Netanyahu barging his way fraternally into the front line of dignitaries. I hope that no one (except the Israeli prime minister) thought he was representing the entire Jewish people, for he looks a proper Charlie; and that is no joke.

*   *   *

The darkest cloud over Europe's future is Europe's past. This is not necessarily the past that Europe imagines for itself. Europeans are in the habit of thinking that for centuries they have been in the vanguard of the human race, showing the way forward to a backward and wayward world. France's *mission civilisatrice* is well known, but every European state that planted its feet on the soil (and the neck) of other countries has harboured a similar idea of itself. Each has groaned, to a greater or lesser extent, under the 'White Man's burden': the burden of imposing rule on other people in their own lands for their own good, the burden of extracting their minerals and other resources (including human) for the well-being of the native population; in short, the extraordinary burden of being obliged to conquer, to subdue and to exploit for the sake of the advancement of humanity as a whole: to *civilize*. And even if Europe today modestly plays down the civilizing role it has played in the world, humanity, so deeply in Europe's debt, has not forgotten. Perhaps, though, it remembers it differently.

Habits of thinking die hard, as do structures of unequal power. It would be nice to think that the past is passé and we are free to plan the European future from scratch. But this is a dangerous illusion. The past is too recent not to be present. Moreover, it is not past: it has merely metamorphosed, adapting itself to changing circumstances. Since the end of the Second World War, denizens of former colonies of European states have emigrated to the former metropole, where they have enjoyed a similar status to the status they once had in their countries of origin under imperial rule. Call it the return of the repressed. If they used to feel like 'guests' in their old home, subject to terms and conditions laid down from on high (and from far away), now they feel like (unwanted) guests in their new home, where they are anything but co-owners: where they are told they are under a 'duty to integrate', as if the onus were purely on them, rather than being shared by everyone who lives there; as if they have to make themselves fit an existing template; as if the template belongs – as it always did – to others, not to them. Take, for example, those French Muslims of North African extraction who, as the anthropologist Paul Silverstein put it in 2007, 'feel excluded from a nation whose citizenship they nominally hold'. In other words, they belong *formally* but not *fully*. He goes on to say that they experience their lives in France 'as a post-colonial continuation of … colonial forms of exclusion and violence'. The colonial periphery has not disappeared: it has merely changed location, moving to the European continent from its offshore sites in Africa and Asia. It has come home to roost. It is the then in the now.

So, when we broach Europe's future, we begin not in the *present* but in the *present-past*. This is the tense of our enquiry. If we ignore the past and the painful task of reckoning with it then the question 'How can people live together in difference?' becomes merely sentimental – and ceases to be political. In the present-past, this question is not only about bridging differences of culture, it is also about overcoming the disparity in status written into the script of colonial history, whether that history is remembered the way Europe imagines it ('the White Man's burden') or the way non-Europeans experienced it. In a way, it comes to the same thing. When you are standing on the top rung of a ladder and looking down, the view is not the same as it is for someone on the bottom rung looking up; but (with a nod to Heraclitus) it is still the same ladder. However, when it is the ladder on which colonizer and colonized stand, there is a slight difference. One view, the view from below, is veridical: it corresponds to reality, the stark reality of undergoing occupation and oppression. The other view is a delusion of grandeur.

*   *   *

Most of the 'migrants' knocking on Europe's doors today, seeking a safe haven and a new future, hoping to set up home, wanting to belong here, are not, by and large, coming from territories that once were colonies of the countries to which they seek admission. But they are, so to speak, in the same boat. It was different again with my grandparents; but not *so* different that I cannot join the dots of *their* experience to the experience of refugees today, or *my* experience to the experience of the third generation of other immigrant populations, and draw out a line of thought about the future. Jews lived on the European periphery for centuries, even if that periphery was inside Europe rather than across the ocean, and racist 'exclusion and violence' was as much a feature of life on the *internal* periphery as on the *external* periphery of the colonies. Not that there is a single narrative that can be distilled from all these histories. But, in the end, whatever routes have led us to the here and now, we meet in the same question, the question at the heart of this essay: 'How can we live together in difference?' 'How can we make each other feel at home?'

I do not have an answer, but I do have a suggestion as to where an answer might begin: focusing on the first-person plural: 'we'. Who does 'we' comprise? Consider the singular: me. I said at the outset that I am writing not as an academic but as myself, identifying myself as Jewish. What does this mean? It does not mean the same for everyone who calls themselves a Jew. But to me it means something which, unlike my cap and gown, I cannot hang on the hook outside the door. I take it wherever I go. It is non-disposable. It is true that Baruch (in the story I told earlier) emerged from his 'Jewish bubble' when he immersed himself in the world of the students' union. But he did not leave his Jewish identity behind; and this is as integral to the point of the story as is his emergence. What is it that he – I – did not leave behind? A miscellany, some of which is fairly superficial and some not. The latter includes a collection of texts, a set of references, styles of argument, a sensibility, a vocabulary, stories, symbols, humour, historical memories, ways of thinking, approaches to life. These are the *marrow* of Judaism; and the word that sums them up is not 'religion' but 'tradition'.

'Tradition' is not a word that gets a good press in modernity. It is associated with closed minds and rigid rules. I am using the word for want of another. The way I am using it brings me back to Stuart Hall, to whom I referred in the opening paragraph: the man who gave us the question about living together in difference. Traditions, he observes, are not so much bodies of doctrine as 'repertoires of meaning'. In other words, they contain resources for thinking. In this sense, a tradition is more like an atmosphere you breathe or a well upon which you draw than a cage that imprisons you. Those same resources are resources for rethinking the tradition itself. Some traditions are older and richer than others but none exists in splendid isolation. As our paths cross on planet earth, our traditions cross-breed. Some are more open and flexible, some have ossified. But the trouble with traditions that have ossified is not that they are traditions but that they have ossified. For, in the sense in which I am using the word 'tradition', no one is without one. Knowingly or otherwise, each of us draws upon one or more 'repertoires of meaning' when we do our thinking and our living. In an incredible shrinking world, each person comprising the 'we' is like me: different.

*　*　*

When I told Baruch's story I ended with an image: diverse pairs of hands jointly on the rudder. The image signified a union based

129

on the co-ownership principle of belonging: a union to which its members belonged because the union belonged to them. In closing, let me leave this same image hovering before the mind's eye. It is not an adequate answer to the question at the heart of this essay. But who knows? Keeping this image in mind, setting our sights on a Europe that corresponds to it, might, in time, make a world of difference.

Bibliography

Bowen, John R., *Why the French Don't Like Headscarves: Islam, the State, and Public Space*, Princeton, Princeton University Press, 2007.

Hall, Stuart, 'Conclusion: the multi-cultural question', in Barnor Hesse, ed., *Un/settled Multiculturalisms: Diasporas, Entanglements, Transruptions*, London, Zed Books, 2000.

Hesse, Barnor, ed., *Un/settled Multiculturalisms: Diasporas, Entanglements, Transruptions*, London, Zed Books, 2000.

Lentin, Alana and Titley, Gavan, *The Crises of Multiculturalism: Racism in a Neoliberal Age*, London, Zed Books, 2011.

Levey, Geoffrey B. and Modood, Tariq, eds, *Secularism, Religion and Multicultural Citizenship*, Cambridge, Cambridge University Press, 2009.

Mandel, Maud S., *Muslims and Jews in France: History of a Conflict*, Princeton, Princeton University Press, 2014.

Ravid, Barak, 'Netanyahu: I will go to congress like I went to Paris to speak for all Jews', *Haaretz*, 9 February 2015.

Silverstein, Paul A., 'Comment on Bunzl', in Matti Bunzl, *Anti-Semitism and Islamophobia: Hatreds Old and New in Europe*, Chicago, Prickly Paradigm Press, 2007.

Silverstein, Paul A., 'The context of antisemitism and Islamophobia in France', *Patterns of Prejudice*, vol. 42, no. 1, 2008.

Waldron, Jeremy, *The Harm in Hate Speech*, Cambridge, MA, Harvard University Press, 2014.

Yuval-Davis, Nira, Video conversation with Nira Yuval-Davis in 'Belonging and the politics of belonging', *Patterns of Prejudice*, vol. 40, no. 3, 2006.

9

A Never-Ending Story:
My Belonging Journey

Viola Raheb

With new waves of refugees still coming to Europe, the issue of belonging is growing in importance. So many people across the continent are debating whether these refugees will ever be able to belong to Europe. In many of the debates their cultural and/or religious background is being used as an indicator that they will not be able to belong, or that their 'difference' will at the very least be a stumbling block. But these presumptions are based on a static definition of identity. They overlook the fact that the development of identity is an ongoing process that is driven by meeting and interacting with others as well as by reflecting on who you are. I am not a refugee and I did not arrive in Europe as a refugee. Yet I do belong in this much-debated Middle Eastern cultural and religious context and at the same time I am being perceived by this society as a 'migrant'.

But let me begin by introducing myself. I am an Austrian of Arab, Palestinian Christian background. To put it more clearly, I hold Austrian citizenship, my cultural background is Arabic, or to be more specific, Middle Eastern, my ethnic roots are Palestinian and I was born the daughter of a Christian Palestinian family. The question of my identity or belonging – or anyone else's for that matter – is thus from the beginning very complex, multidimensional, dynamic and as such ever changing. In addition, there are at least two perspectives on the issue of belonging: the way you see yourself and how the outside world sees you – and they often vary, thus creating areas of tension. To illustrate this I'll first share some personal reflections on issues relating to my own sense of belonging.

When Elements of My Belonging Became Important

I was born in Bethlehem to a Palestinian Christian family in 1969. The different defining elements of my identity were being a woman, a Palestinian, an Arab and a Christian. These were not always in harmony with each other; there were always areas of tension between them. While I lived in Palestine I had few problems with the last three elements of my belonging. But the central conflict I faced was being a woman in a patriarchal society, or at least this is what I perceived to be the main area of tension. At certain crossroads in my life, my womanhood determined my self-image as well as the image others had of me. It affected my decision to study in Germany when I was 18, my becoming the first woman to hold the position of Director of the Evangelical Lutheran Schools – a position that was until then always occupied by men – and even my very personal decision to stay single until I was 33 years old and later on to prioritize my marriage over my then very well-advanced career. I felt the tensions associated with these decisions very deeply.

The years I spent studying in Germany between 1989 and 1995 were an important phase in my life. I was 19 when I went to Germany and 25 when I returned to Palestine. In Germany a major change occurred both with regard to my self-image as well as to the image others had of me. All at once my Palestinian nationality stood at the centre of how I saw myself as well as at the centre of how others saw me. Moving from one continent to another brought with it a shift in what I prioritized about my belonging. The political context was the first Intifada taking place in Palestine in 1989. Palestinians were portrayed in the Western media using a dominant stereotype: that of Palestinian children throwing stones. At the same time, valuing your Palestinian identity as an expression of national belonging was almost unheard of, not only at the social level, but also when faced with German bureaucracy. Every time I had to prolong my student visa, German state officials repeatedly confronted me with my official status: 'Nationality Unclear'. This categorization led to my growing longing constantly to emphasize that Palestinians do exist and that I was a Palestinian. But given the way that the history of the Middle East was presented, being a Palestinian often had the bitter taste of being labelled a 'terrorist'. Therefore, as a means of coping and surviving when being asked where I came from, I learned to accentuate a new and until then not personally relevant element of my belonging by stating that I was from Bethlehem. Shifting the geographic focus from Palestine to the little town of Bethlehem had a wondrous effect. Germans, who had their own stereotypical images and mental pictures of Bethlehem, the biblical town of childhood memory, felt at ease and encountered me with a smile, instead of withdrawal or scepticism as was the case when I told them that I was from Palestine. I would then add that Bethlehem is in Palestine, which made being confronted with my Palestinian identity less shocking to some.

But this was not the only difficulty. Most Europeans and Americans have neither met with, nor do they grasp the notion of a Christian Arab or a Christian Palestinian. They think that we have been converted to Christianity either by European missionaries in the Middle East or during our stay abroad. That Christianity is indigenous to the Middle East region, and certainly to Palestine, is seldom recognized. So being a Christian Palestinian was also a puzzling belonging to some. And that was not only the case with 'ordinary' people. Even in the Faculty of Evangelical Theology at the Ruprecht-Karls-University in Heidelberg where I gained my masters degree, some of my professors were astonished to have a female Palestinian Lutheran student studying theology.

And last but not least, I was aware that some attitudes towards me were driven by certain popular images that are connected with Arab women: often either exotic ones drawn from the images of *A Thousand and One Nights* or the products of a stereotype of a suppressed human being presented as trapped in a patriarchal, Arab, Islamic society. And neither case represents who I am as an individual.

These challenges that arose with regard to my identity and belonging had a major influence on me. It may sound weird, but I have become more 'Palestinian' in and through Germany than I was before.

In 1995 I returned to Palestine at a moment and in historical circumstances defined by the 1993 Oslo Accords. The entire socio-political context had changed in the years I was studying in Germany and at the same time, I myself had also changed. My socialization in Germany produced remarkable shifts in my belonging. I was still a Palestinian, Christian, Arab woman, yet I had become a Western-trained academician, whose academic first language was German, which was altogether different from knowing and using German as a means of communication. Having spent almost six years in Germany acquiring different cultural skills, learning a new language, developing friendships and so on, I experienced another change that led me to understand myself as, from then on, belonging to both cultures: Arab and West German.

Some people describe such an experience by saying that they feel themselves forever positioned between two cultures, a description I never use due to its static character. Rather, I used to feel like always being on a journey between these two worlds, to which I felt a sense of belonging; two worlds that were, in reality, totally separate, different, distinct and difficult to reconcile. I felt this reality even more acutely through the way people in each world paradoxically looked at me as belonging more to the other world and less so to their own.

Following my marriage in 2002 I moved to live in Austria. From then on Vienna became my new home. So being abroad is no longer a temporary experience of living and studying in a foreign country, but rather the place where my life is centred. And in the last few years, my sense of belonging has acquired new dimensions. I have become an Austrian citizen, which means that at border crossings I show my Austrian passport and doors open that had so far been closed to me as a Palestinian. At the same time I take part in political life in Austria, I have the right to vote, which I make use of, and I am engaged at various levels of Austrian society. The new challenge in my life therefore became learning to live and act not so much as a Palestinian in Austria, but rather as an Austrian citizen of Palestinian origin. This goes far beyond any shift in belonging arising just from learning a new language.

Becoming More Cosmopolitan: Personal and Political Realignments

Over the last 13 years I have repeatedly experienced my sense of belonging undergoing major shifts. The Arab element of my identity is becoming less of a determining factor. I have learned to see myself more as a cosmopolitan who has absorbed a variety of cultures and traditions through travelling to and living in different places. As such, it is almost impossible to reduce my cultural belonging to something one-dimensional. Yet, as my mother tongue, Arabic still remains central to my identity, more so since the birth of our son.

After a great deal of thought, we made the decision to raise our child as bilingual. Language is not only a means of communication. Rather it functions as a medium through which culture and tradition are transmitted. Though Arabic is my and my son's 'mother tongue' – a deceptively simple categorization with a wide spectrum of definitions – our points of departure differ fundamentally. (I will return to this question below.)

My Palestinian identity has also changed. From being a woman who was born and raised in the occupied territories, I am now a woman who belongs to the wider Palestinian diaspora living abroad. This geographical relocation has been accompanied by a political one. In the past I have hoped for, and committed myself to, a solution to the Palestinian problem based on the establishment of a state in the occupied territories. Today, I still hope for a political solution; one which does not involve completely giving up the right of return for refugees and other Palestinians living in the diaspora. But as a realist who hardly believes such an outcome to be possible, I hope for a solution that at least guarantees the Palestinians control over their own borders, which would then allow us all the right to enter and visit.

While undergoing this political realignment, I have also experienced a shift in my inner attitude. During my life in Palestine when I had to deal with the political context and the everyday challenges of living under occupation, I had what I would call a 'never-ending optimism'. In my 2003 book, *Geboren zu Bethlehem: Notizen aus einer belagerten Stadt* (*Born in Bethlehem: Notes from a Besieged Town*), I wrote: 'We cannot afford the hopelessness'. Today, living in the diaspora, I have developed what I would call the 'scepticism of distance'. The luxury of distance from everyday events, harassments and challenges makes it possible to consider other perceptions and allows space for more self-reflection – or at least let's say it might enable a rethinking of one's inner attitude.

At the same time my perception of my Christian belonging has also changed. One of the first shifts occurred when I was confronted with my husband's experience of this element of his belonging. This was dramatically shaped by the fact that he was born in the Palestinian refugee camp Dbayeh in Lebanon – one of the few refugee camps with a Christian Palestinian population, mostly Maronites – that was attacked by Lebanese Christian Phalangists in 1976 along with two other refugee camps, Tal el-Zaatar and Jisr El-Basha. As a theologian I have worked a lot on instrumentalizing God in war. But this time I was confronted with a narrative of which I was so far unaware. The Lebanese Christian Phalangists believed that the 'Jesus' of the Christian Palestinians in Dbayeh was not the same as that of the Christian Lebanese, although both sides belong to the same Maronite denomination.

I also still find it quite difficult to feel that I belong to the Evangelical Lutheran Church in Austria, which perceives its position as a minority in Austrian society as its destiny. I was raised to acknowledge the potential and possibilities of being a minority and the opportunities it allows to bring about change in society.

So, to put it simply: the various elements of my identity and belonging have shifted and are still shifting, and this is part of who I am, which does not make life any easier.

Two Generations: Towards a Pluralistic Sense of Belonging

As for our son Ranad, who was born in Vienna in 2004 and raised here, he belongs to a generation that also has to struggle with belonging, maybe more so than my generation, given that he came into the world already carrying the weight of multiple belongings. His arrival was one of the most challenging moments of my new life in Vienna. To me it posed the question of the extent to which I, as a first generation migrant, am ready and willing to engage in inter-generational challenges regarding the issue of identity ownership. Of course, I have to acknowledge from the outset that this is my perspective on my son's belonging and as such is the view from the outside.

During my pregnancy, I wrote him the following letter:

Dear Son,

The rhythm of your heartbeats invites me to remember my inner rhythm, which I had forgotten. Your once gentle, once strong knocking reminds me of my challenging personality that does not reveal itself only as powerful, but often expresses itself tenderly. The date of your birth cannot be determined, which makes me realize that everything in this world has its time and that nothing can be forced. To have you in my life means to confidently believe that the world is still in order, as an old saying goes. To have you in my life means to rediscover the miracle of life and to reaffirm life itself anew, through you and with you.

Affirming life is not an easy task for your parents. Your father was born in a refugee camp near Beirut, as a son of a Palestinian family that was expelled from their home in 1948.

Your mother was born in Bethlehem, as a daughter of a Palestinian family living under Israeli occupation. Both parents were born stateless. Both have spent their childhoods and youth in war and conflict, both had to fear for their lives. Both are living today in Austria, which is more out of destiny than of choice.

You will be the only one of us who will be born with a nationality. Under 'nationality' on your birth certificate will be written: Austrian.

This letter is in itself already an expression of intergenerational challenge: my language and perspective reflect my rational, cognitive approach to the issue of belonging, which can never be that of my son, since we will have and already have had different experiences. However, the nationality stated on your passport is one thing; having a sense of belonging to this country and this culture, which is a process, is another. One often-discussed question with regard to belonging is: 'Where is home?' For our son, home is definitely 'Vienna'. But this is not merely a geographical location. I remember one discussion we had together during a visit we made to Bethlehem. We were reflecting on the experiences of the day when my son asked me if, in the future, he would be the one to inherit my house in Bethlehem. I replied positively. He looked at me and said: 'I cannot promise you that I will come to live here. I like being here, but my home is Vienna. I can only promise you that I will come to visit Bethlehem.' In that moment I had to struggle with my tears. I had to ask myself: why would my child have the impression that I would ask him to leave Vienna and go and live in Bethlehem? And then I had to recognize that he felt that same sense of collective identity and belonging I still have for Palestine. When I speak of Bethlehem, I refer to it most of the time as 'home', yet not as a place on a map, more as the place where family and friends are. With my adult, rational and intellectual approach I can build bridges between the various elements of my belonging, but for him as a child, it seems these bridges were yet to be explored. At the same time, the question arises as to how our family narratives affect the notion of home and belonging of our son.

The question of the perception of Austrian society and its agencies of this issue is also relevant. Or to rephrase this from our perspective: how does the interaction with Austrian society influence our perceptions of identity and belonging? This is something often heard when we are asked where we come from.

Our son's answer is always the same: 'My mother is from Bethlehem, my father from Beirut and I am Viennese.' So it seems he does sense that there are different entry points of belonging for us and for him. Yet when asked only for himself, he usually answers: 'I am Viennese', which does not prevent people from immediately rephrasing the question: 'Yes, but where are you originally from?' And after again giving the same answer, another question follows: 'Where do your parents come from then?'

What more does my son Ranad have to say? To repeat again that he was born in Vienna and is a citizen of Austria? Surely the questioner would know by now that he speaks German fluently, even with a Viennese accent if need be. He could add that he attended preschool and primary school and is now in the Gymnasium. Nevertheless, for parts of society none of this seems to be sufficient as an indication of belonging.

Meanwhile, his answers have changed depending on the question or the situation. Recently, a journalist was interviewing my husband and me and asked whether he could also interview our son. The first question he asked him was: 'Do you feel yourself more Austrian or Palestinian?' Ranad did not think for long. He looked at him and said: 'I am both!' So for him it seems possible to have multiple belongings that include two socio-cultural backgrounds, which at first sight do not appear to have much that connects them. Yet explaining this multiple belonging over and over again is a strenuous exercise both for him and for us, since it continually comes up against the prior perception or the definition of the one looking in from the outside.

The issue of bilingualism that I referred to briefly above is relevant here. From early on, we decided to raise our son bilingual. He would speak our mother tongue, Arabic, and German. In the family we speak Arabic with each other. Yet our social life is very much dominated by German, the common language we use with friends, visitors, work colleagues and so on. In order for our son to develop the language skills appropriate for his age, as well as to help him mix with other children in his peer group, we opted to send him to preschool at the age of two. The population of the seventh district in Vienna, where we live, comprises mostly students, intellectuals and artists. Ranad was not the only one in his preschool whose mother tongue was not German. But we were among the few, if not the only ones, who always spoke to him in Arabic, also within the confines of the preschool.

At first he did not speak German at the preschool, although he understood everything. Nevertheless, very often we heard people say: 'The poor kid, you still talk Arabic to him, how can his German develop like this?' The most striking comment came, after about a year, from a mother of a child in the same preschool, when it became apparent that our son's German was at the level of any other child of his age whose mother tongue was German: 'I have really been worried about him concerning his language.' The fact that the woman had a migrant background herself struck me more than her comment. It is not only the image of the so-called 'majority' that bilingualism hinders integration; even migrants themselves often adopt this perspective.

It did not take long for Ranad to start talking to us in German. He also started asking us to talk to him in German if there were others around. He did not want to be different from the other kids, something very normal for his age, but also a sign of simply wanting to belong. For me it is very clear that his main language is German. This is the language in which he is most proficient and most comfortable. As a mother, acknowledging this is essential; therefore, for my part, there was never any sense of competition between German and Arabic, or the fear of the loss of an important element of belonging. As he gets older he is increasingly talking to us in Arabic, also in front of his friends. It took him a while to feel at ease speaking Arabic in public, but now that he does, perhaps it's yet another sign of an inclusive, multiple belonging.

Bilingualism often proved to be very difficult and challenging, for us as parents, for our son, for the school and for the environment at large. At the same preschool, we discovered how little training the educators receive to deal with bilingual children and to understand that being fluent in the mother tongue is of great advantage in acquiring a second language. One day I was talking to the educator at the preschool, while our son was looking at a children's book in the classroom. The educator looked at our son and told him that he was holding the book upside down. For a moment he was puzzled, so I told him this was a German book. He smiled and turned the book in order to open it from left to right. I looked at the educator and asked her if I could give her some advice on this issue. She was very welcoming. I explained that Ranad was bilingual and we read to him in both languages. Therefore he was used to opening some books from left to right if they were German, and from right to left if they were Arabic. The book he had just been holding was one that he had at home in Arabic, therefore he opened it from right to left. The teacher was surprised, as she did not know that Arabic goes from right to left.

But it is not only the issue of language that is challenging with regard to multiple identities. When we were looking for an elementary school for Ranad, I visited almost all those in our area, trying to decide which would be the best for him. On each occasion I asked the question: 'How about religious education?', deliberately formulating it in an open way. Practically every time, and there were many, I was given information about Islamic religious education, although no one asked me which religion we belonged to or which religious education I meant. Every time, the school personnel were surprised to hear that I was inquiring about the teaching of Christianity. After explaining that I was a Lutheran theologian and our son was baptized in the Evangelical Lutheran Church, often the answer was: 'Oh, this is not so easy, as we do not have many Evangelicals in the school. He might need to go to another school in the afternoon for religious education.' So again, the issue of religious affiliation was also very challenging for us. In elementary school, Ranad was the only Evangelical Lutheran in his class. For religious education to be provided there had to be at least three students – quite a challenge. Once it became clear that there weren't three students, some parents and teachers suggested that it would be better if I asked for my son to be released from religious education. Some said it was anyway better for him, since Lutherans were a minority in Austria and as a child he should not feel isolated or different. In Austria the overwhelming majority of the population belong to the Roman Catholic Church. So, when the denomination is a minority one, even religious belonging proved to be very challenging.

This brings me back to my personal belonging. Yes, I was born and brought up as a Lutheran, yet we were also raised in an ecumenical environment. Christian religious education in our schools was ecumenical and not confessional as it is in Austria. I wanted to pass on this ecumenical spirit to our son, so in first grade I sent him to the Catholic service at the beginning of the school year. When he came home he said: 'Mom, they asked me why I am here, this service is only for Christians.' At six years old he was unable to counter such a statement. Now he can. But nevertheless, he does not like to go to the Catholic services any more in the morning when school begins.

I could go on recalling more of the many experiences we went through and are still going through that influenced our senses of identity and belonging. But I believe this is a never-ending story, and it is good that this is so. At the start of this essay I wrote that the question of identity and belonging was for me, from the beginning, a very complex, multidimensional dynamic, and as such ever changing. The challenge of belonging is therefore a life-long process of reflection. I have tried to reflect on some of the significant moments of my particular journey and also on some aspects of belonging relating to the second generation within my family, knowing that by doing so, it offers another perspective from the outside. I have yet to explore the extent of the differences in the perception of identity formation and the construction of a sense of belonging between our first and second generations. As a mother, I am looking forward to the discussions we will have on these issues with our son in the years to come, and I hope that I will be able to listen, engage, understand and respect his perception of his identity and belonging.

Bibliography

Raheb, Viola, *Geboren zu Bethlehem: Notizen aus einer belagerten Stadt*, Trier, AphorismA Verlag, 2003.

Raheb, Viola, 'Shifting boundaries of the self: reflections from the perspective of the diaspora', in Mitri Raheb, ed., *God's Reign and People's Rule: Constitution, Religion, and Identity in Palestine*, Berlin, AphorismA Verlag, 2007.

Raheb, Viola, *Nächstes Jahr in Bethlehem: Notizen aus der Diaspora*, Trier, AphorismA Verlag, 2008.

Raheb, Viola, 'Leben mit Sehnsüchten und Melancholie', in *Rot-Weiß-Rot, Wir erzählen*, Wien, aa-infohaus Verlag, 2012.

Raheb, Viola, 'Multikulturelle Qualitätskriterien: Suchspuren in Kindergarten und Grundschule', in Simone Fuoß-Bühler and Hans Bühler, eds, *Interkulturelles Lernen in der Grundschule-Wer lernt von wem?* Berlin, Cornelsen Verlag, 2012.

10

The Paris 2015 Attacks and the Eclipse of Senses of Belonging in Europe

Umut Bozkurt

I was born two years after the ominous summer of the 1974 Turkish military operation in Cyprus in the last divided city of Europe, Nicosia. I was lucky enough not to have experienced what my fellow Cypriots went through and how they fell victim to the darkest acts of human capability: death, terror, revenge killings, rape of underage girls were the order of the day. My life was defined by war, division and the agony of that long summer. It could not have been otherwise. A country so traumatized and marked with heart-wrenching memories could not but produce children as scarred as itself.

Just like other conflict-ridden societies, the trauma of war was lurking around every corner in Cyprus. There it was when you looked into the face of the woman whose father went missing and who never saw him again. And there it was when you saw the walls of deserted houses in far-away villages pockmarked with bullet holes. Trauma was everywhere and it passed from one generation to another in the lullabies mothers sang to their children, in the stories grandmothers told to their granddaughters and in the sorrow-stricken faces of the relatives who had lost loved ones.

Growing up at a time when we were constantly exposed to nationalist propaganda meant that it was unthinkable that Greek Cypriot children were just like us and did not actually look like aliens with green tails. Nevertheless, I was somehow saved from turning into a bigoted nationalist and for this I am grateful to my father who taught me that what we learned from our history books was a distorted version of history, that 'there are good and bad people' in every ethnic community and you cannot discredit an entire ethnic community and victimize your own.

My outlook on the world was pretty much shaped by this experience. A belief in humanity that surpasses the divisions created by ethnic, religious or national identities is a legacy of those dark days of my childhood where we were seen as nothing but young minds to be moulded in line with the divisive, hateful discourses of the nationalist elites. I would try to subvert this indoctrination in my own way. I remember how my teenage self would daydream of many things including boys, beautiful dresses, becoming a novelist and one day overcoming this division to see reconciliation, coexistence and peace prevail in Cyprus.

My sense of belonging in Europe is also shaped by this very experience. I feel that I do and I do not belong to Europe. It depends on how European identity is constructed. I do not think Europe can be defined as a concrete empirical object such as a continent or a market. Rather, I view Europe as an 'imagined community', as Benedict Anderson would conceptualize it, where citizens are created by education and voting. Europe's existence was not prede-termined because spaces are socially constructed. Europe is being Europeanized. In that sense, the European Union is not a 'historical heritage, or a circumstantial reality', writes the sociologist Claudia Ghişoiu, but a product of a structured project that used political, economic and cultural means to construct 'a new vision for a continental alliance'. In other words, a set of agents helped generate a collective consciousness and promote the acceptance of the 'European idea'.

Yet is there a single European construct? Hardly. Some accounts, such as that by Marinus Ossewaarde, explain Europeanness as possessing 'certain [ancient] Greek habits of the mind, being accustomed to a Roman legal system and sense of organized rule, and having a Christian understanding of religion and the relationship between God and humanity'. Such a construct considers freedom, human dignity, rule of law, democracy, religious tolerance, reason, cultural pluralism and respect for the individual as constitutive of absolute European values. It is interesting to see that the slavery-based city state of ancient Greece is widely considered by some to be 'the cradle of European civilization', yet Nazism is seen as an aberration from core European values, the exact antithesis of the values of the Enlightenment and liberal democracy. It is as if the extreme nationalism and biological racism of the Nazis was far removed from the imperialism practised by European states. Even though Germany was a latecomer, in the words of the historian Enzo Traverso, 'a keen pupil following the two great colonial powers, France and Britain', the central tenets of Nazi ideology such as 'the natural supremacy of the white race, Europe's civilizing mission in Africa and Asia; the view of the world beyond Europe as a vast area to be colonized; [and] the theory that the extinction of the inferior races was an inevitable consequence of progress' were commonplaces of nineteenth-century European culture.

Especially from the 1960s onwards, European identity was constructed as characterized by multiculturalism. Will Kymlicka argues that 'multiculturalism should be situated in relation to larger social transformations of the post-war era':

More specifically, multiculturalism can be seen as part of a larger 'human rights revolution' in relation to ethnic and racial diversity. Prior to World War II, ethnocultural and religious diversity in the West was characterized by a range of illiberal and undemocratic relations – including relations of conqueror and conquered; colonizer and colonized; master and slave; settler and indigenous; racialized and unmarked; normalized and deviant; orthodox and heretic; civilized and primitive; ally and enemy. These relationships of hierarchy were justified by racialist ideologies that explicitly propounded the superiority of some peoples and cultures, and their right to rule over others. These ideologies were widely accepted throughout the Western world, and underpinned both domestic laws (e.g., racially-biased immigration and citizenship policies) and foreign policies (e.g., in relation to overseas colonies). After World War II, however, the world recoiled against Hitler's fanatical and murderous use of such ideologies, and the UN decisively repudiated them in favor of a new ideology of the equality of races and peoples. And this new assumption of human equality has generated a series of political movements designed to contest the lingering presence or enduring effects of older hierarchies.

Kymlicka argues that three 'waves' of such movements can be distinguished. The struggle for decolonization that took place between 1947 and 1965, the struggle against racial segregation and discrimination launched by the African-American Civil Rights Movement from 1955 to 1965 and the struggle for multi-culturalism and minority rights. According to Kymlicka, each of these movements transformed the earlier catalogue of hierarchical relations into relationships of liberal democratic citizenship. The ideas and policies of multiculturalism that emerged from the 1960s onwards changed the way citizenship is understood. In the past it was predicated that the only way to engage in a process of citizenization was to impose a single, undifferentiated model of citizenship on all individuals. Yet the key contribution made by multiculturalism was that 'the key to citizenization is not to suppress these differential [ethnopolitical] claims, but to filter and frame them through the language of human rights, civil liberties and democratic accountability. And this is what multiculturalist movements have aimed to do.'

Today, many observers emphasize that a multicultural Europe, where immigrants are encouraged to keep their cultural traditions from their homeland while embracing values of diversity and mutual respect for different cultures, has failed miserably. The multicultural Europe that celebrates diversity has been trumped by the Europe that today is busy turning itself into 'fortress Europe'. I can hardly feel that I belong to this fortress Europe that excludes more than it includes.

The EU reached a dirty deal with Turkey in March 2016 promising it aid, an easing of visa restrictions for its citizens as well as the 'unfreezing' of Turkey's bid for EU membership, in exchange for Turkey increasing its efforts to contain refugees within its borders. This said a lot about the EU's fear of mass migration as it renewed the candidacy of a country tilting towards autocracy and on the brink of civil war.

At a time when the world is experiencing the worst refugee crisis since the Second World War, the EU is striving to take in as few refugees as possible. The UNHCR has revealed that the number of people who fled war and violence in 2015 is likely to break all previous records. The refugee agency announced that the global refugee total had passed the 20 million threshold for the first time since 1992. In the words of UN secretary-general Ban Ki-moon, '2015 will be remembered as a year of human suffering and migrant tragedies.' He added that, in total, more than 5,000 women, men and children had lost their lives this year 'in search of protection and a better life'.

The response of the EU to the deepening crisis has been to fortify its borders. It also put in place a controversial military strategy in summer 2015: monitoring migrant boats in the Mediterranean's international waters more closely in order to break up human smuggling rings. In December 2015, EU leaders promoted the significance of border protection before the European Council summit. The president of the Commission, Jean-Claude Juncker, and the president of the EU parliament, Martin Schulz, organized a joint press conference in Brussels and underlined the importance of protecting the EU's external borders in order to preserve the integrity of the Schengen area. Juncker also added that he expects the European Council to agree with the main thrust of the Commission's recently announced proposal for a permanent European Border and Coast Guard. Refugee organizations voiced their concern that strengthened borders will just push migrants to use riskier routes and will benefit the human smugglers whose services will be in greater demand than ever.

However, Europe is not confronted only with a refugee crisis but with a set of crises: economic weakness, a deficit of democratic accountability, the perceived failure of multiculturalism, the right to citizenship, the increasing radicalization of European Muslims and the rise of the extreme right and xenophobia. These crises pose significant challenges to the sense of belonging to the European project.

The Dynamics Behind the 2015 Attacks in Paris

The murderous attacks in Paris in January and November 2015 tell us a lot about this multidimensional set of crises that is unfolding in Europe.

On Wednesday 7 January, two masked gunmen, dressed in black and armed with Kalashnikov assault rifles, attacked the building of the French satirical weekly newspaper *Charlie Hebdo*, killing twelve people and injured eleven others. After leaving, they killed a police officer outside the building. It was later revealed that the gunmen were two brothers: Chérif and Saïd Kouachi identified themselves as belonging to the Yemen branch of the Islamist terrorist group Al-Qaeda, which took responsibility for the attack. The brothers were later shot dead by police on the ninth following a hostage drama in the north of Paris. On the same day another terrorist, Amédy Coulibaly, having already killed a policewoman on the eighth, killed four hostages at a kosher supermarket in east Paris and was then killed by police when they stormed the building.

On 13 November, Paris witnessed a series of coordinated terrorist attacks that killed 130 people. The attacks included suicide bombings near the Stade de France and suicide bombings and mass shootings at cafés, restaurants and the Bataclan concert hall. ISIS claimed responsibility for the attacks, saying that they were in retaliation for the French airstrikes on ISIS targets in Syria and Iraq. Seven attackers were killed at the time and two more five days later.

So how do we explain these attacks? Since Al-Qaeda and ISIS assumed responsibility, we need to start by discussing the role of Islam in these killings. Can we say that the attacks were inspired by Islam? Does Islam provide ethical justifications for killing? No doubt fundamentalist ideologues and demagogues have utilized religious ideas and images, as a contributor to the Immanent Frame blog put it, 'in crafting worldviews of grand warfare', spreading them through compelling internet videos. The role of religion can be problematic in the sense that it can be used as an excuse for violence. However, it should be emphasized that religion on its own cannot explain these attacks. First of all, Muslims do not form a monolithic community. Nor does their religion define their politics. The arguments that 'Islam is inherently violent' and that 'Islam is inherently peaceful' are both problematic because, as the journalist Gary Younge put it, 'Islam, like any religion, is not "inherently" anything but what people make of it'. In the case of the Paris attacks some actors are using Islam to justify their violence.

Blaming religious beliefs and scriptures without looking at the socio-political and historical contexts leads to superficial explanations. In my view four conditions produced these attacks: the colonial legacy; the stagnation of the French economy and inequality; the failure of multiculturalism and increasing radicalization of European Muslims; and political developments in the Middle East and France's foreign policy.

According to Mark LeVine, the *Charlie Hebdo* killings are 'rooted in generations of violence, hypocrisy and greed' generated by French colonialism. Two perpetrators of the *Charlie Hebdo* attacks and one perpetrator of the November attacks were reportedly of Algerian descent. France's invasion of Algeria in 1830 led to 130 years of murder, expropriation, racism, exploitation and misrule that only ended after a vicious anti-colonial struggle. The bloody war that continued between 1954 and 1962 led to the death of 1.5 million Arab Muslims and many thousands of French men and women. A bloodbath of massacres, disappearances and torture continues to poison the relationship between Arabs and French to this day. In 1961, 200 Algerians were massacred in Paris as they were participating in an illegal march against France's colonial war in Algeria. As Robert Fisk explained in *Counterpunch* in November 2015, 'Most were murdered by the French police, many were tortured in the Palais des Sports and their bodies thrown into the Seine.'

In his 2015 book, *Who Is Charlie? Xenophobia and the New Middle Class*, the controversial French thinker Emmanuel Todd claimed that 'France is a kind of pseudo-republic favouring only the middle class while the working class and children of immigrants have been excluded ... Its economy is faltering, unemployment is sky-high, inequality is the norm.' Since 2008, like the rest of Europe, France has been gripped by the banking and sovereign debt crises. This also led to a political crisis and a questioning of the government's legitimacy, which became a significant factor behind the rise of Marine Le Pen's Front National.

After 2008 the top three French banks, Crédit Agricole, BNP Paribas and Société Générale, became the most systemically risky financial entities in Europe. In the studies carried out by the European Systemic Risk Board, France was warned of the overexposure of these banks and the need for billions of dollars of new funds to keep the French banking system solvent. In 2013, Standard and Poor's downgraded France's triple-A rating. It was clear that global capital wanted to see more drastic measures against French workers. Soon after, the three top banks announced major restructuring plans, which included a few thousand job cuts and plans to withdraw from several activities and parts of the world. In these circumstances, François Hollande was elected as the new president of France in the 2012 elections. Even though Hollande had promised to fight back against German-led austerity measures during his electoral campaign, as soon as he was elected he reneged on his promise and continued with Sarkozy's austerity policies.

The *Charlie Hebdo* attacks also revealed the failure of multiculturalism in France and the increasing radicalization of Muslims. There are about 20 million Muslims in Europe. France is home to around 5 million, roughly 8 per cent of its population, compared with about 5 per cent in both the UK and Germany. The 2015 attacks in Paris need to be understood in the context of France being the European country that has supplied the most jihadis to the so-called Islamic State in Iraq and Syria (ISIS). But the problem is not only peculiar to France. Ruud Koopmans carried out a pan-European study in 2013 that was based on interviews with 9,000 European Muslims. The results were striking. They showed how large numbers believe in many of the ideas championed by ISIS: a return to the roots of Islam; the conviction that religious (Koranic) law stands above all secular laws; a hatred of Jews and homosexuals; and a view of the

West as the enemy of Islam. Moreover, two-thirds of the Muslims interviewed across Western Europe said that religious rules were more important to them than the laws of the country in which they lived.

So why are Muslims being radicalized? If we just focus on the case of France – which has relevance for radicalization in the rest of Europe – a few factors are worth noting. France is home to Europe's biggest Muslim minority suburbs (*banlieues*) where large numbers of unemployed Muslims live, struggling with poverty, segregation, exclusion and marginalization. Some are involved in crime and drugs and serve prison sentences, and some of those are radicalized in the process. What defines this French-born generation is grievance more than anything else. The perpetrators of the *Charlie Hebdo* killings were raised on such rough estates, involved in violence and crime as well as having unstable family lives. Chérif and Saïd Kouachi were orphaned brothers who grew up in foster homes. Amédy Coulibaly was also raised on one of the Paris *banlieue*'s most notorious estates. Both Chérif Kouachi and Coulibaly served time in prison, Kouachi for his involvement in a case involving the organization of jihadis to fight Americans in Iraq, Coulibaly for his involvement in robbery. Prison seems to be playing a significant role in radicalizing France's Muslims. It was certainly the case with Chérif Kouachi who met Djamel Beghal, a jihadi convicted for attempting to bomb the American embassy in Paris in 2001 and introduced by him to Coulibaly.

Clearly, the fate of Muslims in foreign conflicts plays a significant role in radicalizing European Muslims. In this sense the 2015 attacks should be placed in the broader context of wars going on from Pakistan to Palestine. Without a doubt illegal wars, torture, civilian massacres, daily bombings, kidnappings in the Gulf and the Middle East, where the victims have usually been Muslim, informed the actions of the perpetrators. Chérif Kouachi, who was affiliated with al-Qaida, said in a 2007 court deposition: 'I got this idea when I saw the injustices shown by television on what was going on over there. I am speaking about the torture that the Americans have inflicted on the Iraqis.'

At the time France was strongly opposing the invasion of Iraq, so Chérif Kouachi's rage was first aimed at the US. Yet despite major differences at times, French intelligence and security services have worked closely with their US counterparts on jihadis in Libya, manipulating the Tuareg in Mali, or working with the Saudis. For example, the French made strenuous efforts to join forces with the Saudis and Turkey to remove the Assad regime in Syria. Together with Israel and Saudi Arabia, France also cooperated with the jihadis who were later to be formalized as ISIS to create havoc in Syria. Yet France then carried out air strikes on ISIS targets in Iraq.

Making Sense of the Multidimensional Crises of the European Project

The assessment of the dynamics behind the 2015 attacks was revealing in the sense that it also touched on the EU's multidimensional crises: the economy, legitimacy, democracy, citizenship and multiculturalism. Here, I will examine each of these and discuss how they undermine the sense of belonging in Europe, focusing on five interrelated issues: neoliberalism and austerity, the rise of the extreme right, the crisis of legitimacy, democracy and citizenship, and finally the rise of austerity citizenship. And I add a note about Brexit, the UK's referendum vote to leave the EU.

As in the case of France, following the global crisis of 2008, which had severe repercussions on all European economies, governments across the continent instituted austerity measures to force working people to bear the cost of the financial meltdown. Even though a significant reason for the crisis was the recklessness of the bankers, 'the tiered and hieratical system in Europe with Germany, Austria and the Netherlands at the top had sought to present the Eurozone crisis as problems of the fiscal indiscipline of leaders in Portugal, Ireland, Italy, Greece and Spain', writes Horace Campbell. Under Chancellor Angela Merkel, Germany has espoused a destructive austerity policy that has demanded budget cuts and opposed stimulus programmes that could help revive the struggling economies of southern Europe. Consequently, draconian cuts in public expenditure created major problems in societies such as Greece and Spain where unemployment soared to over 25 per cent. Yet despite these measures, it is not possible to argue that the system has stabilized, as Europe is now facing deflation and a deepening of the economic recession.

One of the significant outcomes of the global financial downturn and the austerity measures that were implemented in the aftermath was the resurgence of Europe's far right. In France, Marine Le Pen's Front National (FN) is on the rise. In an environment marked by the weakness of the left and Hollande's inability to resist austerity measures, the FN exploited the fears of the economically disadvantaged and politically deprived, disgruntled citizens struggling with high unemployment, property repossessions and an inability to obtain credit. Le Pen promotes a programme that calls for a moratorium on immigration and the implementation of a 'French first' policy on welfare benefits and employment, as well as restoration of the death penalty. This discourse paid off. In the EU elections of 2014, the FN emerged as the dominant party, receiving 25 per cent of all votes. The FN also won the first round of France's regional elections on 6 December 2015, taking 28 per cent of the vote. Even though it was not successful in the second round, the party is gaining ground.

The resurgence of the far right in France, and also in Germany, Greece, Sweden, the Netherlands and the UK, means that there is a chorus of national leaders who argue that 'the open borders and liberal tolerance championed by the EU are allowing a virulent jihadist virus to infect our countries' and 'the real culprit is Islamic immigrants taking jobs away from the native-born', writes Jacob Heilbrunn. With the success of the 'leave' campaign in the UK's EU referendum, the main plank of Nigel Farage's UK Independence Party, which won 28 per cent of the vote in the May 2014 EU elections, is in the process of implementation. Its criticism of French multicultural policies for creating a jihadist 'fifth column' in the country will no doubt continue. The far right Freedom Party is leading the polls in the Netherlands and the anti-immigrant Sweden Democrats Party gained 13 per cent of the vote in Sweden in 2014. In Greece, the neo-Nazi Golden Dawn Party entered parliament in 2012. Its slogan was 'so we can rid this land of filth'.

The rise of the far right in Europe is evidence of the decreasing support for the EU and the idea of European integration, but the erosion of the sense of belonging to the European project, as demonstrated in data produced by Eurobarometer showing the change in percentage of citizens who trusted the EU between 2007 and 2012, manifests itself more broadly than just as a turn to reactionary extremism. Apart from Finland and Sweden, there has been a marked decrease in the number of citizens of EU member states who support the European project, particularly so in Ireland, Slovenia, Portugal, Spain, France and Greece.

The most pronounced drop in support for the EU was recorded in countries facing a deeper economic crisis. Nevertheless, trust declined even in countries that have not been under direct conditionality or pressure from the EU and the International Monetary Fund (IMF). Declining trust in the EU reveals the crisis of legitimacy the entity has been facing in the aftermath of the 2008 crisis.

The EU decided to deal with the financial crisis by imposing austerity measures on democratically elected governments as a result of decisions taken by a closed group of self-serving and democratically unaccountable decision-makers. Increasingly, Europe is turning into a Europe of markets in 'which non-democratic institutions make use of blackmail and fear to impose unpopular decisions', writes Donatella Della Porta. The problem is that, in the aftermath of 2008, the EU parliament has seen its visibility reduced, whereas the closed group of decision-makers has gradually assumed greater weight in policy-making. The European Central Bank, created to be independent of democratic controls, has assumed enormous power as it decided whether to create money and how to distribute it. Decisions taken with very little transparency were then imposed on democratically elected governments that led to them losing their sovereignty in the process.

Europe's crises of legitimacy and democracy are coupled with a crisis of citizenship. The Marshallian concept of citizenship that had become part of the new post-war consensus is today giving way to austerity citizenship. According to T.H. Marshall, citizenship is a status, given to all full members of a community, that has three main elements: civil (freedom of speech, thought, faith, liberty of the person, the right to own property and to conclude valid contracts, the right to justice), political (right to participate and execute power) and social rights (right to an adequate standard of living, right to education, right to housing). He emphasized that all three elements were interconnected: first, civil rights were gained, followed by political and social rights. Marshall's model became the predominant one for understanding citizenship in liberal democracies after the Second World War.

After 1945 European societies co-opted their working class members by providing them with the basic welfare that necessarily flows from the interconnected rights at the heart of the Marshallian model of citizenship. Yet following the decline of welfarism in the aftermath of the economic shocks of the 1970s, the rise of neo-liberalism and the fiscal retrenchment introduced to tackle the 2008 crisis, the politics of austerity is producing what Nicos Tri-mikliniotis, Dimitris Parsanoglou and Vassilis Tsianos define as 'austerity citizenship'. They argue that 'Citizenship is in this context the specific tool of sovereign governance that regulates the balance between rights and representation and renders certain populations as legitimate bearers of rights while other populations are marked as inexistent', and driven towards illegalization and invisibility. Who are the new 'rejects'? The new homeless who lost their homes after the economic crisis, the unemployed, migrants. The exclusion of the groups who were co-opted into the system in the past leads to destructive social upheaval, such as the attacks carried out by jihadis recruited from the poverty-stricken suburbs of French and Belgian cities.

Furthermore, the imposition of austerity citizenship perpetuates the image of a fortress Europe that is anything but multicultural. Subaltern migrants are blamed for undermining 'our' welfare state. Immigrants are scapegoated due to their inability to integrate into 'our' liberal norms because they are allegedly predisposed towards fundamentalist Islam/criminality/terrorism. Even though it is the neoliberal policies which generate the conditions for the exclusion, marginalization and victimization of migrants, austerity citizenship serves to legitimize the exclusion of certain groups and pushes them towards invisibility.

Without dissecting it at length, the 23 June 2016 UK referendum vote to leave the EU can be seen as another manifestation of the decreasing support for the idea of European integration and the crisis of belonging to Europe. Media reports and opinion polls revealed that a significant segment of the white working class voted to exit the EU, the poorest and most alienated group in British society. And a significant factor for them, and the non-working class pro-Brexit voters, was opposition to immigration and, for many, to immigrants themselves. These voters, still bitter about the effects of the 2008 global financial crisis, felt that the state had left them behind and that solving the problems they face – finding secure jobs, struggling on inadequate pensions, avoiding the poverty trap – required 'taking back control' of their own lives by introducing radical controls on immigration.

The Challenge to People's Sense of Belonging in Europe

I see the 2015 Paris attacks as the Pandora's Box that brought into the limelight the multidimensional set of crises currently facing the European project. These crises pose significant challenges to people's sense of belonging in Europe. The significant decline of trust in the EU, including among countries not under pressure from the EU and the IMF, is not surprising when a group of democratically unaccountable decision-makers run roughshod over the decisions of elected governments and impose unpopular decisions that impoverish millions of people.

My personal sense of belonging in the European project is also undermined as I observe that Europe today is busy turning itself into 'fortress Europe', trying to protect itself from the influx of refugees at a time when the world is experiencing the worst refugee crisis since the Second World War. This is a Europe where xenophobia and the far right are on the rise, European Muslims who live as 'second-class citizens' are increasingly radicalized and the post-war Marshallian citizenship model is evolving into an austerity citizenship that excludes many who were co-opted into the system in the past. It marks some as legitimate bearers of rights while creating millions of new rejects, some of whom carry the potential to engage in disruptive social upheaval.

It is neoliberal policies that generate the conditions for the exclusion, marginalization and victimization of certain groups in society and produce austerity citizenship. Europe remains a political construct that favours the white middle class, while the working class and immigrants are excluded. It persists with an economic model that appeals to the stability concerns of a small number of capitalists at the expense of a faltering economy marked by deepening inequality and high unemployment. As long as this is the case, it is hard to see how the sense of belonging and trust in Europe can be restored.

Bibliography

BBC News, 'Paris attacks: who were the attackers?', 9 December 2015, www.bbc.com/news/world-europe-34832512.

Caldwell, Christopher, 'Immigration and Islam: Europe's crisis of faith', Wall Street Journal, 16 January 2015, www.wsj.com/articles/europe-immigration-and-islam-europes-crisis-of-faith-1421450060.

Campbell, Horace G., 'Manipulation in Paris', Counterpunch, 19 January 2015, www.counterpunch.org/2015/01/19/manipulation-in-paris/.

Ceka, Besir, 'The EU may have a democratic deficit, but national governments are facing an even greater legitimacy crisis', London School of Economics Blog, 29 October 29 2013, http://blogs.lse.ac.uk/europpblog/2013/10/29/the-eu-may-have-a-democratic-deficit-but-national-governments-are-facing-an-even-greater-legitimacy-crisis/.

Chrisafis, Angelique, 'Emmanuel Todd: the French thinker who won't toe the Charlie Hebdo line', Guardian, 28 August 2015.

Cook, Lorne, 'EU turns to Turkey to help manage its migration woes', Associated Press, 27 November 2015, http://bigstory.ap.org/article/08a1483c24054657a81b2eea2dc1afc4/eu-turns-turkey-help-manage-its-migration-woes.

Economist, The, 'The attacks on Charlie Hebdo and a kosher supermarket brought the French together. But the unity may not last', Paris, 17 January 2015.

Esman, Abigail R., 'Radicalization of Europe's Muslims hits a crisis point', The Investigative Project on Terrorism, 23 March 2015, www.investigativeproject. org/4803/guest-column-radicalization-of-europe-muslims#.

Fisk, Robert, 'Charlie Hebdo: Paris attack brothers' campaign of terror can be traced back to Algeria in 1954', Independent, 9 January 2015.

Fisk, Robert, 'Shadows of Algeria: the lost context of the Paris attacks', Counterpunch, 17 November 2015, www.counterpunch.org/2015/11/17/the-shadow-of-algeria-the-lost-context-of-the-paris-attacks/.

Ghişoiu, Claudia, 'Constructing European identity', Romanian Journal of Sociology, nos. 1–2, 2012.

Heilbrunn, Jacob, 'Charlie Hebdo fallout: specter of fascist past haunts European nationalism', Reuters blog, 13 January 2015, http://blogs.reuters. com/great-debate/2015/01/13/charlie-hebdo-fallout-specters-of-fascist-past-haunt-europes-new-nationalism/.

Immanent Frame, The, 'Values and violence: thoughts on Charlie Hebdo', 24 February 2015, http://blogs.ssrc.org/tif/2015/02/17/values-and-violence-thoughts-on-charlie-hebdo/.

Kymlicka, Will, 'The rise and fall of multiculturalism? New debates on inclusion and accommodation in diverse societies', in Steven Vertovec and Susanne Wessendorf, eds, Multiculturalism Backlash: European Discourses, Policies and Practices, London, Routledge, 2010.

LeVine, Mark, 'Why Charie Hebdo attack is not about Islam', AlJazeera.com, 10 January 2015, www.aljazeera.com/indepth/opinion/2015/01/charlie-hebdo-islam-cartoon-terr-20151106726681265.html.

Marshall, Thomas H., Citizenship and Social Class, and Other Essays, Cambridge, Cambridge University Press, 1950.

Ossewaarde, Marinus, Theorizing European Societies, Basingstoke, Palgrave Macmillan, 2013.

Pan European Networks, 'Border safety urged', 17 December 2015, www. paneuropeannetworks.com/government/border-safety-urged/.

Porta, Donatella Della, 'The European Union's crisis of legitimacy and the Greek referendum', Global Research, 9 July 2015, www.globalresearch.ca/the-european-unions-crisis-of-legitimacy-and-the-greek-referendum/5461541.

Safdar, Anealla, 'Number of refugees to hit record in 2015', Al Jazeera, 18 December 2015, www.aljazeera.com/news/2015/12/deaths-remembered-international-migrants-day-151218035026917.html.

Traverso, Enzo, 'Production line of murder', Le Monde Diplomatique, February 2005, https://mondediplo.com/2005/02/15civildiso.

Trimikliniotis, Nicos, Parsanoglou, Dimitris and Tsianos, Vassilis S., Mobile Commons, Migrant Digitalities and the Right to the City, Basingstoke, Palgrave Macmillan, 2015.

Younge, Gary, 'Charlie Hebdo: the danger of polarised debate', *Guardian*, 11 January 2015.

Zeese, Kevin, 'The roots of Charlie Hebdo attacks: colonialism and war', *Popular Resistance*, 11 January 2015, www.popularresistance.org/the-roots-of-charlie-hebdo-attacks-colonialism-war/.

11

Home and Homelessness in Europe

Göran Rosenberg

I must confess to a certain obsession with place, and especially with the place of my childhood. There have been other places in my life, and to some of them I am attached with lasting bonds of memory, but the place where I first saw the world, and saw everything for the first time, and gave everything I saw its first name, has remained a place of incomparable significance to me. Perhaps this is a personal oddity, having to do with the peculiarities of my biography, or perhaps just a matter of character, mine being of a more place-bound variety. There are certainly people who appear to be at home anywhere and who would consider my obsession with place atavistic and obsolete, if not downright reactionary. In a rapidly globalizing world, the attachment to place, and the quest for home associated with it, has often come to be considered a primitive remnant from a pre-globalized era of limited mobility and local horizons, a lingering nostalgia that may all too easily become the source of populist resentment, ethnic nationalism and xenophobic fear. The German word *Heimat*, with its historical connotations of being a cornerstone of Nazi ideology (*Blut und Boden*, blood and soil), undoubtedly impregnates the notion of home with the sentiments of attachment and belonging. And there is no denying the destructive potential of *Heimat* in the history of Europe.

One might perhaps argue that this notion of home is a peculiar product of German culture and history since it seems to have no equivalent in English. 'Homeland', 'fatherland' or 'motherland' may have similar ethnic and nationalist connotations but they lack the specific spatial quality of *Heimat*; an irreplaceable physical and human landscape to which our sense of home is inherently attached. Needless to say, I have no wish to make the place of my attachments the foundation of an ideology or a source of resentment, and even less so a cause for strife and war. But neither do I wish to renounce or suppress a relationship that I believe has formed my life in ways not fully explicable. I would go even further and argue that attachment to place is as intrinsic to human existence as is the need of home.

A home can certainly be many things, but the physical and human environment, in which we evolve into human beings and make our way into the world, is arguably a place that will stay with us and shape us whether we are aware of it or not. The science telling us so is convincing (the lasting effects of early childhood experiences) and so is the story of my father, which tells me that the significance of such a place to a human being will be more conspicuous in its absence than in its presence. To be deprived of it wholly and radically, including the memory of it, or rather the faculty to remember it, will make for a lasting sense of homelessness that has become part of my biography.

In the late summer of 1945, the young man who was to be my father arrived at Öreryd in the southern Swedish province of Småland. It's a very small place situated on an ancient trade route running along the small river Nissan, which flows from the hills of Västergötland to the coast of Halland, and you might easily pass it by without noticing. Perhaps easier done today than 70 years ago when Öreryd was the site of a temporary camp for survivors of the Nazi concentration and extermination camps, and some ten wooden barracks were erected on the common just beneath the white wooden church. During most of the war, the barracks in Öreryd were inhabited by refugees from Norway – more cousins to the villagers than strangers really – but on the very day the war ended, the Norwegians left the barracks and marched to the railway station in neighbouring Hestra, 'with flags flying and music playing', to board the train for home.

The young man, by contrast, had no home waiting for him. No traces of home remained in the world he had left behind, and in the world where he had arrived no home was on offer. He was not even sure that he would be allowed to stay. The Swedish government had agreed to receive people like him on a temporary basis only, as 'transit migrants' or *repatriandi*, which meant that in due time they were expected to find a home somewhere else. If the young man had known the local language, and had thus been able to read the editorial in the leading liberal Swedish daily *Dagens Nyheter* on 15 September 1945, he would have noticed that the continued presence of 'Polish-Jewish refugees' on Swedish soil was a contested matter. 'We are not used to dealing with people so alien to Swedish views and standards', the paper wrote.

Some 70 years later I can report that the young man and the equally young woman who would be my mother, and who had arrived in Sweden a year later as homeless as he, not only remained in Sweden but eventually managed to build a home of sorts, if not so much for themselves, then for their children and grandchildren.

Late in life, when I began writing *A Brief Stop on the Road from Auschwitz*, a childhood memoir of my father whom I had lost at the age of eleven, I soon discovered that what a child may see and understand of a father is very little, and what he may remember is sketchy and unreliable. Young children normally take very little interest in the lives of their parents, busy as they are making sense of their own lives, having to make themselves at home in a world which still surprises them every day. There is a world common to children and parents, of course, a world of emotions and experiences, stories and memories, of a family past to be told and shared, often with actual people to confirm it, and an inherited artefact or two to evoke it. In my case, such a family past was non-existent as far as the eyes of a child could see, which meant that large parts of the world of my father remained invisible. What the eyes of a child could get a glimpse of at times, and the body of a child might store as sensory deposits, to be retrieved as memories much later, were the incessant and at times frantic attempts to survive the loss of that kind of home which spells not only roof over your head but ground under your feet.

In the case of my father, the ground was cut from under his feet in a most thorough and irrevocable manner, leaving him to cope not only with a radical loss of home, but of human value as well. The humiliation and dehumanization of victims was instrumental to the Nazi extermination project. Having survived physical extermination didn't mean that you had withstood the prior mental destruction. After having survived Auschwitz my father had to survive the survival, and as a child I could only get a whiff of what that meant.

There were the inexplicable moments of silence, the sudden whitening of a face, the hardened grip on my arm or hand, the voice of a child heard crying through the wall at night. There was also the glow of ambitions, the flood of plans and projects, the radiance of unreleased energy, the sometimes puzzling mixture of light-hearted playfulness and desperate determination. As I tried to make sense of my childhood memories, adding to them the knowledge of hindsight and perhaps some reflection as well, I saw a man beset by the necessity to restore his value as a human being in others' eyes and his own. To justify his survival, perhaps, by making himself worthy of that life given to him by the most unlikely of circumstances, beyond any notion of fairness. At any rate, that is how, much later, I wished to explain the sometimes frightening swings between boundless cheerfulness and impenetrable silence, and the eerie air of absence and loneliness he radiated as we walked along the quays of the harbour during our last winter together.

The particular story of my father's attempt to regain his foothold in the world in a small industrial town in Sweden may not lend itself to broader generalization. People lose their homes for various reasons and under shifting circumstances and they differ as to their possibilities and abilities to deal with their situation. Surviving the Holocaust made for an extraordinarily harsh experience of multiple and severe losses, in the case of my father eradicating every remnant of home and repressing every memory that might have been attached to it.

Being homeless and yet having memories and people and even artefacts with which to furnish a home to be, is arguably easier to overcome than a homelessness where no such support is at hand. To the extent that the loss of home carries with it the loss of power, position and recognition, it will be a source of personal anxiety and frustration, and eventually a source of social fragmentation and conflict.

*   *   *

During the brief era of triumphant globalization, with its promises of frictionless communications in an increasingly borderless world, it was tempting to declare obsolete the rootedness of human existence in particular settings and circumstances. Human capital was to become as mobile as financial, and human individuals as free to roam the globe as the goods and services they produced and consumed. The perks of the global village would inexorably reduce the significance of place-bound communities.

As globalization began to reap financial turmoil, political disaffection, economic injustice and social dislocation, triumph turned into uncertainty and the demarcation lines of identity and belonging – new and old, inherited and invented, terrestrial and virtual, open and closed – soon criss-crossed the European landscape. Add to this the immediate dislocating effects of rapid and large-scale migration and it is not hard to see why the spectre of homelessness might again come to haunt European societies. And this time around, people will not necessarily have to leave home to sense the ground shaking under their feet.

For the first time in post-war Europe generations are emerging with shrinking prospects for economic and social advancement. They will have to contend with jobs offering less security, lower pay and fewer rights and benefits, thereby running the risk of being locked out of a social order to which the entrance key is a secure and lasting foothold in the labour market. This is not a new social class emerging, with a defined role to play in the economic system, like the vanishing proletariat, but a heterogeneous and divided group of people defined by their very lack of position, power and place in society. To a first generation of migrants, this might still be seen as a transitory state, but to children and grandchildren of migrants – not to mention the children and grandchildren of the long-established working and middle classes – being locked out of their own society might seem like becoming homeless at home. In Sweden, this new form of social exclusion has a name, *utanförskap*, 'outsidership'. While ethnic and cultural otherness remains a most visible and persistent factor in *utanförskap*, and therefore large-scale immigration can all too easily be seen as the root of it, 'homelessness at home' is today a social ill that may afflict young people on every side of the ethnic and cultural divide, since it is caused by far more fundamental transformations in the conditions for creating and upholding a political and social community. At the core of it I see a growing chasm between what a human society must be able to offer its members (home and belonging, not least) and what the societies of an increasingly obsolete national and industrial paradigm are able to provide.

While a more globalized and 'multicultural' social order might seem a logical step for an ever more interdependent and interconnected humankind, there can be no globalization without societies that are able to provide their members with a community to which they can belong and a place in which they can feel at home. Human formation can occur under the most diverse circumstances and produce the most diverse human beings, but it cannot reasonably occur without the intimate physical and emotional interaction with the people who happen to inhabit the particular world into which each and every one of us, without being asked, has been delivered. To feel at home in the larger world we must first make ourselves at home in the small world of our first encounters and impressions.

When Antoine de Saint-Exupéry's Little Prince learns that the world is full of roses like his first rose, he lies down and cries: 'I thought that I was rich, with a flower that was unique in all the world; and all I had was a common rose'. The Little Prince has attached himself to one particular rose, not to all the roses of the world, in the same way as we must attach ourselves to particular people and things before we can attach ourselves to the world at large. And similarly, being disconnected from those first attachments, or losing them in one way or another, might also become a source of longing and mourning for us. Meditating on the prince and his rose, the British philosopher Joseph Raz writes: 'We become aware of the world, if we are lucky, in the bosom of strong attachments, personal and others, which are, for each of us, *unique*, and understood to be so. Gradually the world opens in front of us, and the objects of our attachment lose their uniqueness.'

One could further argue that the modern nation state was made possible by the human capacity to expand hard-wired tribal allegiances to a socially constructed loyalty to what Benedict Anderson called 'imagined communities'. What we have come to understand as justice in a democratic society – equality before the law – may in fact be understood as a larger form of loyalty only. Richard Rorty makes us ponder how we would act if one of our parents or children committed a sordid crime and asked for our protection; we would most likely be willing to perjure ourselves (i.e. obstruct justice) to supply him or her with a false alibi. If an innocent person were wrongly convicted as a consequence of our false testimony, we would suddenly be torn by a conflict between justice and loyalty. If the innocent person turned out to be a friend or a neighbour, the conflict would most likely be more painful than if the innocent person were a stranger 'of a different race or class or nation'. We are then not really torn between loyalty and justice, Rorty argues, 'but between a loyalty to our family and a loyalty to some group large enough to include the victim of our perjury'. If and when the going gets tough, and loyalty to kin may come into conflict with loyalty to a larger group, the larger loyalty might yield: 'Sharing food with impoverished people down the street is natural and right in normal times but perhaps not in a famine when doing so would amount to disloyalty to one's own family.'

*   *   *

'I believe in justice, but I shall defend my mother above justice', Albert Camus famously said in an interview in 1957. His declaration was made against the backdrop of an increasingly cruel colonial and civil war in Algeria, with torture and terror tearing apart the fabric of French Algeria, chipping away at the ground under the feet of Camus' proverbial (but very real) mother, Catherine, a poor hard-working widow, practically deaf and dumb, who came to symbolize Camus' life-long attachment to the home of his Algerian childhood. 'I have never written anything that was not, either directly or indirectly, linked to the country in which I was born', he also said. To be fair, the justice that Camus was prepared to reject for the sake of his mother was the justice of a revolutionary terror striking blindly in the streets and on the buses of Algiers. The plea for his mother was a plea against a war in which he didn't believe.

Camus urged his readers to look for 'the dark and the instinctive' in his work and it seems clear to this reader that deep sensory memories from the landscape of his childhood keep reverberating through his writings, revealing the centrality of home and belonging to his literary and philosophical wrestling with the absurdity of human existence. The true 'crime' (or the existential tragedy) of Meursault, the protagonist of *The Stranger*, who randomly kills an Arab on the shore, is to live only for the moment, with no attachments to anyone, with no sense of purpose, and thus with no past and no future.

Having survived Auschwitz, the Austrian-Jewish writer Hans Mayer changed his name to Jean Améry as a reaction to having been robbed not only of his home but also his language. The language in which he had made himself at home in the world was now the language in which he had been made a stranger in the world and banished from it, and people like him were eradicated. To Améry, the destruction of home and language constituted a state of irreparable homelessness, to be seen as a 'dark and instinctive' undercurrent in most of his writings.

An essay by Améry is titled 'How much home does a person need?' Writing in the language of his homelessness, the word he uses for home is *Heimat*. '*Die Heimat* is the land of one's childhood and youth', Améry asserts. 'Whoever has lost it becomes a loser himself, even if he has learned not to stumble about in the foreign country as if he were drunk, but rather to tread the ground with some fearlessness.' The *Heimat* of Améry is a home that cannot easily be replaced, and the loss of it not easily compensated for.

'How much *Heimat* does a person need?' is how Améry asks his question.

'The more of it, the less he can carry with him', is his answer.

Jean Améry had no home at all to carry with him, and neither had my father. With no links remaining to 'the land of one's childhood and youth', and with a subsequently weakened capacity for attaching yourself to the world, homelessness might become an unbearable state of being, Améry argued, and so it eventually became to him – and to my father. And perhaps it is only by being able to imagine ourselves in such a situation – being abandoned by 'our own' world – that we might fully grasp the centrality of home and belonging to human existence.

Hannah Arendt certainly grasped it. Having been ostracized from the German society to which she thought she belonged, having seen 'friends' and colleagues silently close their doors and her *Heimat*'s state revoke her social standing and legal protection, she intimately knew what it meant to lose one's ground. 'It was as if an empty space [had] formed around one', she told German television on 28 October 1964.

That empty space, the experience of having been made homeless at home, may be seen as the personal backdrop to Hannah Arendt's life-long preoccupation with the scourge of statelessness, the kind of homelessness born out of the twentieth-century division of Europe into sovereign nation states by means of war and ethnic cleansing.

Statelessness was an unprecedented human condition, Arendt argued, leaving millions of people with no home anywhere, at the mercy of societies to which they did not belong. What was unprecedented was not the loss of home in itself, 'but the impossibility of finding a new one. Suddenly, there was no place on earth where migrants could go without the severest restrictions, no country where they would be assimilated, no territory where they could found a new community of their own.' People who were made stateless had not only lost their home, 'the entire social texture into which they [had been] born and in which they [had] established for themselves a distinct place in the world', but also the legal right to re-establish such a place for themselves anywhere else. 'The calamity of the rightless is ... that they no longer belong to any community whatsoever'. In a humanity that was to be 'completely organized' by nation states, the loss of home and political status could 'become identical with expulsion from humanity altogether', Arendt asserted. Being homeless under such circumstances might even be considered worse than being a slave in antiquity, since

> even slaves still belonged to some sort of human community; their labour was needed, used, and exploited, and this kept them within the pale of humanity. To be a slave was after all to have a distinctive character, a place in society – more than the abstract nakedness of being human and nothing but human. Not the loss of specific rights, then, but the loss of a community willing and able to guarantee any rights whatsoever, has been the calamity which has befallen ever-increasing numbers of people. Man, it turns out, can lose all so-called Rights of Man without losing his essential quality as man, his human dignity. Only the loss of a polity itself expels him from humanity.

Today, the expression 'the abstract nakedness of being human and nothing but human' might sound like a description of the ultimate condition of neoliberal individualism, but to Arendt this was a description of the empty space. Any notion of human rights based 'upon the assumed existence of a human being as such', she wrote, would break down at the very moment it was confronted with people 'who had indeed lost all other qualities and specific relationships – except that they were still human'.

Which of course was precisely what happened at the Evian conference in the summer of 1938, when representatives of 32 well-fenced nation states of the Western world firmly closed their respective doors to the rightless and stateless (and thereby systematically dehumanized) Jews of Germany and Austria. For a number of years after the war, millions of displaced persons and refugees, people who were 'nothing but human', were similarly put at the mercy of well-fenced nation states deciding whether to offer them a place from which to re-enter an 'organized humanity'.

'The world found nothing sacred in the abstract nakedness of being human', Hannah Arendt wryly noted.

*   *   *

The European structure that eventually emerged from two near-fatal disasters in less than 30 years may today be understood as the most ambitious and certainly the most legitimate and peaceful attempt in European history to create a common political order for the multitude of peoples on this small and fractured peninsula on the western tip of the Eurasian continent. Having convincingly demonstrated their recurrent capacity for self-destruction, the embattled remnants of Europe seemed prepared to learn the lesson: either they bind themselves together or together they self-destruct. In a speech in Zürich on 19 September 1946, Winston Churchill famously stated that Europe must be provided 'with a structure under which it can dwell in peace, in safety and in freedom. We must build a kind of United States of Europe.' And although no such thing seemed at all feasible at the time, the outbreak of the Cold War would soon provide the Western nations of the post-war European divide with a common enemy, a common cause and a common transatlantic alliance, and thus with the climate of trust and cooperation necessary for a European Economic Community, EEC, to be formed and the goal of forging 'an ever closer union among the peoples of Europe' to be commonly declared in the Treaty of Rome of 1957.

When the Cold War suddenly ended in 1989 and the conditions for a new European order radically changed, the community simultaneously embarked on a policy of enlargement and a policy aiming at a far-reaching economic convergence in order to establish a close economic and monetary union enabling the introduction of 'a single and stable currency' (the Maastricht treaty). It certainly looked as if the European Union (EU) was on a winning streak to build a European order that had a ring of Churchill about it, purporting 'to make all Europe, or the greater part of it, as free and happy as Switzerland is today'. In the prevailing mood of Europhoria at the time, the violent resurgence of ferocious nationalism in the Balkans could all too easily be interpreted as yet another argument for pursuing the European project at full throttle, emphasizing the need to embrace even the fringe of European nation states.

What was not pursued, however, was democracy on a European level. As the EU rapidly widened and deepened, its increasingly disparate member states were to remain the highest level of democratic decision-making and the ultimate source of political legitimacy. The EU would thus increasingly be governed by having elected national parliaments adopt directives and regulations decreed by the non-elected institutions in 'Brussels'.

And herein lay the built-in weakness of the new European order. With European leaders unable or unwilling to create a demos of Europeans and make the EU a democratic federation of sorts, a conflict between nation state democracy and European-level decision-making – 'the democratic deficit' – was inevitable. To put it in terms of this essay: a conflict between an order catering to our need for home and belonging and an order unable to provide it.

This has become increasingly clear as seven years of European plenty have been followed by seven years of famine (with no end in sight), and fast-growing tensions and conflicts are threatening to tear the EU apart. The creation of a common currency presumed a common fiscal discipline that never materialized. The creation of open borders and the free movement of people between widely different social systems presumed a coordination of social policies and practices that were contested from the start, and a common asylum and migration policy that fell apart as soon as it was put to the test. The goal of forging 'an ever closer union among the peoples of Europe' presumed a level of European trust and solidarity that had never existed before and proved hard to create.

* * *

Is this then Churchill's 'tragedy of Europe' playing itself out again? Is this tiny continent of tightly packed peoples and cultures, 'grouped in so many ancient states and nations', historically incapable of creating a common order for their inexorably intertwined fates? And if so, must we conclude that the post-war European order, as it has been conceived so far, must be reconsidered, and if possible reconstructed?

With the real possibility of a structural breakdown of the EU in its present form, I believe that we must reconsider both structure and idea, form and content. The structure cannot be based on a widening fissure between power and legitimacy, and the idea cannot be based on the notion of Europe as home. Europe can never become a home in the sense of *Heimat*, but nor can it become a home in the sense of *Gemeinschaft*, the term introduced by the German sociologist Ferdinand Tönnies in 1887 to denote a human community held together by bonds of love, friendship, neighbourliness and blood, as well as binding traditions of religious, professional and intellectual kinships. In contrast there was *Gesellschaft*, a human community principally held together by bonds of utility. *Gemeinschaft* relations are prevalent in a family, tribe or clan, or any other social circle trusting and warm enough to make us act out of duty or obligation. *Gesellschaft* relations prevail in societies where trust is becoming increasingly depersonalized, making us act from expectations of utility and reciprocity.

Tönnies linked the expansion of *Gesellschaft* relations to the emergence of modern capitalistic society. 'The capitalistic society', Tönnies wrote, 'is the most distinct form of the many phenomena represented by the sociological concept of Gesellschaft'. But since no society could be based on *Gesellschaft* relations only, the emerging middle class society (*bürgerliche Gesellschaft*) of the nineteenth century sought to supplement its expanding sphere of *Gesellschaft* with a corresponding sphere of *Gemeinschaft*, which meant extending 'warm' loyalties to increasingly 'cooler' institutions and relations, making the nation state the *Gemeinschaft* of national capitalism. In some cases it took the moving of borders and people to achieve this symbiosis of *Gesellschaft* and *Gemeinschaft*.

In other cases, like Sweden, the process was mainly democratic and peaceful and created perhaps the most successful modern *Gemeinschaft-Gesellschaft*, the People's Home or *folkhemmet*, in which the state assumed the role of a benevolent *pater familias*, trusted with everybody's welfare, commanding far-reaching duties and obligations of every member of the nation. This had to be based on the creation of common criteria for 'family' membership, determining who should belong and who should not, producing a society with little tolerance for social and ethnic deviation, not to mention strangers. In that sense Sweden was no different from any other nation state based on the imagined community of an imagined nation. The weeding out of 'degenerates' through government programmes of forced sterilization and the suppression of minorities (the Sami) through programmes of socio-cultural adaptation were official policy from the mid-1930s into the mid-1950s, with forced sterilizations ending only in 1976.

The step from being loyal to a family or a tribe to being loyal to a nation state is not an obvious or natural one. History knows many forms of society where tribal loyalties have remained the widest loyalties possible and where the limits of justice have been subsequently determined by tribal feuds and fortresses. History also tells us that once a larger loyalty is established, it might quickly be dissolved into smaller loyalties again.

*   *   *

It seems apparent by now that no European order will be able to emulate the element of *Gemeinschaft* that was instrumental in the building of the democratic nation state. Europe can never become a home to its inhabitants in the same way as Sweden or Denmark, or any other society conceived on the premise of an imagined ethnic and cultural *Gemeinschaft*.

What the nations and peoples on the European continent have at best managed to create and temporarily sustain is a series of European *Gesellschafts*, temporary arrangements of rather fragile political agreements and contracts between numerous competing and conflicting histories, languages, cultures, religions, traditions and memories. Transnational European elites, from crusaders and clerics to financiers and Eurocrats, have all been linked by relations of *Gesellschaft* rather than by relations of *Gemeinschaft* and none of them have managed to provide Europe with a harmonious building for its all too many homes, not even the most democratic and legitimate of European organizations, the EU. On the contrary, with the many homes of Europe being increasingly borderless, large-scale migration reshaping the landscape they inhabit, globalization shaking the ground on which they are built and the spectre of 'homelessness at home' generating genuine fears, the all-too-human questions about who we are and where we belong are again becoming increasingly pervasive and frustrating, and under the present circumstances tend to produce desperate and destructive answers.

'The transition from *Gemeinschaft* to *Gesellschaft*,' wrote Francis Fukuyama, 'constitutes an intensely alienating process that has been negatively experienced by countless individuals in different societies.' The current appeal of radical Islamism to young people of Muslim origin raised in the heart of European societies may thus in part be understood as the appeal of the promise of home and belonging to people caught in the empty space between a *Gemeinschaft* lost and a *Gemeinschaft* deemed inaccessible. 'It makes no more sense to see today's radical Islamism as an inevitable outgrowth of Islam than to see fascism as the culmination of centuries of European Christianity', Fukuyama added, warning that if the wider community fails to satisfy the needs of 'identity', a plethora of narrower communities, more or less imagined, more or less open to each other, promising identities galore, inhabited by people 'more sure about who they are', might again fill the void.

The French sociologist Alain Touraine has coined the term 'demodernization', a process arising out of the failure of modern society to maintain the link between 'the world of economy, market and technologies ... and the world of collective and individual identities'. What kind of social order such a process might lead to in an era of unprecedented global interdependence and interconnectedness, we can hardly imagine, and perhaps don't dare to. How then, if at all, can the current European order be reconstructed to prevent 'demodernization' from gaining momentum?

My answer, quixotic as it might seem at this point in time, is to reconsider the idea of federation, which is still the only idea around for a peacefully negotiated social order explicitly constructed to accommodate multitude and diversity; a European *Gesellschaft*, a structure or a capacious building, in which the all too many homes of Europe, old and new, large and small, could be peacefully accommodated. Reviving and rehabilitating the much-maligned idea of federation is the only way to take the contentious and divisive issue of home and belonging in Europe seriously without abandoning the idea of a common European order. If anything, *E Pluribus Unum*, 'out of many, one', the original motto of the American federation, is more relevant to the European condition, where the historical and cultural diversity is larger and the record of disunity and discord arguably more disastrous, and the need for a common order therefore even more compelling.

In his speech of September 1946, Winston Churchill gave a stark description of the human landscape still visible across Europe: 'a vast, quivering mass of tormented, hungry, careworn and bewildered human beings, who wait in the ruins of their cities and homes and scan the dark horizons for the approach of some new form of tyranny or terror. Among the victors there is a Babel of voices, among the vanquished the sullen silence of despair.' Seventy years later, the Babel of voices can be heard again. There may be no sullen silence of despair, but those voices are shrill, expressing fear and resentment, and telling us that we must take very seriously the possible human consequences of yet another European tragedy.

In this, the only thing we know for certain is that any future of something called Europe is the future of multiple homes and belongings, historically intertwined, inherently diverse, creating for themselves either a common order or a common disaster.

Bibliography

Améry, Jean, *At the Mind's Limits: Contemplations by a Survivor on Auschwitz and Its Realities*, Indiana, Indiana University Press, 1980.

Anderson, Benedict, *Imagined Communities: Reflections on the Origin and Spread of Nationalism*, London, Verso, 1991.

Arendt, Hannah, *The Origins of Totalitarianism*, New York, Harcourt Brace Jovanovich, 1958.

Arendt, Hannah, '"What remains? The language remains": a conversation with Günter Gaus', in Jerome Kohn, ed., *Essays in Understanding 1930–1954: Formation, Exile and Totalitarianism*, New York, Harcourt Brace & Company, 1994.

Azar, Michael, 'The stranger, the mother and the Algerian revolution: a postcolonial reading of Albert Camus', www.eurozine.com/articles/2010-10-15-azar-en.html.

Fukuyama, Francis, 'Identity and migration', *Prospect Magazine*, February 2007.

Raz, Joseph, *Value, Respect, and Attachment*, Cambridge, Cambridge University Press, 2001.

Rorty, Richard, 'Justice as a larger loyalty', *Ethical Perspectives*, no. 4, 1997.

Rosenberg, Göran, *A Brief Stop on the Road from Auschwitz*, London, Granta, 2014.

Saint-Exupéry, Antoine de, *The Little Prince*, tr. by Katherine Woods, London, Mammoth, 1931.

Tönnies, Ferdinand, *Gesellschaft und Gemeinschaft*, Leipzig, 1897. Quotes from *Community and Society*, Transaction Publishers, 1988.

Touraine, Alain, *Can We Live Together? Equality and Difference*, Stanford, Stanford University Press, 2000.

12

The Undiscovered Continent

Doron Rabinovici

What makes me a European? I was not born in Europe but in the Middle East, and I can still remember how at primary school in Vienna I played up the fact that I came from a different continent. Back then I maintained that I was Asian. All the others in the all-boys class were born 'real' Austrians – a term still used today. I was the exception. Someone exotic. No other pupil in my class had already flown in an aeroplane. The whole of Vienna seemed to me to be a place of grey uniformity. Scarcely anyone was foreign or different. I had no idea that the former metropolis of the multinational Habsburg state was once characterized by a diversity that has since been eradicated. The large Jewish community that existed here was in part expelled and in part murdered. Vienna was a city which now found itself in a Cold War no man's land between the two superpowers. We lived in the shadow of the Iron Curtain. Not many from the East got as far as the city on the Danube. Some who did were the Turkish and Yugoslav men who were invited to Austria to take on those jobs that indigenous people did not find sufficiently lucrative. Austria did not yet belong to the Europe which was then called the European Economic Community (EEC), what we now know as the European Union.

I was born in Israel and lived there only in my early years. While not in Europe, Israel is certainly Europe's progeny. Even though we were an Ashkenazi family, in my early years we lived in Sh'chunat Shapira, an area of Tel Aviv that was home to mostly poor, oriental Jews. My father and mother came to Zion as survivors of the

Holocaust: he from Romania in 1944, she from Poland at the beginning of the 1950s.

Was I born a European because European history shaped my family history? That may be so, but could not the same be said for many people who grew up in Morocco, Algeria, Turkey or even Argentina around the same time? Isn't their fate also influenced by European politics and history? Aren't many of them also shaped by the literature, music, art and culture which we associate with Europe?

Anyway, what does it mean to be a European? What is Europe and where is it? We are taught when other continents were 'discovered', which for the most part means being able to say when some European country conquered them and at what point it enslaved, exploited or even murdered their peoples. We hear about the so-called 'natives' and how the Church forced them to adopt Christianity. We read of tribes who were baptized not so much with water as with blood. The maps of the other continents were once full of blank spaces. They were already marked as the possessions of European countries, but seemed at the same time virginal and untouched. Europe, by contrast, pretended to be complete and unsullied.

Nevertheless, one might sometimes think that the continent of Europe never really existed as a common space, but merely as a geographical area in the process of fragmenting into its separate states. After all, it is well known that the notion of 'Europe' is a myth that precedes by many centuries the notion of 'Europe' as embodied in the EU. The Greeks of antiquity believed that Europe was a young princess seduced by Zeus who had assumed the form of a bull. She came from Sidon, which we know was in Lebanon, in the Middle East, approximately that region from which people are now fleeing to Europe. When the child princess climbed on the divine bull's back, he swam with her out to the open sea. She was at his mercy. A reminder perhaps of today's boat refugees? Zeus took the underage princess away to Crete to rape her and the land mass was named after her. The foundation myth of this continent is not a charming bedtime story for children. It tells of violence and abuse. A minor must submit to her kidnapper in a foreign land.

We are consoled by the fact that the bull is actually immortal. *Quod licet Iovi, non licet bovi* ('What is permitted to Jupiter is not permitted to an ox'). The Greeks saw Europe as chosen and elevated by the king of the gods over and above Asia and Libya, as Africa was then called. Here, in their eyes, was the centre of the world. Here they wanted it to remain. Their view still determines our perspective today and leads us all too often to ignore the rest of the world, even though the Hellenistic view was superseded long ago by hard facts. Not only are the other continents, with the exception of Australia, bigger and furthermore home to many more people, but they are discrete land masses. There can be no doubt about their physical integrity. Europe, by contrast, contradicts the common geographical understanding of what a continent should ideally look like. As has often been observed, it is no more than an appendage of Asia; a mere bulge. For this reason it makes no sense to try to align the EU with so-called 'natural borders': they do not exist. They are sheer inventions, arbitrary demarcation lines which became untenable in an age of motorized transport, hi-tech communication and globalized economies.

Culture cannot serve as the dividing line between the continents either. Not only because it does not work as such, but also because the peculiarity, the advantages, indeed the originality of Europe are ultimately the result of its diversity, the wealth of its languages and traditions. From the beginning the Occident, the 'Abendland', as it is called in German (the old Christian West) was a battle cry. Yet it was nothing but a counterpart to the Orient, the 'Morgenland' (the East). Significantly, 'Occident' depicts an empire that boasts of being where the sun sets, while 'Orient' speaks of an empire of the rising sun. Tomorrow seems to be a land in the East. The contemporary crusaders of the old Occident are fighting for an empire with no rising sun, but only a fading light.

The word originated in the fourteenth century, when the New World had yet to be 'discovered' and when it was not known that there were five continents. The earth was seen as flat – just as extreme right-wing populist thought would have it today. Whoever now talks of the Occident does so only to lament its demise, echoing the thinking of Oswald Spengler in his *Decline of the West*. The sole desire of such people is arrogantly to affirm the primacy of a particular culture. Whoever wants to revert back to the old Christian Occident will be thwarted fighting new crusades. A new Europe cannot be discovered in this way. It will always be elsewhere.

The unresolved question of where Europe's soil begins and ends is possibly what lies at the root of this continent's singularity and uniqueness. Perhaps we can define Europe as a continent precisely because it is the exception that proves the rule. It has no geographical unity but is characterized by bulges, isthmuses and meandering coastlines. It consists of peninsulas and islands from the Scandinavian archipelagos to the Italian boot, from Ireland to Cyprus. This physical topography has influenced the development of its internal diversity and at the same time its openness to other continents. Could geography be a reason why so many languages are spoken in Europe? Every bay is its own cultural community. Every patch of land was once its own small state, with its own particular costume(s), music and language. This territorial configuration encouraged contact with other cultures, offering the possibility of trading with and learning from them, but also subjugating and exploiting them.

Fragmentation is Europe's common denominator. A strange interplay has dominated the history of the continent. Every time the world seemed to have been destroyed by war and barbarism, Europe longed for unity. But as soon as integration looked possible, indeed, became almost real, separatism and regionalism reared their heads again. Europe is Janus-faced. It resists uniformity. Whoever wants to unite the continent must respect its infinite variety.

Geographical, national or cultural seclusion do not make for a strong, united Europe. On the contrary, they manifest isolation, resentment, timidity and chauvinism, thereby demonstrating the very weakness many hoped that the EU would consign to oblivion. This ambivalence, already evident from the Greek myth, should not be overlooked. Europe is necessary in order to overcome Europe.

But where is this Europe's border? Who is a European today? The EU holds out to us the promise of supranational citizenship in which skin colour, ancestry and religion should play no determining role. In a Europe seen thus, the abducted princess brought here from abroad by Zeus was perhaps the first true European because she – like so many other Europeans – came from somewhere else.

From the beginning Europe was a political construct that served power interests. The EU is no different. It too has to take into account the facts of the market. At the same time it was about reconciling Germany and France after two world wars. The European project *resulted* from a crisis and has *developed* through crises. It differentiated itself from the Warsaw Pact. It was not a cultural or religious project, for that would have necessitated Austria, Hungary, the German Federal Republic and the German Democratic Republic constituting a united group within it. It was, rather, economic conditions that led to the establishment of the EEC and at first it went quite well. But had it only been about economics, Greece, Spain and Portugal could also have joined early on. However, these states were only accepted after their democratization. So economics is only one factor which makes for a common Europe. From the very beginning, the rule of law and democracy were equally fundamental to the European project. And when the former Eastern bloc states became candidates for membership in the post-1989 enlargement drive they were only accepted once reform of their political systems brought them into line with the so-called 'free West'.

The crises confronting the EU have increased alarmingly in recent years and they cut a swathe right across the continent. Europe is an empire that prides itself on advantages that it is simultaneously abolishing: Europe extols its social policy and engineers its collapse. It praises its health services yet cuts them. It hails its educational institutions only progressively to deprive them of financial resources. The continent celebrates itself as the land of democracy while taking from national parliaments what it still won't give to the European Parliament. Culture and art are lauded only to be made subject to the exigencies of the market. It's important to highlight these contradictions, but it's not my wish to badmouth Europe. The anti-EU, populist agitators are doing this already. And all too often governments make Brussels responsible for everything unpleasant that they themselves have agreed to. No, I would not want in any way to malign the EU. On the contrary, we need *more* Europe.

As the Europe of capital is now a reality, so the Europe of politics has become a necessity. A strong political roof is needed to protect the people and the continent's cultural diversity from the ravages of neoliberalism. The problems we face can only be solved together. The economic crisis, ecological dangers, jihadism and the return of racist movements demand European answers. The terrible murder of 130 victims in the November 2015 attacks in Paris, news of which reached me as I was writing this essay, only serve to reinforce the need for collective action against such threats.

We were understandably scornful when President George W. Bush justified the war against Iraq in 2003 using the slogan 'War on Terror'. And the fact is that under Saddam Hussein Baghdad had no operational relationship with al-Qaeda. The 'old Europe', as US defence secretary Donald Rumsfeld called it, was right when it doubted that terrorism could be defeated by military means alone. But did we foresee that terrorism might conduct open war against us? That selective, isolated attacks might cease and instead an army of assassins would cross several countries and borders, wreaking havoc? That such a war could be declared on us via YouTube and Twitter with not only innocents and bystanders being slaughtered live on camera, but also non-partisan aid workers? It all happened; a terrible reality we continue to experience.

The crimes of the assassins of the self-styled Islamic State (ISIS) are not carried out in secret. Humanity is being subjected to ritualized murder. Mass executions, which include children, are staged and broadcast. Beheadings of women doctors and humanitarian aid officials are celebrated. The sexual enslavement of captured women goes unchallenged. Enthusiastic cheers greet the destruction of churches. Training camps for child soldiers are presented to the press as if they were orphanages or day-schools.

Part of the programme is the extermination of minorities – whether they are Yazidis, Kurds, Muslims or Christians – who are branded as infidels. The goal is ethnic cleansing and genocide.

Terrorism celebrates its atrocities. Its battleground is the international public arena. Its area of operations is civil society. Murderous gangs, armed to the teeth with howitzers, tanks, helicopters and missiles, are pictured travelling from town to town to massacre the inhabitants. A hooded executioner pronouncing judgement in British English and seizing a knife to cut off the head of a hostage is videoed and repeatedly broadcast. The media provide the scene for the criminal enactment of this primitive barbarism. In seeing *what* happens, we are seeing *that* it happens.

ISIS ruled over an empire in which all minorities are persecuted. It invoked Sharia law and dreamt of the caliphate. Initially nurtured by Qatar and Saudi Arabia, ISIS was also secretly encouraged by Turkey. But it would be wrong to confuse jihadism with Islam. We must also differentiate between the various Islamist tendencies and jihadism. High Muslim clerics condemn the theory and practice of ISIS. The majority of Muslims fear jihadi terror.

All the same, the power of jihadism's appeal should not be underestimated. Boko Haram in Nigeria, Abu Sayyaf in the Philippines, Jund al-Khilafah in Algeria and other similar groups have signalled their support for ISIS. Sympathizers worldwide are turned on by its violent videos, which show murderers indiscriminately shooting civilians, playing football with severed heads or nailing people to crosses. Many radicalized followers from all over Europe, often *déclassé* youth, have gone like pilgrims to fight with ISIS.

The EU is based on the credo that everything can be resolved through discussion. But jihadism does not want to negotiate. It has declared a war on us that eschews dialogue and understanding. Its real goal is the end of all coexistence. Not fighting it means leaving its victims, mainly Muslims but also the entire population of cities like Kobani in Syria, in the lurch. Admittedly, neither ISIS nor jihadism itself is likely to be defeated with weapons alone. One terrorist group would only be replaced by another.

Horrified by the attacks on the editorial staff of *Charlie Hebdo*, which were perpetrated in January 2015, I posted on Facebook the cover picture of the magazine from October 2014: a caricature of Muhammad who stands before the jihadis who want to behead him and says: 'I am the prophet, idiot.' Whereupon the masked man with the knife replies: 'Shut up, infidel!' Until then it had been more important to me to laugh about the God of my own religious denomination than about that of others. But now it became even more important to defend freedom of speech in view of the actions of the murderous jihadi gangs. I felt that laughing about God and his prophets was the basis of the Enlightenment. This had nothing to do with anti-Muslim resentment. On the contrary: the *Charlie Hebdo* cover distinguished very carefully between the Prophet and the jihadi murderer. It did not equate them.

I have read many articles in which commentators showed understanding for the racists of the far right, anti-Islamic Pegida movement founded in Germany and accused the entire political left for failing to oppose Islamism out of political correctness – as if banning minarets or headscarves would have helped to prevent the jihadi crimes. Then again, other journalists declared that it was basically the so-called critics of Islam and the right-wing extremists who were responsible for the jihadi terrorist excrescence and would profit from it. Both sides are mired in a culturalist discourse about Islam and Islamophobia. Left and right blame each other instead of mobilizing first and foremost against the perpetrators.

Following the *Charlie Hebdo* murders, *Jyllands-Posten*, the Danish centre-right conservative newspaper, which sparked protests around the world in 2005 when it published controversial cartoons of the Prophet as an assertion of free speech and a rejection of pressure by Muslim groups to respect their sensitivities about their religion being criticized, decided that it was too dangerous for them to publish such cartoons. The left-wing *Charlie Hebdo* itself printed cartoons of the Prophet just when it was important to rebel against Islamist terror.

Meanwhile, defeating the evil spirit of militant Islamism will not be achieved by focusing solely on responding to the individual terrorist attack. Iran, for example, condemned the Paris attack, but only in December a man there was condemned to death by hanging because he had posted a caricature of Muhammad on Facebook. It's clear, therefore, that the deeper ideological context of militant Islam must be fully acknowledged. This weaponized ideology will live on so long as it is not tackled and overcome politically.

The murderers in Paris acted with clear intent. For this reason and others the fight against terrorism should also be pursued in a focused and purposeful fashion, while distinguishing between Islamophobia and anti-Islamism. But it is just as disastrous to lump all Muslims together and equate Islam per se with jihadism as it is to maintain that jihadism has nothing at all to do with Islam. Saudi Arabia, which condemned the Paris attack for sinning 'against the true Islam', had the blogger Raif Badawi, who was condemned to 1,000 lashes for insulting Islam, publicly flogged on the same Friday that the kosher supermarket was attacked. Meanwhile, in Vienna, where I live and write, the government runs an inter-religious dialogue centre that is financed with Saudi money and is named after the country's ruling monarch, King Abdullah.

We are witnesses to the practice of conducting business with Islamic states and of placing all Muslims in our country under general suspicion at the same time. Meanwhile H.C. Strache of all people, the leader of Austria's right-wing extremists and the chairman of the far right Freedom Party, now warns against Muslim antisemitism, although not so long ago he himself posted an antisemitic cartoon on Facebook depicting a Jewish banker with a hooked nose and Jewish Stars of David for cufflinks.

Although there are also fundamental differences, the parallels between antisemitism and Islamophobia are obvious. The fury against the mosques evokes the erstwhile accusations against the synagogues. The campaigns against the Muslim practice of ritual killing of animals (*halal*) resemble those against the similar commandments for *kashrut* in Judaism. What today is assumed about Muslims in Europe is reminiscent of the Grand Sanhedrin that Napoleon convened two centuries ago in France. At that time Jews were suspected of forming a parallel society, which had its own laws and its own schools. It's clear from contemporary reports that even in Napoleonic France the issue was the capacity of Jews to integrate. It was said that Jews and Judaism were not compatible with the Enlightenment.

Today's racists are no different and Austria is not without them. Nowhere is this clearer than in the graffiti scrawled on the wall of the former Nazi concentration camp of Mauthausen in Upper Austria in February 2009: 'What the Jew was for our fathers, the Muslim mob is for us.'

At this historic moment of crisis for the EU, its member states demonstrate little unanimity about what they want it to be. This uncertainty provides an opportunity for many in Europe to foment open hatred against those from whom they want to distance themselves. And Islam is the suitable bogeyman. In the post-Auschwitz world few openly confess to hatred of Jews. Even right-wing extremists in Belgium and Italy like to style themselves as friends of Israel, if only to be able to mobilize better against Muslims. However, it would be naive to think that Islamophobic politics do not also threaten the EU's anti-racist values, which include a taboo on antisemitism. Where there is widespread agitation against Muslims, no Jew and no outsider – ultimately no one – can feel safe.

But faced with jihadi mass-murder, anti-racist appeals are not enough. The EU must take an unequivocal stand against Islamist terrorism, which is waging war against free societies. However, this is no 'clash of civilizations' dividing the Occident from all Muslims and it should also not become one. For if we took that view, we would have already lost – and indeed lost everything we value and everything we are. Neither resentment nor denial of the conflict can help us.

Where the criminal force of ISIS has imposed its rule of terror, it must be defeated by military means. But instead of agitating against Islam in general, the key task is to ostracize those regimes which finance ISIS and to pursue the profiteers who supply it with arms. Only if we act in solidarity with Muslims, who are its first victims, can its death cult and Islamism more generally be defeated.

Without a common European security policy it will not be possible to continue to enjoy this continent's open society. We must defend freedom without in any way surrendering it. It would therefore be wrong to restrict human rights at this time. On the contrary: by extending them we are better placed to defend ourselves. Our struggle should not be one *between* civilizations, but rather one *for* civilization itself. It is life in all its diversity and democracy that the jihadists want to destroy. Our best reply to their terror is to maintain a robust democracy and demonstrate zest for life and moral courage.

The series of attacks in Paris and Brussels between January 2015 and March 2016 has had a significant impact on the discussion of the refugee crisis. Among the effects of the dead assassins in Paris in November 2015 was the Syrian passport of a man originally assumed to have arrived in Greece in one of the numerous rubber dinghies currently bringing to the shores of the continent thousands upon thousands seeking refuge. Those who have always seen asylum seekers as including suspicious intruders were emboldened by this to become even more dogmatically unsympathetic. They exploit the struggle against ISIS to mobilize against precisely those who are fleeing from jihadi cruelty and the civil war in Syria. They want to make us believe that the children who escaped the battles and the waves of the Mediterranean are agents of Islamism. Does anyone really think that ISIS, a movement which sells its sequestered oil and art treasures and which therefore has at its disposal large foreign exchange deposits and heavy weapons, could not find other ways of crossing borders? Haven't these criminals already managed to reach Madrid, London, Boston, Toulouse, Brussels and Paris in order to kill? Don't they even mostly originate from these places? The jihadists hate the idea that a Europe of human rights could offer Muslims a better home than their own empire.

The EU was founded as the antithesis to Nazism. It united in opposition to Stalinist Europe. It did not however submit to the logic of Nato, which also consisted of dictatorships, to fight the communist East. It was not open to the fascist and semi-fascist regimes in Greece, Spain or Portugal. After the end of the Cold

War it embarked on a path of enlargement, drawing on its tradition of resistance to totalitarian regimes to embrace the countries that threw off the communist yoke and show that it was committed to remembering the victims of Nazism. This was the crucial factor in the EU's decision in 2000 to stage a symbolic protest against the coalition between the Austrian People's Party (ÖVP) and the Austrian Freedom Party (FPÖ) by taking diplomatic measures against the Vienna government. The other EU members wanted to have nothing directly to do with the right-wing extremists.

The government turned the 2000 decision of the remaining 14 members into an attack by the EU on Austria, treating it as if it amounted to external interference – as though Austria were not party to the collective agreements that bind the EU's members together. However, the participation of the FPÖ in the coalition was not merely an Austrian matter. From 1995, every government minister, including from the FPÖ, participated in decisions which affected many European countries, indeed the whole of Europe. Thus it was not surprising that European politicians feared such an alliance.

It was clear from the beginning that this dispute was a European matter, the significance of which reached far beyond the borders of Austria. The EU was going through a period of change involving deepening integration, the consolidation of its internal structure and expansion to the East. The action taken against the Austrian coalition sent a signal to future member states about what would not be legitimate in the new Europe.

A procedure for penalizing member states for human rights violations was actually codified in Article 7 of the 1999 Amsterdam Treaty and then amended in the 2001 Nice Treaty and the 2009 Lisbon Treaty. But the symbolic move against the Austrian coalition did not invoke the original Article 7. And more recently, proposals to apply Article 7 to the authoritarian Orbán government in Hungary were rejected by the European Parliament and an attempt to call to account the anti-democratic Polish Law and Justice Party government looks unlikely to succeed. In fact there have been grounds aplenty for applying Article 7 given the many anti-democratic actions in recent years. But instead of decisive initiatives being taken against right-wing extremist developments in some member states, the EU has been decidedly apathetic, to disastrous effect. What was still seen as an isolated scandal in 2000 now threatens to become normality. In many EU states the right-wing agitators and extremists are growing in strength.

These racist and chauvinist populists, who act as defenders of the Occident and of their nations, could lead – as the UK Brexit referendum might – to the demise of the EU and their own countries as well. It's clear that the EU will not be destroyed because of a few hundred thousand refugees but far more likely as a result of surrendering those foundations of human rights and democracy on which it is based. The German word *Außengrenze* (external border), so often heard nowadays, is itself a concept which indicates how fragile the idea of unity in diversity has become. The demand to shore up Europe's *Außengrenze* out of fear of the other can only be advocated by those who have not learned to overcome the internal borders, do not want Europeans to live in harmony and solidarity, and do not want to celebrate and secure these values.

Racists and narrow-minded separatists in the EU have momentum. This is perhaps a perverse result of how a Jekyll and Hyde-like federal Europe is being constructed. We are not Poles, Hungarians or Irish because we are Europeans. We only became Europeans so that we could better remain Poles, Hungarians and Irish. By way of comparison, scarcely anyone on the other side of the Atlantic would think of saying they are only an American because they are first and foremost a Californian or New Yorker. For exactly the same reason no one in the USA would suggest excluding California from the federation when it is mired in state debt. In the EU, on the other hand, Grexit – the departure or expulsion of Greece – was and still is actively considered, even though the massive European economy certainly would not founder because of the debts of little Greece.

It's possible that the rage of all too many Europeans against the EU has not a little in common with the phenomena which ultimately led to the break-up of other, earlier multinational entities such as the Habsburg monarchy. The centre is seen as distant and aloof. The structure which characterizes the empire does not encourage a universalist view but instead strengthens particularist perspectives.

A (pan-)European public is scarcely developing. As I pointed out above, when criticized, some governments are all too ready to ascribe to Brussels all responsibility for the laws they themselves helped to introduce. And in many countries, even if their governments distance themselves from it, chauvinist and racist populism is attaining dangerous levels of support, and doing so in part by successfully masquerading as the nation's voice against the EU.

The foundations of a unified Europe must be defended against both the right-wing extremists and the radical Islamist racists. We do need a European refugee policy, but equally we must have unified security measures. But it would be wrong to believe that Europe can defend itself alone in the face of so many challenges. The euro crisis, national deficits (whether in Greece or Portugal), social tensions, anti-democratic dangers and jihadi terror all demonstrate that we need a vision of a social Europe so that the European project does not collapse in a welter of resentments and violence.

What is it, I asked at the beginning of this essay, that makes me a European? My answer has not much to do with ancestry or origins, geography or homeland. Rather, it is perhaps the *idea and vision* of a democratic and social EU which allows me to say that I want to be a European.

If someone wants to know where is this Europe of mine, the Europe to which I want to belong, given all the problems I have discussed, I am almost tempted to reply that it has not yet been fully discovered. Or to put it differently: we are searching for it. It is both a land still located somewhere in the future and one that is already in sight.

Bibliography

Blom, Philipp, *The Vertigo Years: Europe 1900–1914*, New York, Basic Books, 2008.

Maalouf, Amin, *In the Name of Identity: Violence and the Need to Belong*, New York, Penguin Books, 2000.

And here I don't mean different skies in the same country or a one-shot change of skies as a child. What interests me is growing up with a *constant as opposed to sequential* switch between skies, with the concomitant tension between different worlds, ideologies, cultures and languages. Such tensions include banal differences in daily life but also clashing world views. But perhaps the most disruptive of all, if you're engaged in intellectual life, is the clash of implicit assumptions linked to given national cultures, which often underpin what are presented as properly detached reflections. Most intellectuals are not even aware that these assumptions colour the very questions they ask, for lack of what I would call a third eye.

Lives lived under very different skies are often perceived by those who have led far more static childhood existences as fabulously interesting, even thrilling. But is this really the case? My aim here is to show that there is a quite a bit of *scuro* while growing up in such a *chiaroscuro* setting. The fields may be vast but the depth of field may be hard to fathom. For those who might think that such a fate is reserved only for a few happy members of the elites, think again. Never have there been so many people across the planet who are either compelled or choose to live between worlds. The number of refugees and displaced persons has now reached Second World War levels; the number of immigrants and economic migrants continues to grow. The world, the optimists say, is on the move. Gone are the heavy suitcases of one-way trips. Cheap cell phones for today's indentured servants and satellite dishes on the balconies of many an immigrant's apartment, along with low-cost flights everywhere, help such migrants maintain the daily ties to lands of origin – in all of their ambiguity – which have been swapped for lands of new futures. Everywhere on our increasingly interconnected planet there are children growing up amid the contradictions of fractured lives, straddling divides which determine how they develop and the kinds of adults they will become. Growing up is difficult everywhere, but add different skies to the mix and, I suspect, the task takes on a different dimension: it may slow down or accelerate the process. Either way, maturation will be conditioned by the great variety of light, shade, colour and meteorological surprises cast by those different skies.

I confess that I started thinking *again* about growing up under different skies in the wake of the terrorist attack on the April 2013 Boston Marathon. Although I was of course horrified by the acts perpetrated by the two Tsarnaev brothers, when their lives were described in the press, in a strange and highly disturbing manner I felt that I understood them. They were the product of clashing worlds: familial, cultural, religious, political, even ideological. They grew up in America, trying and failing to make it by the standards of their new country. Their mother had returned to Chechnya and incited them with her virulent anti-American feelings, while urging them to stand up for their humiliated and murdered fellow Muslims. Their return to the homeland of their childhood, their attempts to integrate there, their search for peers whose complex values they could relate to so as to bolster shifting identities, their ongoing dissatisfaction and frustration (numbed by marijuana) – these experiences were shared, minus the murderous violence, by most who are geographically split. Add to this press reports about tense relations with other family members who became immigrant success stories and would have nothing to do with the brothers and their parents, and the terrible cost of unresolved belonging is all too apparent.

I find the terrorist attack by the Tsarnaev brothers highly symbolic. Did they use pressure cooker bombs to commit their murderous acts because of the explosive pressures they felt *within*? This feeling of being torn between competing worlds may also help explain the choices made by the terrorists coming from the UK, France or Belgium who have joined the ranks of ISIS. These are extreme cases where individuals rejected fundamental social and ethical norms, but this malaise affects many more people who will never resort to acts of violence, but instead internalize the pain. For the outwardly fashionable few who will live in the 'Fast Lane', the title of Tyler Brûlé's weekly *Financial Times* column chronicling the consumption trends of the well-heeled international traveller, many more who grow up under different skies will end up confused, hurt, ill at ease and never quite at home anywhere.

Growing up in such circumstances always prompts questioning thoughts about 'the road not taken', the language never fully mastered, the soul that's metaphysically out of kilter with its environment, not sociologically. This is a malaise that those who belong to one or the other side of an identity dilemma cannot fathom. It's felt largely as an inner tension, but becomes far worse when aggravated by external events. I recall the young South East Asian Briton who told me many years ago that he loved the grey skies and the surrounding green fields of his native Birmingham, perfectly rendered in Constable's paintings. Tragically, however, British society would not let him consider these horizons as his own or chose not to believe him when he said they were. He was not allowed to belong, and this feeling hurt more than any blatant discrimination. Then there was the young Dutchman of Moroccan origin who told me that even though he did not agree with the French decision to prevent girls from wearing the *hijab* in school, he at least respected France for having set up a commission to discuss the issues. Whereas in the Netherlands, he could paint himself green and no one would notice because they were uninterested in his presence, happy to have the state toss him welfare checks without ever taking him into account.

Growing up under different skies has many parallels with the fantasy of adoption. Perhaps as a way to imagine a different life with better parents, or simply in reaction to even the smallest punishment, many children sooner or later wonder whether they were adopted. Children who *have* been adopted often spend their entire lives fantasizing over the identity of their biological parents. Recently, DNA testing and a growing number of legal recourses to open those sealed envelopes in distant bureaucratic offices attest to this existential need to come to terms, often with great effort and not always successfully, with that other imagined reality. Those who grow up under different skies ask themselves the same kind of questions. The parents remain the same, but the children wonder about the other life they might have had somewhere else;

the childhood home that was; the world that could have been. The American novelist Thomas Wolfe affirmed that one cannot go home again. But what about those who have more than one home to go back to, and where the contours of those homes blur over time? On what peg can they hang their childhood? Better still, to what secure anchorage can they tie it?

So how does one grow up under different skies? It is not the same thing for the child of temporary residents, diplomats, refugees, exiles, immigrants, expatriates, wandering hippies or cosmopolitans. The temporary resident is on a fixed-term contract; she has a return ticket and the child will return with her when her work period expires. The diplomat's child never really leaves his country but carries it with him, not unlike a turtle with its shell, since his parents are abroad to fly the country's flag. The refugee family is looking to secure life's essentials and a place safe from killing, oppression, persecution and injustice. There is no going back and the price to pay in building a new life is enormous, but there is also something reassuring in this lack of choice. Life is here and now. Nostalgic yearning for the lost land won't help. But there can be a return with a purpose much later, as I shall show. The exile will inculcate in her child a sense of purpose based on the fact that she was punished for her courageous resistance against a terrible regime. The settling of accounts is embedded in the very essence of such a departure, as is the will to return to restore a lost world. The immigrant is looking for a better life in a different and better world and is propelled by one wish: that the children 'make it'. The expatriate moves lightly between worlds in comparative luxury. He has a home to go back to even when he prefers to be footloose. As for the wandering hippie, it is amazing to see how many of their children have only one ambition in life: to have a boring, rooted middle class existence. One final category, the cosmopolitan, completes the list, but I am not sure such a person still exists today. The term implies fluent cultural shifts, innate self-confidence and belonging to an upper class that is not just fashionably comfortable across the globe, but also stands out because of the masses that stay put – and today the masses are no longer static.

What are the questions young people growing up under different skies must address? To begin with, their family circles become far more important than that of the 'one sky' young whose families have stayed put and who can also rely on far larger multi-generational social networks. The family issue is further compounded if the parents come from different worlds or adhere to different sets of beliefs or religions. Do they inculcate their cultural and political values in their children? Whose magnetic north, if they have one, predominates? Are the parents integrated where they live or have they remained marginal outsiders? Should their children protect them, act as bridges to the outer world, absorb their tensions or try to overcome them? In such contexts, do schools offer an alternative? How do the young tackle the frighteningly difficult task of making friends when faced with pre-existing cliques? Later in life finding a partner becomes important and with it comes the question of whose tradition to pursue: that of the parents? Or should you break rules and strike out on your own? Is it really a random choice? After choosing, are tensions transcended or do they remain, barely submerged, ready to surface with the slightest inner conflict? For the immigrant, refugee or exile, origins are not easily shed. Identity matters.

So how can you make a life under different skies? Most obviously, integrate and assimilate; fully embrace the world in which you live. But it's not as easy as it sounds. Today, immigrants are not expected to 'melt together' with other elements of society in a 'melting pot'. Skin colour, religious beliefs and family traditions are seen as positive aspects of diversity. Our *Zeitgeist* no longer expects Jews to have 'nose jobs' or Blacks to straighten their hair or whiten their skin. But not only do identities remain visible, they are given a quasi-mythical significance. Others may feel driven to choose to rebel. This can lead to violence and terrorism, but we should not forget that this is nothing new. Think of the anarchists and revolutionaries of the late nineteenth and early twentieth centuries, imbued with hatred for societies that would not accept them. Some Jews born within the Pale of Settlement and denied a future in Russia itself chose this path.

Far more common is choosing a collective ethnic or religious identity now that other social identities, such as class, have weakened. In societies such as the UK or Canada, which positively encouraged multiculturalism, self-definition through your own group was possible and popular. But for some people, such a collective identity can be a trap for it offers the world a visible, external *persona*, which often hides a divided or as yet unformed inner self.

The opposite of collective identity is detachment and solitude. This may suit great artists and intellectuals, but whether they grow up calmly, much less happily, is another story. Such a choice can also produce solitary and alienated individuals seeking refuge in their own secret gardens, but some gardens are more fertile than others. There are also wastelands where weeds grow and give little solace. Think of the world's manifold forlorn immigrant and refugee encampments.

Finally, there is the pursuit of what I call selective belonging, while appreciating multiple identities. But of all the possible existential solutions this is perhaps the most difficult to achieve. And yet, as I will demonstrate, it is actually the 'happy ending', possibly the only mature outcome of growing up under different skies. During the difficult years of late childhood and adolescence, such a state of being is virtually impossible to achieve or even to aim for. The self is still much too fragile and subject to severe external pressures and contradictions even to envisage it. Imagine an albino having to protect himself from more than one sun.

Of course it's true that native-born young people, who have only known one sky in their lives, are equally susceptible to these choices. But I would add that they lack the added layer of anguish that youth shuttling beneath different skies will experience. The native-born who goes abroad for the first time faces the prospect of an exhilarating and liberating feeling of discovery. For the young person growing up under different skies, the familiarity of travelling to other places breeds alienation and even torment. There is something astigmatic in the contemplation of your other sky.

I'm thinking of all those Americans of Indian origin who Manu Joseph has described in his *New York Times* columns. They maintained a strong Indian identity in their American world and during the heyday of India's booming economy chose to return. They were attracted by what were often cushy jobs, the financial opportunities and the call from 'home'. But it did not take them long to return to the American homeland. Penetrating India proved to be impossible, for every encounter jarred their nerves and made them understand that they no longer belonged. They discovered that their deepest values were different.

If you're lucky enough to live in a Western pluralist democracy, such attempts at life in the other country can offer a sense of psychic closure. You return fully able to embrace the most open, and thus the friendliest sky. But what happens when you are forced to go back to the country with the greatest tensions and problems, to abandon the liberating Western experience, for reasons such as a denied visa or family pressure, and find yourself back inside a more confined, even stifling setting? And what happens when the coming and going is between Western countries where, to the outsider, the differences seem minor, even invisible, or if visible, part of the local colour?

Freud spoke of the 'narcissism of small differences', but in the case of those growing up under different skies, the differences are not small. They take on monumental proportions as symbols of an elusive self. Anthropologists may study and catalogue such differences but those who absorb them from childhood know they have a way of accumulating, even snowballing into major internal dissonances. And worse still, these dissonances are completely undetectable to those on the outside.

There are three areas in which these differences make themselves acutely felt: in the tensions between family and the local environment; in the problem of language; and in the raising of children. Distancing yourself from your parents is an integral part of growing up. But for those living under different skies, the process is longer and fraught with anguish. For in separating yourself from parents you are also separating yourself from the other sky. Politics and geography thus turn the act of growing up into a matter of existential choice. This is ideal terrain for therapists. I can think of no better description of this dilemma than the novelist Gary Shteyngart's autobiography, *Little Failure,* even though his was 'just' a one-way immigrant experience. The Soviet Jewish boy who attended Jewish schools in Queens, New York City, and dutifully followed his parents into the Republican Party finally emerges as a left-wing writer married to a WASP and living in a house in bucolic Connecticut – but this is after many experiences with drugs and countless psychotherapy sessions.

In contrast, refugees and a few select immigrants often make other choices. They want to go back and make a difference. Fatuma Dayib is a 1990s Somalian refugee who became a Finnish citizen, was studying at Harvard when I saw her on television recently and was determined to go back to Somalia to run for president even though it might cost her life. In effect she had only one relevant sky in her life: the others were incidental. The same is true of those Chinese temporary residents, mainly students, who absorb what they need and want from American universities without letting themselves be influenced (or distracted) by the very different democratic political and cultural environment before going back home to their Chinese sky. As for an example of just how far the exile can remain uncompromisingly attached to the homeland, one need only think of Alexander Solzhenitsyn who lived several decades in Vermont without ever learning English, too absorbed by his Russian sky.

The problem of language lies at the core of the many skies predicament. Psychological research shows that bilingual children have more versatile and adaptable brains and a greater ability to learn other languages. But it also shows that you are a different person in a different language, for words are the tip of the iceberg of cultural references. I remember seeing a video in Stockholm's Museum of Folk Art in which a woman of Suomi origins, who had moved from the north of Sweden to Stockholm where she pursued a brilliant career, was filmed describing her life in Swedish on the balcony of her Stockholm house and then repeating the same story in Suomi in front of her family house in Sweden's great north. The words she used might have been the same, but the woman was not.

Her facial expressions and body language were totally different. Her tone of voice was determined and positive in Swedish and much more languid and melancholy in Suomi. It was as though identical twins had been raised in two different families, in two different languages and in two different cultures: each culture being its own universe. The result for those growing up under different skies is one of disorientation and permanent frustration.

But not only is there the issue of which language captures your inner essence, there is also the problem of languages not totally mastered. Monolinguists will envy anyone who is bilingual or trilingual in childhood, but ask such a multilingual person how they feel deep inside and you will be surprised to learn that many of them pine for 100 per cent mastery of a single language that suffuses their being from the top of their heads to the tips of their toes, a language which could encompass all of their existential experiences; the kind of language which is the indispensable tool of poets.

From my very early childhood I grew up speaking Italian at home, French at school and English in the streets. But these neat categories morphed into something far more complex when I spoke Italian to my children, French to my husband and English to the academic world. To this day I know and feel that something essential gets lost in the switching of linguistic gears. There are simply too many inner feelings I do not formulate for the simple reason that I don't know in which language to formulate them (I am not talking here about academic writing). What happens when you don't have one delicate *madeleine* to take you back to your past but rather, all at once, outlandish American, pink coconut cupcakes, refined French Saint Honorés and beautiful Italian *Crostate*, each a window on to a parallel universe? Perhaps I should write up these impressions in three different languages, but is that really feasible without such an exercise becoming a pedantic linguistic experiment?

Furthermore, language takes on deep psychological connotations when entire families move. Do the parents continue to speak to their children in their native language? Or do they switch and choose to speak the new language to them in what remains a foreign idiom, the equivalent of wearing thick gloves and caressing a child? Languages can also be symbols of suffering or humiliation: the German language Jewish refugees gave up and never spoke among themselves or their German-born children; the Sicilian dialect that stood for family warmth but also for poverty and oppression. These unspoken shards leave as many traces as the spoken ones. They condition the lives of children when they enter school and face teachers and classmates who do not carry similar invisible baggage. For anyone growing up under different skies these are not abstract questions. They go to the very heart of one's most intimate self-expression.

Fortunately these linguistic dilemmas evaporate with time. They do not contaminate the next generation. The children of those who grew up under different skies enter life largely freed from this linguistic dilemma. The reason is simple: they are most likely to have been born and to have lived inside a more stable linguistic setting. My children *also* speak Italian and English but it's a plus not a source of existential conflict. In the case of foreign words and phrases passed down in non-multilingual families, they might accompany children's lives like old sepia-coloured photos: tender mementoes bereft of all anguish. Much has been written about the desire of third-generation immigrant offspring to find their family's roots, but this has most often not been the product of a split identity. When I was in Tallinn shortly after the collapse of the Soviet Union, I met a young American of Estonian origin who had chosen to return 'home'. She had opened a soapstone boutique in the high part of the city and was proud to have lived up to her grandparents' dream of return. She told me her Estonian sounded funny and antiquated to those who lived in the city and when I questioned her she confessed that the reality was not quite what she expected. In brief, she was contemplating returning to America, her true home. Conversely, during one of my visits to Berlin, a taxi driver told me he was from Palestine. When I asked from where, he proudly announced 'S'fath', the Arabic pronunciation of the Israeli city (Safed in its English transliteration) pronounced *Tsfat* in

Hebrew. He grew up in Lebanon but had never set foot in Palestine. Nevertheless, his mental sky was there.

Growing up under different skies brings with it a quasi-inevitable romanticization of the country where you don't live and a tendency to downplay the virtues of the country where you do live. This constant see-sawing of emotions most often ends in disillusionment. These are feelings that are not really shared by those who grow up in one country. You can prefer the East Coast to the West Coast of the USA, the Rhineland to Berlin or northern England to southern England, but these are choices about variations within what is broadly the same culture and language, not unresolved tensions about *which* culture and language you should inhabit.

Growing up, becoming an adult under one sky can be hard enough. Most make it. They relinquish the adolescent's singular focus on the self and learn to see themselves in relation to others. It's far more difficult when faced additionally with a conflicting dual national or collective belonging. You either find some equilibrium *within* that duality, or build yourself anew out of the diverse cultural choices available in a heterogeneous society. This is not to ignore that adulthood also involves negotiating the complexities of life as embodied in family, friends, acquaintances, professional contacts and the wider society. Under different skies, these are not so much concentric circles as ripples in a pond, spreading out into ever larger circles. Throw two stones close to each other in a pond. The ripples will overlap, complex undercurrents will develop and nature's geometry will give way to a seemingly unmanageable chaos … until closure comes as the ripple effect finally fades.

And one final issue, which is a near inevitable consequence of such divided origins: thwarted pride. Whether consciously or unconsciously, in the name of individual or collective origins those with torn identities feel the need to stand up for the identity they consider the most fragile, or the one deemed to be inferior. Such pride is a complex emotion which has little to do with patriotism. It is a defensive stance, a rallying around the totem pole, a way to give dignity to one's own divided soul. But collective pride is often misplaced, at times politically wrong and frequently ridiculous.

Above all, it greatly slows down the process of growing up for it provides protective sanctity where clarity and relativism should prevail.

How do you finally grow up given these complex circumstances, the conflicting pressures of different skies? Here are some tips. The list is not exhaustive and of course reflects my own personal experiences.

Accept complexity. This may be painful. If so, try curbing it by sharing experiences with other strangers. Minimize the natural desire to belong by extolling multiple belonging, even if you don't really know how to bring it about. Accept familial choices, but transcend them. Acquire an internal compass so that you control your latitude and longitude coordinates and avoid shipwrecks. Pick and choose from your backgrounds while also retaining an understanding for what is discarded. Cultivate the ability to stand outside yourself but also learn how to jump in. Learn when to be a bridge or a dam in relation to each culture's positive or negative aspects. Cross borders at will while realizing that they won't disappear because they correspond to an ingrained human need. Embrace life as a whole rather than segment it. Above all learn to move on, a complex term that applies to anything from broken romantic relationships to frustrated work conditions, but in this case it means changing skies: set your own horizon.

None of this will be easy, no matter where you live. There is an implicit and often not so implicit demand that people with complex origins conform. They are expected to prove their loyalty by adopting the identity of their 'native' peers. 'We' in the West demand and expect that 'our' Muslims condemn the horrors perpetrated elsewhere in Islam's name. Some will make full acceptance of Jews conditional on their ceasing to support Israel uncritically. If you're culturally 'different', you may be expected to abandon this or that custom. 'Society' will deem such familial or ancestral principles to be repressive and retrograde, so little consideration will be given to the strong feelings people may have not to betray their cherished traditions. Globalization is making such problematic belongings commonplace, but this does not mean that they are any easier to overcome. It is very difficult to grow up as an individual while relinquishing your community or communities.

Does this imply that wanting to cherish and stay connected to more than one world leaves you with a split personality? I am told that psychiatrists now tell their schizophrenic patients that they must understand that the others 'out there' have only one (limited) reality, whereas they, the patients, have more than one. In order to communicate with others and relate to the outside world, they are told to keep their other inner worlds to themselves. There is only so much that others can understand. Show restraint in what you impose on them.

When you can rely on the camaraderie of others with similar complexities, it is a welcome and precious gift. Unfortunately, it's rarely there when you're growing up and unable to articulate the pain of non-belonging. And besides, everyone else seems so much stronger than your own fragile self. Quietly accepting this fact is perhaps a sign that you have indeed managed to reach maturity under different skies. There is one consolation though: any symbolic scars you acquire do not pass inexorably from one generation to the next. The heavy baggage of complex belongings grows lighter with time.

I have found solace in an old proverb from Normandy, my adopted country home, so distant from the blue Italian and American skies of my youth. The Normans call a perfectly blue sky with no clouds, a sky that bodes no change, a 'stupid sky'. Perhaps that is the essence of all growing up: to cherish the continuing change that life brings, to embrace clouds and to welcome the coming storms.

Bibliography

Conrad, Joseph, *Under Western Eyes*, London, 1911.

Hoffman, Eva, *Lost in Translation: A Life in a New Language*, New York, Penguin Books, 1989.

Lahiri, Jhumpa, *The Interpreter of Maladies*, New York, Houghton Mifflin, 1999.

Pinto, Diana, *Entre Deux Mondes*, Paris, Odile Jacob, 1991.

Rahman, Zia H., *In The Light of What We Know*, London, Picador, 2014.

14

The Profound and Ambivalent Nature of Belonging in the EU

Montserrat Guibernau

Varieties of Belonging

Belonging is a personal experience that connects us with others who we consider close to and familiar with our own way of living in the world. It means attachment, compromise and identification with a specific community and culture in which the individual feels comfortable with the way things are done, life is organized and rules and norms are defined.

In terms of how we live our lives, belonging implies responsibility to fulfil a number of duties and expectations that speak of our values, those we love and those who love us or have loved us. Belonging evokes the significance of community as a space in which individuals feel safe, and find solace and support. Yet this is a space which does not necessarily imply co-presence. However, it could also become a space in which the individual may feel overwhelmed by the pressure to conform and obey; a space that could foster the development of an oppressive environment and which therefore points to the profound and ambivalent nature of belonging.

Belonging is often perceived as rewarding because it contributes to the avoidance of feelings of aloneness that regularly remind us of the existential anxiety connected with our own awareness of having a limited life; a life of struggle and love, but also a life of uncertainty and pain. This pain is generally borne in silence as our busy routines distract us from showing such feelings. Belonging allows connection with others and also emphasizes expectations of solidarity and a shared purpose.

I was born by the shores of the Mediterranean and my sense of belonging is marked by memories of a distant past: summertime by the sea with my parents, my brother Toni and my grandparents in my home town of Vilanova i la Geltrú in Catalonia. Growing up in the Mediterranean, for me family values have always been strong, and together with land, culture and historical experience, they constitute the pillars of social life. During these formative years I discovered the multifarious Mediterranean millenary culture that has grown out of the variety of the peoples of Europe. I have always been fascinated by the enormous wealth of cultural diversity in Europe and particularly admire art created across the Mediterranean lands and islands from Cadaqués in northern Catalonia to Halki and Napflio in Greece. But my sense of belonging also bears the imprint of memories of the past, my understanding of the present and my hopes and fears for the future.

Since its inception, Europe has stood as an example of the struggle and endeavour to value the arts and advance democracy and good governance, from its cradle in Athens to contemporary struggles for democratization and technological, social and political progress. My sense of belonging to Europe, and specifically to the European Union, connects with the key aims of the EU's founding fathers – to prevent another great war and the misery associated with it – and the ideas of social and political integration which they developed to achieve those aims. But I have deep concerns, especially since the economic crisis, about the lack of solidarity that pervades most of our attitudes, the absence of compassion in a world ridden with violence, a world in which authoritarian politics and fundamentalism, especially of the religious variety, are increasingly playing a more influential role. This is also a world in which division hampers progress; an environment within which tolerance is losing ground and is often portrayed as weakness.

The multifaceted nature of belonging is such that it does not connect automatically to making the rational choice about tolerance and compassion that would allay these deep concerns.

After all, belonging is an emotion, and this explains its tremendous power, a power that goes beyond rationality and, precisely for this reason, is considered as a challenge and a threat to rational behaviour. Belonging is somehow portrayed as uncomfortable to those who, for various reasons, have never experienced the positive consequences of community whenever these exist and contribute to the empowering of European peoples.

We are, and have been for many years, often confronted with situations in which belonging is not a matter of choice, but the outcome of an imposition grounded largely on political and cultural power. Sharp boundaries are established between those who belong and those who do not, between insiders and outsiders, those 'to be trusted' and 'the rest'. This is a response to the desire to control and exert power over a physical space, virtual or imagined. On some occasions, the limits of belonging established by these boundaries or frontiers are the outcome of formal agreements or obligations. Once set up they have the power to separate physically those located inside from those outside the boundaries. This is a condition that simultaneously generates rights and duties within a bounded space.

We tend not to be given the opportunity to choose whether we belong to one or the other side of the border. Others are often predisposed to decide for us by invoking tradition, family, historical accident, war or international treaties. These criteria are generally not static so that, throughout history, the limits of belonging have changed and they continue to do so. It is important to remember that peoples make borders and that nations are not eternal. This is the European reality, going back centuries.

Borders seek to assert a clear distinction between those who belong and the 'others', often defined as 'strangers', 'potential enemies' or 'current enemies'. Only those who belong are entitled, according to their status, to enjoy rights and duties within the limits marked by the borders. In this context, the community's survival depends upon its ability to maintain the border and establish the criteria of inclusion and exclusion of people. In so doing they signal the difference between those who deserve the community's trust, so that they can access it, and those regarded as 'alien', 'too different to belong'.

Borders possess a symbolic character and emerge as a response to the demands of social interaction. However, neither all borders, nor all of their components are visible and identifiable to the naked eye. They exist in the minds of people and peoples that benefit from or suffer the consequences of their existence. The harshest borders are those generally defined as 'invisible', or even 'non-existent'. In spite of having no physical form, they continue to play a key role in decisions as to whether to exclude the different simply because they 'do not fit', 'do not understand' or 'do not speak', 'look' or 'think' like the majority.

In the global age, frontiers are never totally hermetic or strictly unchangeable. Where they appear longstanding and stable their very nature makes them fluid and permeable; able to accommodate a certain degree of ambiguity and anomaly that allows them, and those who control them, to respond and react when subjected to intense pressure.

Often the illusion or the fiction of continuity and constancy hides or disguises 'fuzziness', where that 'fuzziness' comprises narrow spaces of dialogue and negotiation of difference in the margins of the status quo, which have the capacity to foster change. For example, this is how the denial of women's rights to participate and engage in public life, which was maintained for many centuries, as if it represented 'continuity', was challenged and breached, leading eventually to the attainment of women's rights to vote and access the labour market and education at all levels.

At present, traditional frontiers are being challenged by the consequences of globalization. Among them I consider the emergence of the digital era that grew out of the communications revolution as the greatest transformation agent of our time, triggering enormous challenges.

Belonging in the digital age has acquired a transient nature due to the fast-changing perception of the relationship between 'self' and 'other'. Formal belonging requires time and effort and involves making a decision about actions, ways of life and expectations. But on occasion, belonging assumes a number of taken-for-granted actions, attitudes and behaviours. However, both ways of belonging imply permanence, stability and fulfilled expectations. The digital age challenges these models because one of its primary characteristics is impermanence.

Although digitality provides secure devices, it also, and more significantly, allows for fast-constructed and fast-eliminated messages. And the devices used for this communication are susceptible to total destruction at the push of a button. The immediate communication being undertaken, frequently in the form of addictive behaviour, consists overwhelmingly of the proliferation of short, often inconsequential messages. The individual can feel easily swamped by the speed and sophistication of the technology and some are excluded from it altogether.

Even for those who master this new environment, its impact does not necessarily result in a sense of greater democratic equality, more freedom and stronger bonds of solidarity among those claiming to belong to the same community or group. On the contrary, the kind of models of belonging now proliferating in the digital age are characterized by a strong emphasis on *individual* – as opposed to *collective* – values and ways of life.

Europe Divided

I have already expressed my concern that authoritarian politics and fundamentalism pose a serious challenge to the Europe of tolerance and social and political integration, to which I feel a sense of belonging. Looking at this more closely, specifically at the way that the rise of radical right populist parties reflects a marked increase in public disaffection and disenchantment with the established political parties and the political system in general, and challenges liberal democracy, we can see that they demand the power to impose belonging or exclusion in our societies, undermining or removing belonging as a matter of choice. These forces of populist authoritarianism represent the resurgence of ethno-politics, which establishes a sharp distinction between 'members' and 'strangers', those who belong and the rest. It is precisely the centrality attributed to 'difference' as a reason for 'exclusion' that is already encouraging the resurgence of non-democratic forms of nationalism across the West.

The rise of populism is both connected with the failure to manage modern societies successfully and the will to control and limit them. It is also associated with what a significant number of citizens describe as a 'need for order, leadership and a sense of purpose', which partly emerges as a response to what is perceived as an unruly world in which ordinary citizens do not matter, and are insignificant and disposable.

Since their inception, modern liberal democracies have successfully managed to empower individuals by improving living conditions and progressively introducing universal suffrage, granting human rights and expanding access to goods, welfare and education; also by making available a range of lifestyle choices, travel, ideologies and religions. This is changing, and division rather than solidarity is gaining ground in Europe.

The economic crisis has played a central role in this drama, prompting a serious setback to the European project; one from which it may not recover. Whatever the long-term consequences, the EU will anyway be forced to reform and change its nature, but it is still too soon to predict whether a return to solidarity or deepening division will prevail among Europeans. The times when countries from Southern, Eastern and Central Europe were queuing to join the EU has come to a halt. The allure of peace, economic prosperity and the creation of a single market has been diminished by the economic crisis, and now Europeans have become sharp critics of the EU.

The EU's image as a prosperous area, proud of creating the euro and always eager to promote enlargement to the East, acted as a magnet to attract countries in Central and Eastern Europe. However, the crisis has emphasized stark differences among Northern and Southern European countries while increasing poverty and accentuating social differences capable of seriously limiting life-chances at a time when social mobility is much more difficult than ever before in the EU's history.

In turn this has generated resentment against immigrants and weariness of diversity. The refugee crisis triggered by war in Syria and rising instability in the Middle East has brought to the fore the complexity of offering a balanced, just response to thousands of migrants willing to seek access to Europe.

Modern liberal democracies have become multicultural and the diversity that this entails is proving difficult to manage. The global economic crisis has drawn attention to social inequality, bad financial management accompanied by lack of responsibility and the urgent need to control the power of the markets. The rule of markets – impervious to ethical values or principles other than making maximum profit – is constructing a dislocated society in which the nation state seeks to retain power and influence by recasting itself, under pressure from global forces, by prompting the proliferation of mechanisms of global governance and the creation of international and transnational regulatory organizations.

In search of legitimacy to rule and preoccupied by generating a sense of belonging among its citizens, the nation state struggles to regain their trust, yet this is indispensable if democracy is to survive. We are living through a period defined by a downgrading of democracy where the word 'democracy' remains, but its original content has been impoverished, its original meaning overridden by abuse. For instance, the dynamic, progressive nature of democracy is often turned into an ossified set of principles presented, by some, as 'static'. This is the case when some EU member states refuse to engage in dialogue with substantial sections of their own citizenry while the EU remains silent, choosing its prerogative of non-intervention in the so-called internal affairs of member states, thus condoning lack of dialogue and weakening democracy. Evidence, perhaps, that to a significant extent considerations of power and geopolitics account for political and economic decisions.

In this context, the basic tenets of liberal democracy – social justice, deliberative democracy and individual freedom – are being challenged by the rise of new radical right populist parties and religious fundamentalism. Their power emerges out of an ability to construct an alternative frame of reference for individuals who feel disenfranchised and dissatisfied within their own communities.

It is important to note that in the twentieth century the West had already fought against authoritarian and totalitarian regimes: Fascist Italy, Nazi Germany, Franco's dictatorship in Spain and Soviet Communism are cases in point. In a similar manner, modern society has already fought against fundamentalism – be it of a political or religious nature – by leading a socio-political transformation rooted in the values associated with the Enlightenment, which resulted in such key achievements as the spread of liberal democracy, human rights, ideas of social justice, universal suffrage and the emancipation of women.

The new radical right political parties across Europe are opposed to certain types of immigrants, particularly Muslims, critical of the status quo and against elites. Initially these parties were ignored by mainstream political parties that considered them as beyond the pale. However, their ability to attract support and obtain political representation in quite a few generally affluent societies, such as Sweden, Finland, the Netherlands, Italy and Austria, among others, has changed this initial trend.

The new radical right is an example of a return to tradition in so far as it seeks to re-establish and preserve the idea that 'pure identities' are still viable through the exclusion of those deemed 'too different' and 'unfit' to belong. By assigning membership of nation, country and society based upon ethnicity, advocates of the new radical right close down the possibility of belonging by choice. This represents a setback to democracy and clearly stands in opposition to the emancipatory politics promoted by the EU.

The novelty of the new radical right stems from its adoption of the discourse of the emerging identity politics to suit its own interests; in this respect, in spite of its links with the traditional extreme right, it is able to offer a fresh message. A protest against the elites, it promotes preservation of the 'majority' culture and the integrity of national identity, understood as part and parcel of European identity. It justifies itself by appealing to the fear disaffected populations have of a world hostile to Western values and culture. It brings ethno-politics to the forefront and contributes to a revival of ethno-nationalism.

In spite of its extremely critical view of the functioning of liberal democratic systems, the new radical right does not advocate their replacement by some kind of fascist-style political system. On the contrary, at least theoretically it stands in favour of a radical *regeneration* of democracy. In this respect it is sometimes referred to as a promoter of 'hyper-democracy'. Programmatically, the new radical right's doctrine, writes Hans-Georg Betz, 'involves a claim for genuinely popular participation and representation by means of radical reform of the established political institutions and the whole political process'. In line with this, it defends the use of referendums and open lists (where voters choose individual candidates from the list provided by each party and individual candidates are elected according to the popular vote) in elections. It seeks to undermine and discredit projects and policies associated with the political establishment in such areas as immigration, multiculturalism, affirmative action and political correctness. So far, it has managed to overcome the traditional split between left and right by combining strong resentment against the establishment and potent demands for democratic reform with the use of protest and identity as mobilizing agents. Such a strategy stands in sharp contrast to the glaring inability to accomplish ideological renewal displayed by most traditional parties, which are unable even to undertake critical self-assessment.

The far right populist parties turn the principle of preserving Western values into a call for 'national preference': meaning citizens should enjoy priority access to social welfare and to the protection of their own culture and language to the detriment of foreigners. Thus a sharp boundary should exist between those who belong and those who do not, with citizenship bestowed on the former, while the latter should be excluded from the social, economic and political rights associated with it. According to this line of argument, new radical right parties portray themselves as defenders of those citizens who, in their view, have become vulnerable and marginalized within their own societies, because they lack the skills or the ability to thrive and prosper in a competitive environment brought about by globalization. It should be stressed that support for what these parties offer is not restricted to blue-collar workers and the lower middle class in poorer countries.

Against Diversity

Clearly the radical right's appeal is as a force defending those who see themselves as the victims of diversity. While the diversity of political ideas, religious and ethical concepts, definitions of democracy and social justice has been seen as a fact of life and positively promoted in the EU, for citizens succumbing to far right ideas diversity means non-selective immigration, 'too many Muslims', Islamic fundamentalism, a lack of loyalty – in short, as I mentioned above, a threat to Western values and culture. But the questioning of diversity is by no means confined to the far right. EU politicians and bureaucrats are fully aware that significant questions and conflicts about how to manage diversity within the modern nation state have emerged. For example, should individual loyalties be allowed full expression even at the risk of injury to collective unity? Can the nation state require loyalty from those who do not accept its tenets? Where should the limits of tolerance be located? Can tolerance extend to encompass the potent force of a rising Islamic fundamentalism which is gaining support, is associated with the use of violence within the EU and beyond, and, like all fundamentalisms, opposes dialogue, maintains a strict hierarchy and rules, and demands unquestioned obedience and loyalty at any price? And anyway, what are the causes of growing fundamentalism and the radicalization of those citizens whose loyalty does not appear to be attached to the society in which they have been born and raised? If they situate their sense of belonging elsewhere, is this an unacceptable threat?

In so far as the issue of migration is central here, it's widely acknowledged that establishing common legislation that applies to migrant workers from Africa, Asia and Eastern Europe is one of the major challenges faced by the EU. It raises questions about moral and economic principles and brings to the fore national differences and interests. The radical right populists would like to deny European citizenship to such people. But current EU regulations specify that European citizenship is solely granted to those who are already citizens of an EU member state, which would appear to make this a battle they would have to fight country-by-country. However, in the future it is possible to envisage the establishment of some kind of European citizenship – detached from membership of a specific nation state – allowing for the free circulation of some individuals entitled to restricted economic, political and social rights probably linked to their status as 'free-floating labourers' within the EU. But would this have the kind of impact on the accommodation of immigrants into Western societies that would appease the far right?

Let's be clear: the loyalty of immigrants cannot be fostered when the conditions required to nourish it are absent. A weak sense of community and a strong emphasis on difference based upon ethnic, social, religious or other attributes invoked as arguments to justify discrimination, together with excessive levels of inequality, represent major obstacles to the integration of immigrants. Inability to access the labour market causes frustration and resentment.

Loyal behaviour may be forced upon some individuals. However, this is likely to be short-lived. And the structures and institutions used to impose loyalty will become weaker as individuals decline to conform and go in search of new attachments – if possible – of their own choice. To many it may sound old fashioned to speak of loyalty; modern societies and their emphasis on individuality have fostered an environment within which many of them have never had a personal experience of genuine loyalty. Attributes associated with loyalty, such as long-term commitment, altruism, solidarity, readiness to sacrifice one's own interests for a higher aim and faithfulness, no longer prevail. On the contrary, today individuals prepared to move and change allegiances are described as 'flexible' and ready to adapt to an ever-changing marketplace and working environment. This makes trust much more difficult to achieve and, as a consequence, the bonds of community become weaker and

and the uncertainty accompanying such strong feelings encourages the retreat to one's own community and, often, the rejection of 'aliens'. In this context the EU faces a serious threat of regression to inward-looking societies reluctant to trust others, wary of those considered too different and unable, or not permitted, to belong.

To be effective, a sense of belonging should fulfil two conditions: to be shared by a substantial part of the population and to be capable of instilling loyalty towards the nation as well as feelings of solidarity towards fellow citizens. I regard these as indispensable attributes for fostering a sense of community among fellow citizens and necessary for constructing a cultural basis for the nation state. Nonetheless there is a degree of ambivalence in the way in which belonging is experienced: for some it acts as a shelter, while for other it becomes a source of anxiety.

All citizens simply do not experience a sense of belonging in a similar manner, or focus their feelings of attachment upon the same elements or with the same intensity. Yet positive belonging assumes that a sense of common purpose involving a shared fate generates an emotional bond among fellow citizens, who thus favour solidarity and social cohesion. Sharing a sense of belonging does not imply a homogeneous citizenry since a certain degree of difference remains a constant. In modern societies, through the process of choosing, belonging is turned into a consequence of free will, which implies a degree of personal commitment absent from assigned forms of membership where individuals are 'expected' to conform to a series of norms, habits and behaviour in the name of tradition.

Currently most Western liberal democracies are multinational and/or multiethnic and contain some groups that regard themselves as 'others', detached from both the nation and the state by reason of choice, exclusion and marginalization, as well as because of economic, social or political factors. Whenever the proportion of alienated people within a nation state grows and turns into what I call a 'significant group' – that is a sizeable number of citizens ready to act together as a political actor – the legitimacy of the nation state is questioned and its sense of community, social cohesion and ability to build a common future is fundamentally challenged.

In such situations a democratic nation state is expected to react by seeking some kind of accommodation of internal differences through the building of inclusive, democratic political institutions and also by engaging in dialogue and responding to the demands of the 'significant group'. However, in some cases the nation state may decide to ignore demands for greater democratization which often include the rights and status of minorities. All will depend on the level of popular support obtained by the 'significant group', and the willingness of both parts to negotiate and reach a peaceful agreement. Of course, geopolitical and strategic arguments connected with the interests of the international community will have to be weighed and are bound to play an important role in the final outcome.

Identity too is a significant factor in determining the outcome of the confrontation between the alienated and the nation state. By identity I mean the set of attributes that make each person unique. This is a definition, but it also points to your identity being an inter-pretation of the self; it provides a sense of purpose and meaning in life. It is constructed over time and subject to transformation and change. A shared identity is an attribute of those who define themselves as belonging to the same nation; but each individual experiences that belonging in a different manner.

In modern societies, identity can be constructed by the individual out of free choice. However, this is not always the case; important differences become relevant when boundaries are decisive in establishing a distinction between insiders and outsiders, those who belong – and can be trusted – and the rest. This state of affairs is currently being exploited by the populist nationalism continuing to emerge in Europe in the shape of political parties that are fully integrated within the democratic system, but which tend to exploit fears of an economic and cultural takeover by immigrants (legal and illegal), refugees and asylum seekers, attracted by the EU's wealth. This poses a fundamental challenge to both democracy and prospects for a political union.

Sharing a sense of belonging does not imply a homogeneous citizenry since a certain degree of difference remains a constant.

If the EU is to prosper as a political institution firmly grounded upon democratic values, we have to work towards the construction of a shared sense of European identity, not only and not primarily because of the economic benefits it will bring, but also because of the values of democracy and social justice at the heart of the EU project. In addition, European identity should be promoted in order to develop further a sense of belonging to the EU as a supranational political actor leading the currently incipient emergence of an EU identity.

The economic crisis has revealed stark economic, political and cultural differences among European peoples. As a result, division prevails over solidarity and the proliferation of the stereotyping of 'others', 'foreigners' and the 'different' illustrates this. Failure to advance political and economic integration threatens the continuity and role of the EU as a unique political institution firmly committed to furthering democracy in a world in which democracy is talked about but hard power prevails.

One of the greatest challenges the EU faces concerns the degree of internal freedom and diversity to be tolerated. In some instances, demands for homogeneity may clash with demands for recognition, in particular if democratic principles are to be upheld. In the quest for political aims, sharing a common identity stands as a powerful asset. Numerous examples confirm the strength of collective identity as an instrument for political mobilization. The relevance of identity establishes visible and invisible boundaries among European citizens; it points to the value attributed to those elements that matter because they are valuable and meaningful to particular communities.

The consolidation of an EU identity requires the political will among EU members to build a shared project for the future, based on a vision encompassing socio-economic progress, commitment to liberal democracy and the pledge to replace conflict by consensus. The EU should foster reciprocal trust among its peoples and fight disintegration and decline, while promoting values of unity, trust and solidarity.

Bibliography

Bauman, Zygmunt, *Modernity and the Holocaust*, London, Polity Press, 1989.

Betz, Hans-Georg, 'The growing threat of the radical right', in Peter H. Merkl and Leonard Weinberg, eds, *Right Wing Extremism in the Twenty-First Century*, London, Frank Cass, 2003.

Gilbert, Paul and Andrews, Bernice, eds, *Shame: Interpersonal Behavior, Psychopathology, and Culture*, New York and Oxford, Oxford University Press, 1998.

Guibernau, Montserrat, *Nationalisms: The Nation-State and Nationalism in the Twentieth Century*, Cambridge, Polity, 1996.

Guibernau, Montserrat, *Nations Without States: Political Communities in a Global Age*, Cambridge, Polity, 1999.

Guibernau, Montserrat, *Catalan Nationalism: Francoism, Transition and Democracy*, London, Routledge, 2004.

Guibernau, Montserrat, *The Identity of Nations*, Cambridge, Polity, 2007.

Guibernau, Montserrat, *For a Cosmopolitan Catalanism*, Barcelona, Angle Editorial Press, 2009.

Guibernau, Montserrat, *Belonging: Solidarity and Division in Modern Societies*, Cambridge, Polity, 2013.

Mény, Yves and Surel, Yves, eds, *Democracies and the Populist Challenge*, London, Palgrave, 2002.

15

Questioning Belonging in the Post-Diasporic Museum

Hanno Loewy

I remember that evening well. It was 9 September. We were all fairly exhausted. It was pouring with rain. The Berlin Jewish Museum was to be opened to the public in two days. But that particular evening was given over to politics and the elite of the republic. More than half of the federal government was expected.

When Chancellor Schröder and his cabinet arrived they hurried through the exhibition. The curators were lined up, ready to answer questions. But by the time the retinue got to the twentieth century, the questions had long dried up. The clock indicated it was time for everyone to congregate in the hall of the old Supreme Court building next door, which had been the Berlin City Museum since 1969. Initially, the plan was to build an extension housing a Jewish section. But in the end the City Museum became the entrance to the new Jewish Museum, the most surprising turn of events that a museum project has ever experienced.

In the hall the tables were set, ready for the hundreds of guests attending the gala. The curators had to look elsewhere for something to eat since the politicians' security personnel had taken shelter from the rain in the marquee near the museum and discovered the staff buffet.

The *Frankfurter Allgemeine Zeitung* published the guest list under the headline: 'The founding assembly of the Bonn Republic'. The year was 2001.

Foundations

The history of the museum as the custodian of cultural heritage has always been the history of how nations were invented. Was that what Krzysztof Pomian meant when he spoke of the museum as the 'quintessence of Europe'? For him, museums were temples of secularization in which 'relations between past and future [would take] ... the place of relations with the hereafter', in which art would replace religion. Yet this image of a world demystified by historicizing it – the means by which Pomian understood the Enlightenment manifesting itself in a museum and saw it as a quintessential European institution – suffered cracks even before the twentieth century. From the beginning this image concealed the other side of this new cult.

Gottfried Fliedl has described in detail a different day, the dramaturgy of which linked the first national museum on the European continent with the new body politic, the people (*Volk*): 10 August 1793. On this day, the anniversary of the storming of the Tuileries, the celebration of the unity and indivisibility of the republic, the Museum Français was opened in the Louvre in Paris. As Jacques Louis David expressed it in the National Assembly, it was for the 'treasures of the nation' and the 'right of all people to their enjoyment'. On this day the new democratic constitution was proclaimed. And a national celebration drew many thousands of Frenchmen on to the streets of Paris where they formed a procession, which eventually culminated in the deputies swearing an oath to the new order.

While the British Museum, which opened in 1759, was not meant for the 'common people', but for an educated and well-mannered audience, the Museum Français, by contrast, was supposed to channel the destructive energy of revolutionary iconoclasm, intent on paving the way to utopia by demolishing everything standing in the way of a new course that supported the state. More precisely it aimed to transform the old centre of power, the royal palace, into a house of the people, and the achievements of a cultural elite collected there for a social elite into the culture of the people.

In place of a commission from God, which was accepted as the basis of the privileges and obligations 'divinely vested' in the nobility, the revolution brought about the establishment of a new form of community: the right of each individual to happiness. Yet even in 1793 this promise no longer seemed to suffice. The past should no longer just be discarded. Now it was a matter of possessing it in its totality and interpreting it anew. 'The fury of destruction', Gottfried Fliedl writes, was now 'countered with a politics of heritage which culminates in the foundation of an authority dedicated to the preservation of historical monuments and of museums. ... This heritage arose from processes that contravened the law and were shaped by violence like secularization, confiscation, expropriation etc., in order then to become the property of the people.'

Yet it was not just the people who thus acquired possession of this 'heritage'. The heritage also took possession of the 'people'. Or more precisely: those who now decided what this heritage should consist of. With the national museums there came into being alongside the cult of the divine, which ultimately survived the revolutions, the cult of culture. The nations of Europe engaged in a competition that did not only mean war, violence and a struggle for power, resources and territories, but also an ever more passionate search for new legitimacy, beyond the privileged proximity to God.

Museums offered new cultural resources to this competition of 'nations'. The magic word that resounds today throughout Europe, 'identity', originates here. And while in the institution of the museum the authors of these great new tales of nations, later also of local communities, religions and ethnicities, concealed themselves in the anonymity of a collective authorship, draping themselves in the garb of the public that they professed to represent, the critical public, as constructed through discourse in the learned societies and salons, reverted back to the worship of material things, the celebration of that which cannot be changed: cultural heritage.

To quote Gottfried Fliedl once again, the museum is 'as one with respect to power and identity: not a neutral place. ... Museum stories are compositions, they have a particular validity, yet the museum maintains the opposite, namely the general applicability of its objects and stories.' What is collected, researched and displayed in a museum claims canonical value, and that is never an innocent decision.

Benedict Anderson described in detail how, in functioning to form identity and canon, museums invent and legitimize the nations of Europe. Admittedly from the 1990s the debate in museum circles has also revolved around the crisis of these 'certainties' provided by museums. They have been subjected to productive questioning in view of migration, transnational relations, and 'transcultural' and 'hybrid' identities.

The optimism associated with this has long since given way to a certain scepticism, in view of the mutually reinforcing effects of the competing forms of identity politics in Europe, which are intent on achieving cultural, political and social separation. This competition is no longer only one between nations. More than ever majorities and minorities in the migration societies seek resources in the struggle for recognition and social hegemony, not least in the field of symbolic politics, whether that is the politics of religion or cultural heritage. The cards in this struggle are distributed unequally but the rules of the game undermine the democratic public and replace it with the paternalism of demography, the assertion of a 'natural' authority within bounded communities.

As early as 2000 Sharon MacDonald pointed out how a high regard for hybrid or 'hyphenated' cultures could also strengthen this culturalism that is built on ethnic 'purity': 'Articulating postnational, transcultural or "hybrid" identity is a difficult matter … it easily runs the risk of unwittingly "freezing" identities, precisely contrary to its ambitions.' This may be a problem for museums, as would 'setting "hybrid" or "fluid" identities against an implicit "pure" identity and conceptualizing the non-homogeneous as inherently "potentially conflictual"'.

With the Jewish Museum in Berlin – a 'historically contaminated place', to use the words of Aleida Assmann – the idea of a national museum that goes beyond a commitment to forms of pluralism has indeed achieved a different, new and unsettling quality that appears both fascinating and problematical. Fascinating because it attempts to create a site that can confer a sense of identity on an empty space, on those 'voids' that Daniel Libeskind designed as the central axis, in a building which demonstratively appears broken and fragmentary (even though we eventually tried to fill it in an almost encyclopaedic way in order to counter this *horror vacui* with something). To establish one's 'own' identity by remembering the experience of the 'other' tests the paradigm of national memory and also the image of multiculturalism.

And at the same time this kind of negatively established identity, produced by means of negative memorials, or 'counter-monuments', as James Young called them, in many variants, itself proves to be problematical in so far as it purports to create a national community. For in no way does this kind of inescapable empty space always generate an openness to the experience of others. It can also swallow this up like a black hole. The empty space of the memory of the crimes, namely the inability of the perpetrators to regret their crimes (which was the really shocking thing about the Nazi trials), proved to be the nucleus of a possible community which can only materialize by excluding the 'other'. When we opened the museum I was reading Dostoyevsky's *The Devils* at the time. And it seemed to me that this book revolved around a single disquieting idea: namely that nothing could create an indissoluble community so much as a communally committed murder.

Thus the opening of the museum on 9 September 2001 took place under an ambiguous star: the sign of a paradoxical acceptance of responsibility for crimes committed, built on empty spaces; and a vexed pride in the fact that precisely for that reason a new community could be constituted.

The next day was relaxed. Collectors and lenders, colleagues from other institutions, friends and advisers came to marvel at the biggest Jewish museum in Europe. And for everyone who had been involved in this adventure, it was a day for resting and catching one's breath before the expected baptism of fire the next day. On 11 September the public would be allowed to take possession of this newly created social space, a 'Jewish space' in all its ambiguity. But as we know, things turned out differently.

At lunchtime, over dessert in the offices of the American Jewish Committee, we were looking out at the new high-rise buildings on Potsdamer Platz when the first reports from New York came in. An aeroplane had flown into one of the Twin Towers. We were able to watch the second one live on-screen. The post-war period was over.

Ambiguities

Peter Sloterdijk once called museums the 'school of alienation'. 'Whoever ... feels at home in a museum has found the place in the middle of the world where one can exist as if one were not here anymore.'

If it holds for museums that what is one's own can become alien and the alien become familiar, this is even more so with respect to *Jewish* museums. Even what they should be called ignites endless debates, at least in Europe, where most of the Jewish museums appeared after 1945, not under the auspices of Jewish organizations but through public processes where various interests in 'Jewish heritage' were brokered, often in a conflictual way, and then expressed spatially. So sometimes there is recourse to circumlocution designed to forestall simplified identities. In Warsaw today there is the Museum of the History of Polish Jews; in Amsterdam, the Jewish Historical Museum which is part of the Jewish Cultural Quarter; in Augsburg the Jewish Cultural Museum; and in Laupheim the Museum of the History of Christians and Jews. Ultimately, colloquial speech eventually ensures that these are turned into 'Jewish museums'. And the ambiguity of such a concept, which oscillates between the attribution of the range of artefacts and the attribution of identity, is in itself constitutive for these museums. They share some of these ambiguities with other museums and at the same time push them to their limits. No other museum went so far doing this as the Jewish Museum of Vienna. When it opened its core exhibition in 1996, it contained 22 holograms that projected the illusion of images of something lost in space.

Cultural museums are a product of the historical processes of secularization and democratization. The cabinets of curiosities of those who wielded power were opened up to the people and sacred art was opened to secular view. Nevertheless the fury of the Enlightenment created new gods. And so the museums of 'the people' became museums of 'peoples', the museums of the nation became national shrines. In the second half of the nineteenth century common cultural roots were invoked and hence a superior unity that went beyond the political claims of the social movements. The museums of democracy became temples of a secular cult. And indeed in this way they also became the battleground and instrument of those wanting to bring new nations and regions into play with their own political claims to recognition and power.

With museums functioning as places where 'identity' is invented, everyday culture, the value of the humble and average, the allegedly 'typical', came into focus. Just as what was taken by rulers and imperialists from foreign cultures gradually converged with 'one's own folklore' and thus began through the medium of folklore to conjure up a quasi-natural order of cultures and territories, so newly created regional and local history museums now dignified everyday objects and at the same time made them unfamiliar. Attempting to grasp conceptually the aura of an object as the flash of meaning, the object that we dignified by placing it in a museum is at this moment also alien to us. Although physically close, it withdraws from us when it is removed from its everyday context and placed in a significant space. The more we seek to link our desire for identity with these things, the stranger they become to us.

The tension between sacred and profane is indissolubly maintained in the museum. What was brought from churches and cloisters to the museum in the course of secularization is only part of a cultural history. And what found its way into the museum from the mundane, everyday culture was mythologized and imbued with an aura of national culture which can be reminiscent of religious devotion.

The tension between past and present is addressed in an equally ambiguous way in the museum. Thus displaying objects in a museum bestows on them a presence that celebrates physical continuity, removes them from time, confronts us with the direct presence of the past and at the same time transforms them into something that they never were.

However, a museum is also a place where we can view things in a room and that means also from two (or even more) sides. It is the movement of visitors in the room which gives rise to a sometimes narrative, sometimes discursive context, in which conscious and unconscious decisions can at any time create new associations and subsequently dissolve them. The museum can be a place in which one can – unlike in the reception of most cultural media – enter immediately into a dialogue about this difference, a dialogue and a series of decisions which interfere directly in the reception of the medium itself. Consequently it is important to see the space that the museum offers as an ensemble of possibilities which grants the visitor real freedoms to bring to bear their own experiences, to relate them to the contemplation of objects and to communicate with other visitors. Admittedly, one mainly tries to do the opposite. Everyone wants to tell stories and hence string the objects together like words, create clarity, explain, direct and educate, when it is precisely the ambiguity of the object that accounts for its quality. Meanwhile there is a new magic word: 'participation', but instead of more openness to the interpretation of objects, in many exhibitions it distracts attention from them even more.

Nevertheless in the spatial despotism of a museum a tension remains: namely that between the narrative intention of the curators and the wilfulness of the visitors who find their own way through the exhibition and thereby, alone or in negotiation with others, form their own network of relationships and produce a discursive space that is repeatedly created anew.

Ultimately every object is trapped between biography and history. Each belongs to the particular web of meaning that a human life constitutes, from whose context it has now been removed. And at the same time, as a social object it belongs to a history that already existed before the object came into an individual's possession, from which it has now again – voluntarily or forcefully – been torn. Historical fractures are what fill museums with objects.

The Jewish museums, too, resulted from the break with religious tradition and its reinvention as 'cultural heritage'. The first ones to be founded around 1900 'owed' their existence to the dissolution of traditional, everyday religious practice, to the dissolution of ways of life that had come under pressure economically and politically, and to migration: from the rural communities to the towns and subsequently the mass emigration from East to West. All these caesura that were perceived or suffered by individuals sometimes as catastrophes, sometimes as new departures, transformed a concept of religiously based Jewish tradition into a question of identity and culture. At the same time, because of the collapse of traditional extended family structures in the course of migration, urbanization and economic mobility, the most important medium of identity and culture, namely the family, faced new competition in the form of the products of mass culture, and ultimately also from museums.

The first Jewish museums resulted mainly from the sponsorship of Jewish communities or related cultural associations: from Vienna 1895, through to Berlin 1933. They were community museums which had in common the attempt to preserve a particular Jewish tradition as universal Jewish culture and at the same time inscribe it in the cultural heritage of the various nations of which they also felt a part. Hence the displaced objects from a disintegrating traditional way of life became bearers of a newly constructed cultural tradition and a particular historical identity, and at the same time a guarantee that, in the process of assimilation and acculturation, their particularity would be preserved.

The promise of the Enlightenment, for which they had always been advocates, was not fulfilled. What remained after the Shoah was a more radical homelessness than the one that had characterized the objects in the museums founded before 1933. Now the idea of the Jewish museum in Europe had itself become homeless and hence stood for the diaspora as such, in its destroyed reality as in its still unfinished utopian potential.

Yet before we try to understand what connects Jewish museums in Europe today with the existence of a post-diasporic diaspora, it is necessary to take a look at Jewish museums which have apparently left the diaspora behind them.

The first one that occurs to me is basically not a Jewish museum at all, since it claims to be the 'Israel Museum', and is always so called. After recently being magnificently extended and redesigned, three wings await its visitors in Jerusalem, each with completely different themes, rhetoric and presentational styles. The 'comprehensive tour' first introduces the visitor to the 'land' and the various cultures that inhabited it, drilling deep into a history that logically concentrates on the building's archaeological collection. You discover that the territory of Israel and Palestine was always a place where paths crossed and every culture left its mark.

The third section displays Israeli and international art. The second and central section, however, is devoted to 'Jewish Art and Life' and presents the richness of Jewish religious and secular everyday culture across the centuries and different parts of the world. At the centre of this section is the cycle of Jewish festivals and their ceremonial art. Alongside Shabbat and synagogue building – wholly in the style of colonial museum traditions, the complete interiors of synagogues from all over the world have been transferred to Jerusalem – this is not least a gallery for a vast collection of Chanukah lights which, through its spatial dominance alone, imbues this previously rather insignificant Festival of Lights in the diaspora with the significance given to it after the Holocaust and the unyielding spiritual and military attitude of the Maccabees in Israel and in the Zionist-religious calendar. The High Holy Days by contrast – not least the highest, namely Yom Kippur and its ethical dimension of self-doubt and self-criticism – are almost completely overlooked.

In the centre of this disproportional presentation of the Festival cycle a video projection forms the real focus of the entire museum. On the one side, set back between the walls of a cube open on two sides, an early work of the film and installation artist Yael Bartana focuses on Remembrance Day for the fallen Soldiers, *Yom Hazikaron*. The siren and the two minutes in which life every year comes to a halt connects the fallen soldiers explicitly with the victims of the Holocaust. The same ritual is performed on Yom Hashoah only six days before. On the other side of the same wall, however, a video work about Israel's Independence Day, *Yom Haatzmaut*, links 'national sovereignty' with the collection of Chanukah lights. The whole installation corresponds with the poor presentation of Yom Kippur on the next wall. Yom Kippur, one discovers, has meanwhile become for many Israelis the commemoration day for the fallen of the 1973 Yom Kippur War.

Thus at the centre of this national museum is the retrospective identification of the nation with an unavoidable catastrophe and its reinterpretation as a sacrifice on the way to a hard-won sovereignty – and thereby also to the legitimation of the hegemony of one part of the population over that other part, the Palestinians.

This banishment of the 'other' to the borders of visibility is taken to extremes in Yad Vashem, the second 'national museum' in Jerusalem. Visiting the historical exhibition today you first encounter fleeting, fading film images of the European diaspora before following a gently sloping path through the story of the annihilation. The path meanders through dark rooms and leads again and again across the central axis, lit from above, and then from half way it imperceptibly begins to rise once more. After this alternating immersion in dark chapters and regular encounters with light from above offering hope, the visitor steps on to an imperial balcony with a splendid view of the Jerusalem Forest down in the valley and some of the western parts of the city on the hilltops opposite. Of course no one learns here that on the next hilltop stood the village of Deir Yassin, whose population was massacred in 1948 by Zionist paramilitary groups under the command of Menachem Begin. Deir Yassin became the central symbol of the Naqba and hence the object of continuing debate about the events of the civil war of 1948. So the stage management of the Shoah eradicates the traces of the catastrophe of the Palestinians, precisely when the gaze is directed to it. Anyone who actually approaches the remains of the village on the hill opposite, however, soon comes up against a security fence. Since the beginning of the 1950s the

Jerusalem mental asylum has been accommodated in the village's few restored houses.

In a completely different way Jewish museums in the USA construct Jewish identity as part of a multicultural fabric, as many Americans like to see their country, and conceive of themselves as 'identity museums', part of an ensemble of showcases that open up the various American communities to the wider public.

The picture that most of these museums project of Jewish life is also one in which the diaspora is superseded, in this case, however, by single-mindedly elevating the 'American dream' as the fulfilment of Jewish universalism. At the same time Jewish museums in the USA understand themselves as 'community museums', and unlike those founded in Europe before 1933 (and perhaps the Paris museum founded in 1946) they see their brief as being not only to preserve material culture and transform religious tradition into cultural heritage, but to offer a testing ground and stage for Jewish concepts of plural identity designed to keep this Jewish heritage fresh and attractive.

This leads us back to Europe, to the post-diasporic diaspora and to the challenge that Jewish museums can pose to the cultural self-representation of European nations, European 'majorities' and European 'minorities'. And even more so because in Europe, unlike in the USA (and on the continent more than in the British Isles), the claim is still made that there is a bond between culture and territory, which, despite European integration, has been rediscovered as a bulwark against migration.

Putting aside its implosion in Israel into a banal cult of the land, fertility, superiority and being the chosen people, Judaism has always been both particular *and* universal, people *and* religion, tribe *and* idea, obstinately keeping to one's own *and* permanently touching everything else, acquiring new aspects *and* jettisoning others. And at the same time it is always the 'other' *and* the 'self'.

Jewish museums that take this ambiguity seriously are located constitutively on the border of belongings. They deal with the past and present of a minority, including its religious dimensions, which at the same time represents a source of the majority cultures of Europe and large parts of the world, of Christianity and of Islam. They reflect the 'self' in the 'other' without having to specify whose 'self' and whose 'other'. Culturally and territorially, they question belonging, identity and separation more thoroughly than their supporters, and at times also their public, might appreciate. They do it in various ways, sometimes consciously, sometimes instinctively. They have gigantic empty spaces at their centre or, as in the planned Jewish museum in Cologne, they turn the symbolic order of history upside down because the entire archaeological excavation area in the old city, from the Roman palace ruins to the Christian Middle Ages and beyond, will in future be accessed via the Jewish museum, as if the key to understanding all history lay buried in the ghetto.

Every one of these museums deals in its own way with this interplay of voids and excessive elaboration, the reflection of one's own identity needs in the image of the 'other', the defensive manoeuvres and changes of perspective. And they depend on their supporters and involved lay leadership who are sometimes more, sometimes less exposed to the interests of the public or Jewish communities, sponsors or political bodies. They exploit the longing of parts of society for recognition, they urge and challenge, lure tourists and provoke debates, but they always do this on the border between the 'self' and the 'other'. The coordinates of this border have certainly changed dramatically since 9/11.

In view of the cultural struggle raging in Europe against the new 'other', namely Islam, which is becoming increasingly like a fantasy of a threat, a new role has been ascribed to the Jewish communities of Europe and also to the Jewish museums. They have become 'our others', the role model of 'successful integration', the proof of our own tolerance. This is so even in Moscow where a coalition of Putin, some oligarchs and the Hasidic organization Chabad, which does missionary work among insufficiently religious Jews, founded a 'Jewish Museum and Tolerance Centre' that has meanwhile become the third-largest Jewish museum in Europe. But what kind of 'tolerance' is it that serves to legitimize all possible resentments against those who do not conform readily and successfully. There is therefore growing pressure on organizations 'representing' Jews in Europe – and museums are also seen as such – to line up as part of a 'Christian-Jewish Occident' and turn the new minorities of Europe into objects to be educated and disciplined. As if European Jewish history contained no abyss that poses many disturbing questions for the model of assimilation.

That these questions can also be posed in a radical way without creating new resentments was demonstrated by a small Jewish museum that went about its work in the shade of the big cities, albeit exactly in the middle of the German-speaking lands of Europe, between Germany and Lichtenstein, Switzerland and Austria. Hohenems was soon to become a mythical place for museum colleagues in Germany and Austria, a secret tip-off whispered meaningfully to each other, if only so that one could picture where it was. Even in the early 1990s colleagues there were attracting notice with projects like the 'Ems Crescent', a monthly supplement to the local newspaper about Muslim immigrants. They dispelled all kinds of myths and discussed whether the former synagogue, abused as a fire station, could perhaps in future be better utilized as a mosque. They projected the histories of Jewish houses on to the façades in the old Jewish quarter in front of thousands of people. And they playfully grappled with propaganda and touristic myths about Israel.

The place: a little town that was sometimes sentimental, sometimes at odds with itself and thereby unexpectedly productive. In the town: an abandoned villa on one of the two main streets which once, as the Israelitengasse (Israelites or Jew's Lane), formed the counterpart to the second main street which bore the name Christengasse (Christian's Lane). Nudging up to all boundaries and repeatedly overstepping them, the museum located there approached the contradictions of its existence in an ironic way.

This was what drew me to the place. In 2004 I began working there.

Arrivals

Hohenems lies on an imaginary map in an innocent somewhere, on the border between an Austrian Habsburg empire that is no more and the Swiss confederation, in the anti-tariff air of the *Heimat* of smugglers and a more or less legal border traffic. The border on the Rhine between Austria and Switzerland is still perceptible even if there is something inherently unreal about it; an EU external border which one can cross when walking or swimming in the Alter Rhein. When the imperial count of Hohenems permitted twelve Jewish families to settle there by means of a letter of safe conduct in 1617, his territory was a small buffer state between Habsburg Austria and the Confederation. Something still remains from this state of non-belonging – in a town once split between 'Jew's Lane' and 'Christian's Lane'.

For me, this place with several borders became a space of belonging in a puzzling and inspiring way. My parents, German Jews, returned from Israel in 1956 with the idea of going to East Berlin. Belonging for them was a political question that framed their personal emotions about home and heritage in a way that was not uncommon then. Today, with the insistent quest for roots and 'identity', these more fluid ideas about personal, political and traditional self-interpretations seem to speak of a distant world. That my mother grew up 'Protestant' with a Galician Jewish father made their story even more complex. And that her life was uprooted by the Nazis and her family was expelled from Germany in 1934 and went to Lemberg turned all fantasies about 'identity' upside down. She finally became 'Jewish' on the steamer to Palestine – the boat as a *mikveh* was a phenomenon pretty common for some German Jews at that time. As a consequence of these detours my upbringing as a German Jew in West Germany (my parents luckily never made it to East Berlin) took place outside of the post-war Jewish community framework in Frankfurt (that was mainly Polish Holocaust survivor-based, and always saying 'let's go to Israel').

I did not 'belong' completely to the Germans, or to the Jewish community. We celebrated Christmas (not even 'Chrismukkah') with a 'Jewish communist' in the cradle, as my mother put it. In the end, for me 'belonging' became a 'belonging' to the asking of open questions. And a museum seemed a good place to live that idea. It took a while to find the right place for exploring this fantasy. In 2004, in Hohenems, it became reality.

From the beginning the Jewish Museum in Hohenems was an experiment that linked themes, time periods and places in a provocative, troubling, sometimes ironic way. It often openly challenged the ideas its visitors brought with them. And at all times it fostered local, regional and global networks which permeated each other in surprising ways, just like the political, social and cultural reality of the present.

Hence it is simultaneously a regional critical museum of local history and a diaspora museum that operates worldwide, a place of concentration and dispersal. It serves – through reunions and collection, a genealogy database and research – as a hub for a global community of descendants that engage in the playful idea of belonging to a global tribe. And it committed itself to the task of confronting and discussing current questions about migration and acculturation and the conflicts associated with them. It was deliberately political, looking beyond questions of how Austria or Germany can 'overcome their pasts' and even beyond questions of Jewish history. Cooperating frequently with civil society partners, the museum broached fundamental current issues concerning the relationship between 'homeland', 'foreignness' and socio-economic reality. In following this path the museum also did not shy away from using irony to circumvent politicized controversies that were loaded with resentment. With Muslim and Alevi immigrants, mainly of Turkish origin, making up about 20 per cent of the population in the towns of the region, it was self-evident that cultural institutions serving the public would also endeavour to target migrants as a group. Indeed for a long time the Jewish museum was one of the few established cultural operators which took seriously this part of its potential public.

In a Jewish museum the visitors encounter themselves reflected in the 'other'. And this applies as much to the non-Jewish visitors as to the Jewish visitors. It produces an opportunity to dare to confuse them and present them with choices; not to instruct them, but to stimulate their curiosity. And that also means jettisoning the fear of ambiguity. For this to happen the museum must see itself as an 'open space', as a place where various concepts of identity, self-images and interpretations may clash, and cultural hegemony may be questioned; where one is not 'invited' symbolically to participate in the exhibition but rather participation is an integral part of the projects from the outset.

The wind of change was blowing. So, instead of berating Muslim men who would not shake hands with women, we engaged critically with the problematical relationship between sexuality and purity laws in *all* religions. Instead of accepting that identities have fixed boundaries, we considered the cultural fertility and also the negative aspects of conversions. Instead of making objects into fetishes of a new cult, we unsettled visitors by questioning whether a certain object was actually real, art or fake. Instead of propagating the myths of Jerusalem ('Israel's eternal capital city', 'holy city', 'centre of the world', the 'place of Judgement Day'), we presented the fatal effect of these myths on a city that was torn apart. Instead of celebrating famous Jews in pop culture or the tradition of 'Jewish music', we drew visitors into a vortex of memories of their own musical rebellions and addressed the birth of pop culture from the perspective of the abandonment of traditions and ways of life. And instead of setting the myth of a 'Jewish state' against the diaspora, we familiarized our public with the reality of an Israeli multiplicity, which left them with one pressing question: how can Israel ever become a civil society if it does not finally consider what all the people who live there can share and not just what's good for the Jews, thereby excluding a quarter of the population? And not to forget the Palestinians who live outside the borders of the state but within the reality of the Israeli occupation.

Instead of posing questions to which we already know the answers, we prefer to pose questions to which we ourselves are seeking answers. These are questions that go beyond Europe and embrace, among many others, the Hohenems diaspora. Perhaps this stubborn insistence that Jewish existence still remains more than ever a diasporic one derives from a European sensibility. It is indeed not a sensibility that prompts belief in a promised land.

Bibliography

Anderson, Benedict, *Imagined Communities: Reflections on the Origin and Spread of Nationalism*, London, Verso, 2006.

Assmann, Aleida, *Geschichte im Gedächtnis: Von der individuellen Erfahrung zur öffentlichen Inszenierung*, München, C. H. Beck, 2007.

Dostoyevsky, Fyodor, *The Devils*, first published in the Russian Messenger 1871–2.

Fliedl, Gottfried, 'Haus der Geschichte: Mein "nein" dazu', 2015, http://museologien.blogspot.co.at/2015/10/haus-der-geschichte-mein-dazu.html.

MacDonald, Sharon, 'Museums, national, postnational, transcultural identities', *Museum and Society*, vol. 1, no. 1, 2003.

Pamuk, Orhan, *The Museum of Innocence*, London, Faber, 2009.

Pomian, Krysztof, *Collectors and Curiosities: Origins of the Museum*, Cambridge, Polity, 1990.

Sloterdijk, Peter, 'Museum: Schule des Befremdens' and 'Weltmuseum und Weltausstellung' (1990), in *Der ästhetische Imperativ: Schriften zur Kunst*, Hamburg, Europäische Verlagsanstalt, 2007.

Young, James, *At Memory's Edge: After-images of the Holocaust in Contemporary Art and Architecture*, New Haven and London, Yale University Press, 2000.

16

The Accidental European

Nira Yuval-Davis

I was not meant to be a European. I didn't plan it. My parents didn't want me to be one; and the 'others' were either indifferent or did their best to ensure I would not be. And yet, here I am, having lived in Europe for more than half of my life, embedded in different ways in Europe and, with all my reservations, I seem to prefer living here – even with 'permanently temporary belonging' – than anywhere else, and mourn the Brexit result of the 23 June 2016 referendum. However, before I can discuss my European belonging, I first need to consider what is Europe and the what, how or where of my belonging to it might be.

As Etienne Balibar argued in a *New Left Review* article in 1991 – though I heard him talk about this in 1990, at the first conference in Germany on racism following the collapse of communism, to which we were both invited as speakers – the notion of 'Europe' lost its stable meaning after the fall of the Soviet Union. After the Second World War leading politicians in Western European states that had suffered egregiously from Nazism saw, against the background of the emerging Cold War, the necessity of building social democratic welfare states and determined that the construction of project 'Europe' was required in order to strengthen the cooperative effort being undertaken to achieve these new cultural-political ends. This 'Europe' encompassed those member states of Nato generally located in the territories over which the Roman empire ruled after it split from the Byzantine empire (with the exception of Greece – the only Greek Orthodox, rather than Protestant or Catholic, country – but the one constructed as the cradle of Western civilization).

Before 1989, the physical parameters of this European landscape and its counterpart on the other side of the 'Iron Curtain' were widely regarded as immutable.

But the collapse of the Soviet Union created contradictory pressures in the definition of the borders/boundaries of Europe. On the one hand, there was an expansionist incentive to incorporate all the countries that geographically belonged to Europe and economically and/or politically might fit into it. On the other hand, this meant enhancing individual and collective inequalities within Europe in a way which eventually created nationalist backlashes across the continent. This was aggravated by the fact that poorer European states, particularly those which joined the euro, were not given enough autonomy to deal with their economic problems, but at the same time were not part of a united political economy. Free movement of people within Europe was welcomed by neoliberal economies, but at the same time also created a backlash of autochthonic extreme right political movements. As Carl-Ulrik Schierup and his colleagues described it, these developments created 'the European dilemma', which forced states and governments to choose between promoting national and European solidarities on the one hand and universal social justice in their welfare state policies on the other hand. These tensions were enhanced with the 2008 global economic crisis and especially when wars and ecological disasters started to drive large quantities of displaced people from the Global South into Europe. In the summer of 2015 this flow of humanity became so serious as to prompt some countries to start threatening to resurrect national European borders even within the Schengen zone.

When political values and economic markets stop being naturalized as signifiers of European borders, there is a growing pull towards a culturalist/religious definition of Europe. If the cultural discourse on Europe since the Second World War was constructed mainly around civic notions of democracy – although Muslim migrants as well as Turkey, the Muslim member of Nato and country of origin of many of Europe's 'guest workers', were always ambivalently framed in terms of outsiders/insiders –

more recent right-wing discourse, such as that of Viktor Orbán, the Hungarian prime minister, switched to talk explicitly of the Christian character of Europe and 'the danger of the Islamization of Europe'. In an opinion piece in Germany's *Frankfurter Allgemeine Zeitung* he wrote: 'Those arriving have been raised in another religion, and represent a radically different culture. Most of them are not Christians, but Muslims. That is an important question, because Europe and European culture have Christian roots. Or is it not already and in itself alarming that Europe's Christian culture is barely in a position to uphold Europe's own Christian values?'

The growing securitization discourse and the transformation of multiculturalism into 'everyday bordering', Europe's growing, dominant technology now being used to control diversity and diversity discourse, are managing to create mutations of the notion of 'Europe' (of which Brexit is one disturbing signifier) at a worrying rate. Dealing with these mutations is a great part of what has preoccupied me in the last few years both professionally and politically, and I'll return to these and the phenomenon of 'everyday bordering' later on in the essay, and explain them more fully. However, before doing this I need to explain how I, a child born in Tel Aviv in Mandate Palestine, came to live in London, and thus occupy a certain specific spatial, as well as political and cultural, situated European belonging. But in order to do so, I have to start from exploring another aspect of my multidimensional, marginalized and ambivalent European belonging in another corner of Europe – Lithuania, one of the post-Soviet parts of the EU's expanding 'Europe', where my parents were born and grew up during and after the First World War.

'Becoming European'

As I mentioned at the beginning of this essay, I was not meant to be a European. On the contrary, I was born a *Sabra* (after the name of the cactus used in Palestine to mark the boundaries of fields), a name given to the new breed of Jews born in Palestine and educated by the Zionist settlers there. I was supposedly rooted in my land

and country, cleansed of all traces of the negatively stereotyped 'diasporic Jew' by having grown up in the Zionist Yishuv (the Jewish community in Palestine prior to the declaration of the state of Israel) – like the cactus fruit: rough and thorny on the outside, soft and tasty on the inside. But my birth as a non-European, non-diasporic Jew was ideologically constructed as a political protest that went even deeper.

My mother, who followed my father from their Lithuanian *shtetl* to settle in Palestine in the early 1930s, went back to Lithuania with my sister to visit her family and then returned to Palestine in the week the Second World War started. Another day or so delay and her way back would have been blocked. She would have ended up, like the rest of our families and community in Alitus, being murdered, with her remains, like theirs, under the asphalt covering the huge mass graves in the woods next to the town. And I would not have been born. My birth, in the middle of the war, was part of a mass response to Ben-Gurion's call to produce babies in Palestine to compensate for those murdered by the Nazis and lost to the cause of Jewish immigration and the regeneration of the Jewish nation.

My mother never went back to Europe. Nor did my father, except to London, at the end of his life, after I moved to live there. I once asked him if he wanted to visit the town of his birth again, and he vehemently rejected the idea. And although, like many Europeans, he was multilingual – he spoke German, Russian and Lithuanian in addition to Yiddish and Hebrew – he never learned English. His emotions were wholeheartedly invested in the 'homeland' in Palestine he helped to build as a socialist Zionist, first in a kibbutz, then in town in the cooperative movement and finally, at the age of 50, as an accountant, working more or less with the same firms that converted from cooperatives to private capitalist companies. Before he died, following a stroke he suffered during the week Israel invaded Lebanon in 1982, he whispered to me that he never dreamed that the utopian society he thought he was helping to build in the Land of Israel would become such a nightmare. It was the first time we talked about Israeli politics since the terrible arguments we used to have when I first started to develop my non-

and then anti-Zionist politics in the mid-1960s and shortly after the 1967 war. But that's another story.

I never dreamed I'd end up living in London for more than half my life. Although I felt claustrophobic in Israel since becoming a teenager, and wanted to see the great wide world, I was also becoming gradually aware of and uncomfortable with the nature of the settler society in which I was living. But I never imagined living permanently outside Israel except, maybe, in the USA, where our only surviving relatives outside Israel were living and where my sister went to live in her late twenties. Europe was definitely not an option.

I got married in 1965 and became a British citizen in 1966. My husband's father was born in the UK, so he was entitled to a British passport, and as his wife I was too. Although the British authorities were not happy about my becoming a British citizen as a result of such flimsy connections, back then, in the 1960s, it was legal. It was only due to the tenacious efforts of an eccentric great aunt of my then husband who spent days and weeks in Somerset House and found the divorce papers of my husband's father from his first English wife, thus giving my husband the status of a legitimate son of his father's second Czech-Israeli wife, that I was asked to swear allegiance to the British Queen in the British consulate in Jerusalem and was given a British passport.

I was very happy to receive this second passport – it represented freedom. When my then husband and I travelled around Europe with our Israeli passports during our 'honeymoon' – at the age of 22 it was my first time abroad – we were stopped at every border, our passports and visas (which we had to acquire separately in Israel prior to departure) were checked and we had to endure the suspicious gazes of our fellow travellers whose passports were not as confining as the then Israeli passport. Nobody stopped us with our British passports. We were 'Europeans'.

I left Israel in 1969 to pursue postgraduate studies in the USA, intending to return to live in Israel or stay in America for some years, at most. I remained for three years, but as a result of a combination of personal, relational and political reasons, I found myself living in London from the end of 1973 in a kind of permanently temporary state.

Of course, 'becoming' British or even 'European' was not that straightforward. In the days of the pre-1981 British nationality law, when I was travelling with my blond toddler son from Israel back to London, especially during the summer, with my dark tanned skin I was often mistaken for his 'nanny' and put in the separate queue of the 'controllable' (i.e. ex-colonial) passport bearers rather than the queue for the 'straight' British subjects to which I formally 'belonged'. It is still not straightforward, because of Britain's ambivalent relationship with Europe, as well as my own ambivalent relationship with Britain.

Virtually from the first day I came to live in the UK, as an anti-Zionist Israeli, living temporarily in London, I was determined to be engaged not only in the politics of exile, but also to become involved in the local political landscape – not because I considered myself as 'belonging' to Britain, or Europe, or even then to London and Hackney (although in later years I discovered that I had become quite a strong local patriot), but because, as a humanist and a socialist feminist, it was important to become engaged in political struggles for social justice wherever you find yourself living. Although I became a member of the libertarian leftist organization Big Flame for a while, it was no coincidence that my main local political activism was originally as a member of WING – Women, Immigration and Nationality Group.

My personal, political and academic preoccupation with issues of borders and boundaries has persisted in different ways since the days I started travelling outside Israel (as well, of course, as experiencing borders in Israel when growing up and since the 1967 war and the beginning of the Occupation). And it continues to this day with my membership of a large EU research project, Borderscapes, leading an international team studying 'everyday bordering'. But I try to continue to act also on the local level, even if it's only to cook – as I don't have time to train as an advisor – at the local Hackney Migrants Centre. My other main political involvement, national and international, which also started in

Israel (in the League Against Religious Coercion), has been in the organization founded in 1989 in the wake of the 'Rushdie Affair', Women Against Fundamentalism.

Returning to the issue of 'Europeanness', there is no doubt that one major parameter of my relationship to Europe, one existential mode of my belonging, is in terms of its borders and boundaries, and this will underlie the rest of my narrative in this essay. However, when considering the question of my European belonging, it is constructed on double bifurcated axes of ambivalence: first, in relation to my identity as a Londoner, and second, as a diasporic, Ashkenazi Israeli Jew.

On Being a Londoner, 'Anglo' and a European

Since coming to live in London, I have worked in two of the 'new' London universities: Greenwich and East London. Although a couple of times I briefly considered moving to work outside London, I never really wanted to leave the capital. My sense of belonging never expanded to the whole of the UK. Although I found it hard adjusting to live in large, anonymous, multi-centred London, the rootedness I could discern in small university towns outside London seemed to me always exclusionary. It was when I stepped outside of London, and I told people that I was from the metropolis so as not to start the complex discussion about Israel/Palestine when I didn't feel like it, that people started asking me about my accent and where I'm 'really' from. At the same time I felt that my status as a single mother was being made an exception rather than the rule, as it was in my neighbourhood in London.

Therefore my London belonging was, in a way, one layer in a multi-layered construct that skipped the UK but was part of a cosmopolitan, global cities belonging (reinforced by my three years former residency in the USA where I discovered, after leaving Israel, what it was to live in a pluralist society), which was bounded by the English language being common to them all. Although, of course, as my American niece likes to point out whenever we have more than a brief discussion, there are as many words in English and American that separate us as those which unite us. This Anglo-Western project of belonging has also had an Australian component. When I first travelled to Australia for a lecture tour in the early 1980s, I was fascinated to discover how much the social circles I mixed with there contained elements of belonging from my previous countries of residence: American friendliness, British left politics and the settler society social relations of pre-1967 Israel. Rather than a positive choice in itself, it was 'accidentally' remaining to live in London after returning from Australia that provided me with the place from which I could easily travel to all those locations where I've built intimate bonds of belonging. The more places I visited and bonded with, the more this Anglo-global framework of belonging continued to expand. But it became most active for me politically in the variety of global feminist forums, including the NGO forums in various UN conferences, in which I have taken part since the 1990s.

This global network of groups included some women from other European countries, but interestingly, Europe was much more marginal in them than countries in the Global South, such as Sri-Lanka and Peru, as well as Anglo-Saxon countries, especially in my fields of activity: the international research network on women in militarized conflict zones and women against fundamentalism. And yet I've also been involved in European political forums, most importantly the European Forum of Socialist Feminists, which changed its name (before ceasing to be active altogether) to the European Forum of Left Feminists after demands not only by feminists from ex-state socialist East and Central European countries, but also from South European states in which the dominant political parties called themselves 'socialist'. Naturally, the conflict in former Yugoslavia occupied a central role in our work on women in militarized conflict zones.

Exploring How Borders and Boundaries Affect People's Lives

It was during the 2000s that my European belonging started to take centre stage in my multi-layered life. It was nurtured by the growing number of visiting professorships I took up in different European countries: mainly the Netherlands, Germany, Sweden and Denmark. In each of these places, I not only forged a new set of close social relations and gained insights into their local issues, I also came to understand better their different and yet common European belonging. However, what was also becoming clearer was that being part of the Schengen zone allowed them to construct a European identity of a different kind and a less ambivalent nature than that prevailing in the UK.

However, it was not until I became involved in the EU Borderscapes research project in 2012 that I had an opportunity to examine more closely situated constructions of European belonging and non-belonging and how they relate to the growing dominance of 'everyday bordering' as the dominant technology to manage diversity and discourses in diversity – a 'front' on which the UK is leading many other European countries. It is not incidental that the drive 'to control our borders' was an hegemonic narrative in the pro-Brexit campaign.

I've always been fascinated with issues of borders and boundaries. As I mentioned earlier, growing up in pre-1967 Israel this was only natural, but I was also aware that other people's experiences were very different. In the early 2000s I carried out a small research project in which I contacted people in various professional, political and personal networks and asked them to send me an email telling me how they experienced borders and boundaries as children, how this has changed and how it has affected their lives. I received many fascinating responses which enabled me to develop theoretically the notion of the 'situated imagination' as well as to write about gendered constructions of these situated gazes at borders. (It was part of my growing dialogical, intersectional, epistemological approach, which sees 'the truth' as encompassing the differential views of the world of the different people who take part in different social encounters.) As a result of that I was invited to give a keynote presentation at a conference at the University of Eastern Finland where important work on issues of borders and bordering was being carried out. Among the responses I received to my questions about borders, I discovered that Finnish people were very sensitive to such matters, having grown up with contrasting constructions of borders – completely permeable on the Swedish side, completely opaque on the Soviet side.

So, when border studies scholars from that university applied to the EU for funds to carry out the huge project on EU Borderscapes, I was approached and asked to lead the international work programme, which studied bordering from an intersectional perspective focusing on the everyday. Becoming more aware of the different situated gazes of the people my team studied in such countries as the UK, Germany, Spain, Finland, Russia and the Ukraine, each with its different relationship to 'Europe', have helped to deconstruct further for me the notion of 'European belonging'. In our specific ethnographic studies in the UK in Dover and London, the articulations of this complex and ambivalent relationship were particularly poignant, especially in the context of the EU referendum, as well as more generally in Europe, as a result of the refugee crisis, to which – as I mentioned above – some countries are responding by threatening to re-establish national borders, also within the Schengen zone.

Everyday Bordering

The research project has been rich and stimulating and has developed and stretched my knowledge and understanding of bordering, belonging and 'Europe' in a variety of ways. However, I want to conclude this essay by describing the notion of 'everyday bordering' which we found to be developing as the dominant technology for managing diversity and discourses on diversity, undermining convivial pluralist, multicultural social relations. It is developing all over Europe (and other 'Northern' countries) but Britain plays a leading role in this.

What we mean by 'everyday bordering' is that rather than questions about borders being confined to international frontiers, or even to major entry and exit points in a country, bordering practices are being applied everywhere, every day and by more and more sections of the population. Employers, landlords, educators, health workers, bankers and so on are all asked to play the role of unpaid and untrained border guards. And in the UK, the passing of the 2014 and even more so the 2016 Immigration Acts made failure in these duties subject to the payment of huge fines or even a prison sentence. At the same time more and more people are suspected of being illegal (or at least illegitimate) crossers of borders. These regulations are supposedly part of the 'anti-terrorism' drive and are aimed at making us safe, but actually their effect is to deprive people of their sense of entitlement and generate suspicions of and within communities, neighbourhoods and even families. And the whole process is highly racialized. I experienced this personally before going to examine a PhD submission at a London university when I was asked repeatedly in emails to produce my passport to prove I'm legally entitled to work in the UK – although it was widely known that I was a staff member of another university in the UK (and have been since the early 1970s).

Clearly, the technologies of everyday bordering are not just – or even mainly – about security. Rather, they are about a political project of belonging, which is aimed at appeasing the growing autochthonic politics of the right. Paradoxically, although this political project is associated in the UK with those who wanted the UK to exit from the EU, it is a mirror image of the growing, populist anti-diversity right all over the EU. As I wrote in my 2011 book, *The Politics of Belonging*, it is important to differentiate between belonging and the politics of belonging. The latter comprise specific political projects aimed at constructing belonging to apply to particular collectivities, which are themselves being assembled in these projects in very specific ways and within very definite boundaries.

Belonging is about emotional (or even ontological) attachment, about feeling 'at home'. While, as Alison Blunt argues, 'home is a material and an affective space, shaped by everyday practices, lived experiences, social relations, memories and emotions', part of feeling 'at home' has been described as being in a 'safe' space. Ulf Hannerz claims that home is essentially a contrastive concept, linked to some notion of what it means to be away from home. However, even more importantly in the political project of belonging, which is informing contemporary everyday bordering in Europe, it is also linked to views of who has a right to share the home and who does not belong there. Belonging tends to be naturalized and part of everyday practices. It becomes articulated, formally structured and politicized only when it is perceived to be threatened in some way.

Finding ways to resist the growing naturalization of the 'common sense' of everyday bordering is becoming my mode of European belonging: a political project of belonging that aspires to continue to nurture convivial pluralism and diversity in our everyday lives. I left Israel because I could not bear to live in an ethnocracy. I do not want to find that what attracted me to live in Britain, especially now that the country voted in the 23 June 2016 referendum to leave the EU, is going to be lost. And I'm following with growing, impotent dread what is happening in my 'homeland', Israel. I do not want the social and political mutation of everyday bordering, which has now become ubiquitous, to get even stronger.

Bibliography

Balibar, Etienne, 'Es gibt keinen Staat in Europa: racism and politics in Europe today', *New Left Review*, 186, March/April 1991.

Blunt, Alison and Varley, Ann, 'Geographies of home', *cultural geographies*, vol. 11, no. 1, 2004.

Collins, Patricia H., *Black Feminist Thought: Knowledge, Consciousness, and the Politics of Empowerment*, New York, Routledge, 2000.

EU Borderscapes project, www.uel.ac.uk/cmrb/borderscapes/ and www.euborderscapes.eu/.

Fenster, Tovi, 'Belonging, memory and the politics of planning in Israel', *Social and Cultural Geography*, no. 5, 2004.

Hannerz, Ulf, 'Where we are and who we want to be', *Public Worlds*, no. 10, 2002.

Sahgal, Gita and Yuval-Davis, Nira, eds, *Refusing Holy Orders: Women and Fundamentalism in Britain*, London, Virago Press, 1992.

Schierup, Carl-Ulrik, Hansen, Peo and Castles, Stephen, *Migration, Citizenship, and the European Welfare State: A European Dilemma*, Oxford, Oxford University Press, 2006.

Sridharan, Vasudevan, 'Hungary: Prime Minister Viktor Orban says Muslim influx threatening Europe's "Christian roots"', International Business Times, 4 September 2015, www.ibtimes.co.uk/hungary-pm-says-muslim-influx-threatening-europes-christian-roots-1518413.

Yuval-Davis, Nira, 'The contaminated Paradise', in Nahla Abdo and Ronit Lentin, eds, Women and the Politics of Military Confrontation: Palestinian and Israeli Gendered Narratives of Dislocation, Oxford, Berghahn Press, 2002.

Yuval-Davis, Nira, The Politics of Belonging: Intersectional Contestations, London, Sage, 2011.

Yuval-Davis, Nira, 'Intersectional contestations', in Sukhwant Dhaliwal and NiraYuval-Davis, eds, Women Against Fundamentalism: Stories of Dissent and Solidarity, London, Lawrence and Wishart, 2014.

Yuval-Davis, Nira, 'Want to know how to kill a multicultural society? Turn its ordinary citizens into border guards ', Independent, 15 December 2015, www.independent.co.uk/voices/want-to-know-how-to-kill-a-multicultural-society-turn-its-ordinary-citizens-into-border-guards-a6774151.html; https://vimeo.com/126315982.

Yuval-Davis, Nira and Stoetzler, Marcel, 'Imagined boundaries and borders: a gendered gaze', European Journal of Women's Studies, vol. 9, no. 3, 2002.

Yuval-Davis, Nira and Stoetzler, Marcel, 'Standpoint theory, situated knowledge and the situated imagination', Feminist Theory, vol.3, no. 3, 2002.

Yuval-Davis, Nira, Wemyss, Georgie and Cassidy, Kathryn, Bordering, Cambridge, Polity (forthcoming).

17

Belonging to the Contact Zone

Nora Sternfeld

In his 2006 book *The Time that Remains: A Commentary on the Letter to the Romans*, Giorgio Agamben writes about Paul. He describes him to readers as the figure who reinvents belonging paradigmatically. For Agamben, however, the road from Saul (as he was known before his conversion) to Paul is not interesting simply because here is someone who turns his back on his own sense of belonging. According to Agamben, Paul does not merely leave Judaism behind him but rather deconstructs the notion of a simple separation between those who belong to it and those who do not. Agamben describes this as 'dividing the division'. The further division Agamben introduces is between 'the Jew according to the flesh' and 'the Jew according to the spirit'. This means that there are now 'Jews who are not Jews, because there are Jews who are Jews according to the flesh [circumcision], not the spirit, and [non-Jews] who are [non-Jews] according to the flesh, but not according to the spirit'.

Paul thus produces a third category: the remainder, a new form of subject that is neither a Jew nor a non-Jew, but a 'non-non-Jew'. This remainder cannot be merged into the binary division. Rather it demonstrates that within the division there is more than just Jews and non-Jews.

Agamben illustrates this by means of a diagram: each side of the Jew/non-Jew binary division is divided by a further division, between flesh and spirit. In the process a new kind of non-belonging belonging arises: that of the non-non-Jews.

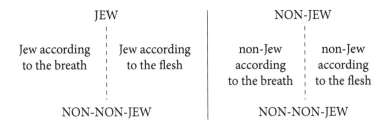

According to Agamben, the significance of this 'division of divisions' is that 'it forces us to think about the question of the universal and particular in a completely new way, not only in logic, but also in ontology and politics'. What then is this completely new perspective on universalism that Agamben proposes? It concerns a universalism that is not based on one big whole but on the constitutive non-identity that lies within every identity. Unlike Alain Badiou, in his *St Paul: The Foundation of Universalism*, he is not of the opinion that Paul is a universalist in the pure sense, transcending any identity. Rather, he calls attention to the fact that Jews and non-Jews are not possessed of one-dimensional identities. When you divide the division you reveal the remainder between every people and itself, between every sense of belonging and itself.

Against this background, in this essay I seek to think about living together – a form of coexistence for which belonging is neither the only criterion nor is it something that must be denied or completely abandoned. If such coexistence were successful, it would not mean that everyone could delight in an ideal world of togetherness. Rather, what I am talking about is a process full of conflicts, misunderstandings and difficulties on all sides of the divisions that come into play. But when dividing the division, something is nevertheless also shared in the remainder. I would like to illustrate this with an anecdote.

Performative Alliances

In April 2013, together with artists, theoreticians and students at Aalto University in Helsinki, I initiated a procedural project which involved looking at what would happen if nothing was clarified in advance, or anticipated and set out in schedules and project rationales. We opened an empty exhibition entitled 'Taking Time' that was supposed to be able to grow over the course of the two weeks it lasted. It dealt with the interfaces of four topics – time, capitalism, art and activism – and we read, discussed, gave presentations, made plans and sketches and immersed ourselves in what would come out of it artistically and intellectually.

Much of what we discussed and experienced and also what emerged artistically in the process was certainly relevant for me. But the most important experience emerged out of the preparations we were making for the closing day of the project, to which I had invited Roy Brand, a curator and philosopher who was then the director of the Bezalel Academy of Arts and Design in Jerusalem and works on time-based art. A discussion began among those on the project mailing list about whether a lecture by an Israeli who comes from a public institution in Israel should be boycotted. As the person who had invited him and initiated the project, I was in a difficult position as I specifically wanted it to be possible for conflicts to surface and be discussed. At the same time I did not want to encumber the many international students at the university in Finland with the ballast of my youth in Austria – neither the associated experiences of antisemitism nor the reflections on structural antisemitism which I developed there. I therefore decided to formulate my position on this question as clearly and succinctly as possible and sent a one-sentence email to the mailing list: 'I propose that we do not judge any of the people in the project by where they come from and where they work but rather by what they say and do.'

The topic was on the agenda when we met together for a plenary session on the same day I sent the email. I was prepared for a long discussion and had mentally mapped out the various directions it could take. However, something unexpected happened that cut short the discussion. After a short presentation of the issue, the first person to speak was Ahsan Massood, an art student from Pakistan. He said that it was explicitly stated in his passport that he was not allowed to travel to Israel and that he would therefore never have the opportunity to say something informed about the country. So whatever his views about Israel, he knew all too well what it meant to be judged and excluded on the basis of his origins. Ahsan rejected this approach and therefore vehemently supported attending the lecture by Roy Brand. He himself would definitely be there. Almost simultaneously, a fellow student, Sepide Rahaa, a feminist artist from Iran, had also indicated that she wanted to speak. She agreed with Ahsan and made it clear that she would find it completely unacceptable if someone were excluded merely because he was Israeli. She too underlined this by referring to her own humiliating experiences of being automatically associated with Iran and its policies, with which she obviously did not identify.

From the outset then, the discussion was changed so radically by the clear solidarity of the two students that it was no longer possible to maintain the typical fracture lines that characterize boycott debates. Some critics left the room so that they would not have to participate in any decision-making, but all eventually came to Roy Brand's lecture. That moment was important for me and created a strong bond between me and the two students.

Since then I have asked myself what united us. On the one hand it seems to have been the experience of 'non-belonging', and on the other hand the ability not to have to 'belong' to every conceivable political boycott. An additional possibility is the connection to a geographical region and the shared refusal to allow yourself to be defined by national enmities. But what probably connected us most of all was the moment itself – the act by which we saw ourselves connected together across existing belongings: the performativity of the alliance. And I can definitely say that for me this moment was an experience which changed my position to that of trusting in the potential of the 'contact zone' and also changed me personally.

Altogether, we experienced many conflicts in the course of the project. Not all were resolved amicably and, in discussing the interfaces of art, activism, time and capitalism, we addressed many issues and argued a great deal. This was fully intended because the project was all about how something could be carried out in the particular kind of space we had created. I had conceived of this space in the sense of being a 'contact zone', the concept developed by the two post-colonial theorists, Mary Louise Pratt and James Clifford, in the 1990s. This concept is important for my understanding of belonging

What Are Contact Zones?

Pratt and Clifford describe contact zones as social spaces, in which diverse social and cultural positions come into contact and have to coexist – more or less conflictually – and be negotiated. The comparative literature scholar Pratt uses the term – in keeping with the subject of her research – primarily in conjunction with Western expansions and ethnographic explorations. For her, the term 'contact zone' comes from linguistics. In her *Imperial Eyes: Travel Writing and Transculturation* she writes:

> I borrow the term 'contact' here from linguistics, where the term contact language refers to an improvised language that develops among speakers of different tongues who need to communicate with each other consistently, usually in the context of trade. Such languages begin as pidgins, and are called creoles when they come to have native speakers of their own. Like the societies of the contact zone, such languages are commonly regarded as chaotic, barbarous and lacking in structure. (Ron Carter has suggested the term 'contact literatures' to refer to literatures written in European languages from outside Europe.)

Clifford emphasizes that the term can be expanded to social differentiations, such as in a city. With this background, it is suitable for describing divided spaces in a culturally diverse society. In *Routes, Travel and Translation in the Late Twentieth Century*, Clifford, whose research is in museum theory, writes:

> The notion of a contact zone, articulated by Pratt in contexts of European expansion and transculturation, can be extended to

include cultural relations within the same state, region, or city – in the centers rather than the frontiers of nations and empires. The distances at issue here are more social than geographic. For most inhabitants of a poor neighborhood, located perhaps just blocks or a short bus ride from a fine-arts museum, the museum might as well be another continent. Contact perspectives recognize that 'natural' social distances and segregations are historical/political products.

Although the two post-colonial theoreticians might not have had our Helsinki 2013 experience in mind, the idea of the contact zone still seems productive for understanding the context in which cities, museums and exhibitions negotiate their existence in today's culturally diverse societies. With it, it is possible to imagine connections between different positions, but without making appropriating or unifying assumptions. The term describes shared/divided social spaces of contact and challenges existing concepts of community at the same time. Expressed in German with the double sense of the word *geteilt* – shared and divided – it is thematized in post-colonial theory in reference to borders and conflicts. It undermines notions of 'authenticity' as well as those of 'powerlessness'. This means that different histories, references and power relations can come into view, but without having to assume or construct cultural differentness at the same time.

Hierarchies are neither considered here as the sole factor producing meaning, nor are they disregarded. For even though everyone within a contact zone is influenced by specific conditions and power relations, but nevertheless not wholly determined by them, it becomes possible to envision a power of agency in theory and practice. This possibility of agency is available to all participants in a contact zone – albeit in different ways against the background of existing asymmetries of power relations. Contact zones are thus power-charged spaces of agency.

In these divided/shared spaces, actors interact with one another under different conditions. What is productive about the concept is that the formation of the subject is not presumed substantially to precede the contact, but instead first emerges through joint agency and negotiation: it is based neither on the Western humanist idea of seemingly universal, equally acting people, nor on the culturalist notions of a predetermination due to origin. In the theory of the contact zone, subjects and actors are therefore not constructed essentially – in keeping with an interaction of a preceding culture or social position – but rather in process and in relation to one another. According to Pratt in *Imperial Eyes*: 'A "contact" perspective emphasizes how subjects get constituted in and by their relations to each other. It treats the relation among colonizers and colonized, or travellers and "travellees", not in term of separatedness, but in terms of co-presence, interaction, interlocking understandings and practices, and often within radically asymmetrical relations of power.'

A further level of the contact zone, which is often misunderstood or forgotten in the use of the term, is that of conflict. An encounter in unequal power relations obviously holds much potential for conflict. And these are not repressed in the term, but are instead an integral component. For Clifford, the contact zone – which he even refers to once as 'contact (conflict) zone' – thus enables an analysis of the museum as a place where conflicts have become sediments. In *Routes, Travel and Translation* he writes: 'When museums are seen as contact zones, their organizing structure as a collection becomes an ongoing historical, political, moral relationship – a power-charged set of exchanges, of push and pull.' In this way, contact zones are no longer seen merely as powerful spaces, but rather as organic structures, in which different social struggles are reflected as ongoing processes of fighting for the power of interpretation. This results in a conclusion within the terms of hegemony theory, to the extent that organic structures are involved, which are the results of struggles within power relations. These are also not immutable, but can be called into question and redefined.

In *Profession 91* Pratt describes very beautifully and vividly the experience of the contact zone in a learning context: 'Along with rage, incomprehension, and pain there were exhilarating moments of wonder and revelation, mutual understanding, and new wisdom

– the joys of the contact zone. The sufferings and revelations were, at different moments to be sure, experienced by every student. No one was excluded, and no one was safe.'

Divided and Connected

To think of society as a contact zone therefore does not mean denying conflicts. In her most recent book, *Notes Toward a Performative Theory of Assembly*, Judith Butler considers forms of living together. Like Hannah Arendt she points out that we share a world which connects and separates us. And like Lévinas she reminds us of the responsibility that goes with it. She writes: 'every communitarian ground for belonging is only justifiable on the condition that it is subordinate to a non-communitarian opposition to genocide'. Thus for Butler (and Arendt) belonging always means being part of a world in which we live together with many others who are not of our own choosing. Consequently, according to Butler there is an undeniable interdependence in this world, which is the basis for the responsibility she demands. However much we strive for independence, Butler writes, we are nevertheless vulnerable and dependent on each other – interdependent. As she convincingly makes clear, we are born dependent on people and things and we die dependent on people and things. Interdependence commits us to each other although it is anything but easy and without friction. Rather it is hard and involves a fair amount of anger. Butler makes this refreshingly clear: 'Inevitably, we rail against those on whom we are most dependent (or those who are most dependent on us), and there is no way to dissociate dependency from aggression once and for all.'

Taking the world as a contact zone thus means thinking of it in terms of conflict. But it also means that the contact zone must not be defined completely without reference to the (powerful and often deadly) lines of conflict and belongings that already exist. The history of the project in Finland that I described is only one of many opportunities for diasporic individuals to experience encounters that at any given time in the contact zone cut across, run in parallel with, or simply follow a different course to, lines of conflict based on land or place of origin. They make possible forms of reference which are not defined by the logic of nation states. That does not have to be the case but can be so. I would like to think of it as the potential of agonistic politics and educational work in culturally diverse societies, and in this connection briefly introduce the concept of agonism as understood by Chantal Mouffe.

Mouffe starts from the assumption that society is riddled with political antagonisms – violent conflicts and us/them distinctions. These are necessary for politics, but as friend/foe dichotomies they make any kind of community impossible. In *On the Political*, Mouffe writes: 'Antagonisms express themselves in the most diverse ways and it is illusory to believe they could be eliminated. Hence it is imperative that they have the possibility of agonistic expression in the form of the pluralistic democratic system.' According to Mouffe, they are therefore domesticated with a view to possible coexistence and a capacity to negotiate. Mouffe calls this kind of sublimated antagonism 'agonism'. As she explains it:

Conflict, in order to be accepted as legitimate, needs to take a form that does not destroy the political association. This means that some kind of common bond must exist between the parties in conflict, so that they will not treat their opponents as enemies to be eradicated, seeing their demands as illegitimate, which is precisely what happens with the antagonistic friend/enemy relation. However, the opponents cannot be seen simply as competitors whose interests can be dealt with through mere negotiation, or reconciled through deliberation, because in that case the antagonistic element would simply have been eliminated. If we want to acknowledge on one side the permanence of the antagonistic dimension of the conflict, while on the other side allowing for the possibility of its 'taming', we need to envisage a third type of relation. This is the type of relation which I have proposed to call 'agonism'. While antagonism is a we/they relation in which the two sides are enemies who do not share any common ground, agonism is a we/they relation where the conflicting parties, although acknowledging that there is no rational solution to their conflict, nevertheless recognize the legitimacy of their opponents. They are 'adversaries' not enemies. This means that, while in conflict, they see themselves as belonging to the same political association, as sharing a common symbolic space within which the conflict takes place. We could say that the task of democracy is to transform antagonism into agonism.

Mouffe speaks of a 'kind of conflictual consensus', 'which opens up a common symbolic space to opponents as "legitimate enemies"'. This common symbolic space should thus be linked to the idea of the contact zone. It can thereby be seen as a space for negotiation which is based on conflict – but on conflict that is also domesticated – and is suffused with concrete, assertive, but not immutable power relationships.

Marie-Eve Morin and Jean-Luc Nancys write about the role of agonism in the project of radical democracy: 'The political task seems to consist in creating a place where differences of opinion and arguments can be expressed. Hence this agonism is nevertheless founded on a minimal consensus, namely the demand that one recognizes the value of agonistic democracy and plays by the rules of the contest [*Agon*].' Agonism thus needs a space and a framework in which its rules can be established as a basis for understanding. This in turn is itself achieved agonistically within the hegemonic relationships and as such is changeable. As Mouffe writes: 'The fundamental difference between the "dialogic" and the "agonistic" perspective is that the latter has the goal of achieving a thoroughgoing change in the existing power relationships and creating a new hegemony. For this reason the agonist perspective can be described in a real sense as "radical".'

If we now go beyond Mouffe and think of this space of agonism together with the concept of the contact zone, then it experiences a decentration, where multiple aspects of a situation are taken into consideration – such that existing rules and narratives are constantly redefined by the marginalized and read differently. Agonist negotiation can thus be seen as taking place in various places in society because we know from the concept of the contact zone that where one side has power, the other side may indeed experience powerlessness, but also always has agency. Thus wherever hegemony is established, we can say, thanks to Mouffe, that this agency can thus also be used to domesticate the antagonism agonistically.

Agonistic disputes in today's conflict zones can run along various lines of conflict. As the history of the project in Finland demonstrates, these can sometimes even be transformed into diasporic solidarities which cut across divisions of belongings. This can happen repeatedly, as two further examples reveal.

Within the context of Büro trafo.K, an independent centre that does research and educational projects at the interface of education and critical knowledge production, which I co-founded, I was involved in a project working on 'contact zones in history teaching'. This involved the mediation of history in a culturally diverse society in such a way that young people could formulate their own questions about the past. Two students, Mario Talaić and Milos Stanišić, worked on Yugoslavia in the Second World War, a topic clearly important to them and, they said, one that had barely been covered in school. So they collected a lot of material on the history of the concentration camp in Jasenovac and the massacre by the Wehrmacht in Kragujevac, which had never been mentioned in class.

As well as protesting about how this history had been marginalized, they also undoubtedly wanted to highlight its relevance. As a result, they posed two research questions – 'Why did the Balkan War begin? Are there connections with the Second World War?' – and discussed them with each other. In so doing they broached different Serbian and Croatian perspectives on the origins of these conflicts, but evidently formulated their research from a shared diasporic perspective of having a common interest in the subject. They presented the results of their research on this question in a conversation with the Austrian political scientist Walter Manoschek that was recorded on video and in a memorial at the school where the project was displayed. This is how the conversation ends:

Mario Talaić: In the Second World War there were also the partisans. They fought for the people, for the Yugoslavs. Croats, Slovenes, Serbs – they are the Yugoslavs. And in the Balkan War there was nothing like that.

Milos Stanišić: You have just said that partisans were for the people. That is true. But after the Second World War they also suppressed people.

MT: But it was better that the partisans, that is the Yugoslavs, provided the leadership than the Cetniks or Ustase. You must also think that. Otherwise things would look [very] different today.

Walter Manoschek: What Mario meant if I understood it correctly: during the Second World War there were not only nationalist groups like the Serb nationalists (the Cetniks) and Croatian nationalists (the Ustase), but there was also over and beyond these nationalities a group for whom it did not matter if you were Bosnian, Croat, Serb, Jew. And that was the partisans. Thus a supra-ethnic group. It is completely correct that this was lacking in the 1990s. No one fought to keep Yugoslavia together any more.

MS: In the 1990s what was important was that if you are Croat, you are Croat. If you are Serb, you are Serb. If you are Bosnian, you are Bosnian. There was division. I saw a film about a father with two sons. They were 18 or 19 years old and had to make a decision: either you go to the partisans or to the Cetniks. If the father went to the partisans and the son to the Cetniks, they became enemies. Families were destroyed in this way. They shot at one another and no longer saw themselves as father and son but as enemies. And that is really somehow the saddest thing.

MT: There were also concentration camps in Croatia which were set up by Serbs. There, neighbours killed each other.

MS: In the Balkan War many friendships disintegrated. At that time one only saw that he is Croat and I am Serb. I cannot be friends with him. That is really sad. When you have lived together for 50 years and at a stroke are manipulated by politicians into forgetting everything after 50 years, I find that truly the saddest thing.

MT: What is also sad is when one goes out into the street, sees someone and I ask where he comes from. When he says: 'I am from Serbia.' And I say: 'I am from Croatia.' Then sometimes one also sees things differently. But fortunately times have also changed. We will still remember it. Perhaps everything will be like it was before, perhaps not.

MS: For 50 years we were united.

MT: Like brothers.

My second and final example is a project initiated by Joujou, a young Palestinian woman who lives in Berlin: 'Palestine Loves Israel'. This very improbable statement is one in a series of 'declarations of love' that defy the logic of wars and which began with the Peace Factory in Israel. Joujou explains that she founded the Facebook page 'Palestine loves Israel' when she heard about 'Israel loves Iran', the initiative which led to the setting up of the Peace Factory website. The idea is to use contacts, especially social media, to create forms of understanding and attachment which can effectively neutralize the seemingly insurmountable mistrust that is sustained by a continuing state-of-war atmosphere and its accompanying propaganda. On the Facebook page of 'Palestine loves Israel', Joujou insists on respectful reporting in which lives cannot be dismissed and grief can be shared.

All three examples reveal how, in the contact zone, other potentially fruitful divisions become conceivable, or how there can be value in a reawakened awareness of previously suppressed forms of political conflict. One outcome of Mario and Milos's project on Yugoslavia in the Second World War, the collapse of the Yugoslav state and the Balkan War of the 1990s, was that, long after the events in question, there is once again room, at least in their conversation, for discussion of the left-wing, anti-fascist position of the partisans. And in the case of Joujou too, the division, this time between Israelis and Palestinians, is divided by another division: that between mere national positions and transnational claims for peace. Through dividing these divisions, positions become possible in the contact zone which can only emerge together, when powerful, existing differences are not recognized in a performative way. Thus a space opens up for new conflicts in which all participants can change together, in which no one has to abandon their sense of belonging, but also no one can be reduced to it.

Europe's Crises, Deconstructing Belonging and Building New Solidarities

What does this all mean for Europe today? How might it be possible to think of Europe as a contact zone?

I live in a Europe in which flight from war, oppression and starvation is as commonplace as racist attacks; a Europe which guards its borders by force and accepts daily fatalities as a result; a Europe in which people seek refuge and somehow make their way despite facing structural racism and violence. In this Europe fascism is gaining political ground everywhere and spreading ominously. The wars in which some European states are engaged are not without repercussions: terrorist attacks seem almost commonplace and are creating fear. I live in a Europe which has drawn few conclusions from its colonial history. In these circumstances I find it hard to see belonging as the context in which I want to consider Europe's positive prospects when it is precisely how belonging can be and is being deconstructed that I wanted to describe.

Europe is a migration society writ large, and the problems it faces, which I have just outlined, reflect the actual experiences of such a society: conflicts and contradictions, which cannot be explained away by reducing them to pre-existing fracture lines, but rather reveal possible diasporic interactions in which divisions, other than those artificially created by fascisms, wars and borders, become conceivable and expressible.

So that there is no misunderstanding, however, I stress that I am not arguing *against* existing approaches to Europe's travails, but *for* a politics that makes it possible for a new approach to emerge that is capable of undermining the old fracture lines. For contact zones make possible new, productive fracture lines and new solidarities. I plead for the creation of alliances as contact zones, in which approaches that invoke an anti-fascist Europe struggle agonistically to oppose fascism together with those who want to see its colonial history and racist present clearly revealed and rooted out. I plead for alliances as contact zones which make it possible to conceive of a peace in Israel/Palestine, while neither consciously concealing the history of violence nor denying the experience of either racism or antisemitism. I plead for alliances as contact zones which reject the national fracture lines that even today run through Austria and which can bring equality, anti-racism and feminism together in one struggle. These unexpected connections that cut across the fracture lines admittedly may not be that well known in contact zones, but they are commonplace enough. They are the basis for a different kind of hegemony in a different world.

Bibliography

An extensive discussion of the Taking Time project can be found in a text of the CuMMA Paper Series: Giulia Palladini, Nora Sternfeld, 'Taking time together: a posthumous reflection on a collaborative project and polyorgasmic disobedience', Helsinki 2014, https://cummastudies.files.wordpress.com/2013/08/cumma-papers-61.pdf.

Agamben, Giorgio, *The Time That Remains: A Commentary on the Letter to the Romans*, Stanford, Stanford University Press, 2005.

Badiou, Alain, *St Paul: The Foundation of Universalism*, Stanford, Stanford University Press, 2003.

Butler, Judith, *Notes Toward a Performative Theory of Assembly*, Cambridge, MA, Harvard University Press, 2015.

Chisholm, Michael and Smith, David M., eds, *Shared Space, Divided Space: Essays on Conflict and Territorial Organization*, London and New York, Routledge, 1990.

Clifford, James, *Routes, Travel and Translation in the Late Twentieth Century*, Cambridge, MA, Harvard University Press, 1997.

Morin, Marie-Eve and Nancys, Jean-Luc, 'Denken des Singulär-Plurals oder Das notwendige Zusammensein', in Elke Bippus, Jörg Huber and Dorothée Richter, eds, *Mit-Sein: Gemeinschaft – ontologische und politische Perspektivierungen*, Zürich, Edition Voldemeer, Springer, 2010.

Mouffe, Chantal, *Uber das politische: Wider das kosmopolitische Illusion*, Frankfurt am Main, 2007. English version: *On The Political (Thinking in Action)*, Abingdon, Routledge, 2005.

Pratt, Mary L., 'Arts of the Contact Zone', *Profession 91*, New York, Modern Language Association, 1991.

Pratt, Mary L., *Imperial Eyes: Travel Writing and Transculturation*, 2nd edition, New York, Routledge, 2008.

Spivak, Gayatri Chakravorty, *Outside in the Teaching Machine*, New York and London, Routledge, 1993.

More on the Büro trafo.K history mediation project at http://trafo-k.at/projekte/undwashatdasmitmirzutun.

Video of Balkan war discussion: https://vimeo.com/15126186.

For more on the Peace Factory see http://thepeacefactory.org/palestine-loves-israel/.

An interview with Joujou for Shtetl Montreal during the Gaza War in the summer of 2014: http://shtetlmontreal.com/2014/07/31/lovers-in-a-dangerous-time/.

18

The Unfinished Business
of Our Own Belongings

Antony Lerman

Until a few years ago the concept of 'belonging' was barely part of my vocabulary. Now I wonder how I ever managed without it. Looking back on my life, I can see how something I took for granted as a child and young teenager was far less securely embedded in my sense of who I was than I ever imagined. Belonging is a powerful human emotion, driven, I believe, by what lies at the heart of the word: 'longing' – an ambiguous emotion, both ineffably sad and hopelessly optimistic. Such that you can be drawn to the notion of belonging, only to want to distance yourself from it. Or attracted by it, only to know or discover that you can never have it. If, as I do, you need to acknowledge that you must live with these complexities, with the continued, unfinished business of your own belongings, then it seems to make sense to see belonging as a journey without end rather than a quest for a destination. But it has taken a lifetime – or reflection on a lifetime – to reach this conclusion.

* * *

I was born British and Jewish in 1946 and for most of my childhood and teenage years saw no contradiction between the two. And although the word 'European' would have meant nothing to me until I studied history at grammar school in the early 1960s, you could say that a sense of Europe *was* being instilled in me from a very early age because I had had, for the time, an extraordinarily rich experience of vacations in Western European countries.

Life was grim for most people. The war had bankrupted the country and rationing was still in place. It was an age of austerity. And yet my childhood memories from the late 1940s and early 1950s, growing up in a small, semi-detached, red-brick house on an estate on the unmarked border between the middle class London suburb of Golders Green and the more urban area of Cricklewood, with its large Irish immigrant, working class population, were of a comfortable, secure and loving home. I was seven when my maternal grandpa died and we moved a quarter of a mile up the road to live with my grandma in her more spacious mock-Tudor house. When grandpa died, my father took over the running of the family bespoke tailoring business based in the East End. It must have been reasonably successful. We were not wealthy and I was aware of few extravagances, but we seemed to want for nothing. I thought holidays in Belgium, Holland and France – Normandy coast and the Côte d'Azur – were what any child of my age would be enjoying. Seen from a Jamesian, *What Maisie Knew* perspective, I was at the centre of *my* world; I felt that I was at the centre of *the* world. *And* I was a Jew. Could any other child be so fortunate?

If you read irony in those last two sentences, you would be wrong. As a Jew, I knew, from a very early age, that I was different. Different, but not 'other'. Different, but included. My Jewish world was interlaced with and not separate from the social, cultural and physical dimensions of the wider society. It functioned as a way of maintaining Jewish religious identity, but even though it was centred on mainstream orthodoxy, its thrust was assimilationist. My parents, like all of their Jewish friends, first- or second-generation working class, immigrant stock, were focused on making a good living in commerce and business, and giving their children the opportunity to advance through good education. Photos of their visibly foreign-looking parents show them dressed in typical Jewish *shtetl* clothes: the men with skull caps and side-curls, full-length kaftans, with the fringes of their Jewish ritual vests visible over their trousers; the women with head scarves or wigs, and modest, dark, full-length dresses. But in photos from the 1950s, my parents and their friends hardly look any different from the general population.

Although the word 'integration' was not current at the time, that was precisely what the gradual abandonment of Yiddish and the visual attributes of Eastern and Central European Jewish life was leading to.

So I never felt like an outcast. No one told me that I didn't belong, that I was there on sufferance only. Yes, I knew antisemitism. I recall a headmaster at my primary school, where around one-third of the pupils were Jewish, ridiculing the Passover story in morning assembly as an example of Jewish perfidy. Parents complained and the man was quietly relieved of his duties. When I was about ten years old, one break time a boy in my class began praising Hitler for what he had done to the Jews. Without hesitation, a group of us – Jews and non-Jews – rounded on him and a little manhandling put paid to his nonsense. I don't recall he ever repeated it. But this was about the sum total of the anti-Jewish rhetoric I can recall from those days.

It was only later in life that I learned just how thin was the wall constructed by my parents to separate us from the immigrant experience, how they had so successfully brought us up to be English Londoners, while the strands, the traces, the bloodlines connecting us to life in the old country and the early years of struggle in poverty in the East End were still manifold, even as they were shrivelling and withering in so many ways of which I was not aware. It never occurred to me that there might be some cost to my parents in following this assimilatory path. Our close family lived mostly in London and had no experience or memory of the Holocaust, although many of them went through very hard times during their East End years, living in poverty and an anti-alien atmosphere that intensified before the First World War and took a more explicit antisemitic form afterwards. And almost all of their parents – my grandparents' generation – were fleeing anti-Jewish persecution in the Russian empire when they arrived in Britain at the end of the nineteenth century and the beginning of the twentieth. Add to that the three-and-a-half years my father spent in German prisoner of war camps after being wounded and captured in the retreat to Dunkirk in May 1940, and it's perfectly understandable that many in this immigrant population had a lot they would want to put behind them in order to create as clear a path as possible for their children to assimilate in British society.

Victor Jeleniewski Seidler, writing about the 'disavowal of Jewishness' among some in the generations of Jews coming to the UK from sites of persecution between 1880 and 1939, speaks of 'forgetting as a path to belonging'. 'Often parents who have migrated from different lands and carry histories of loss have wanted to conceal these painful histories,' Seidler writes, 'to give their children more opportunity to belong.' It's a truism to say that what I became is in great part the consequence of my parents' choices, but looking back, knowing much more about their pasts and guessing what they might have 'wanted to conceal', I realize that who I am has also been determined by what they chose to forget.

I could have been a poster boy for the assimilationist model. Penniless, strictly orthodox, paternal grandfather, with no skills or profession, arrives in Britain in 1901 from Zhitomer in what is now western Ukraine, fathers seven children, lives in poverty for more than three decades and dies in 1944, never having mastered English. Father, born in 1918, is moderately successful in business, and climbs into the middle class. Second generation son goes to grammar school and becomes the first in his family to go to university.

Only the poster remained unfinished. When I was 13 I joined a Zionist youth movement, eventually became a committed Zionist and decided that Israel was where I believed I belonged. In 1970 I emigrated to Israel before completing my university education, became a citizen of the Jewish state, lived on a kibbutz, served in the army and planned to spend the rest of my life working collectively with other Jews to contribute to the Jewish national revival and build a socialist society. I was voluntarily turning my inclusive, Jewish, religious-cultural difference into an exclusive, Jewish, ethno-national difference.

This was a caesura. It did not feel like that at the time because the process of becoming a Zionist took place over a decade. Nevertheless, it was a clear rejection of the 60-year assimilatory path taken by my grandparents and my parents, a rejection of their choice of a pluralist model of belonging – just as Britain was moving towards a *de facto* multiculturalism. For Jews who wanted to preserve Jewish identity, the only solution was to return to the 'homeland' and regenerate the nation. Assimilation was tantamount to national suicide. The Jewish diaspora would wither and die. Jewish nationalism offered an uncomplicated, singular belonging, an opportunity to participate in the Jewish return to history, to end the diasporic period of Jewish powerlessness.

*   *   *

So how did this happen? Why would I want to break from the assimilatory path of my Polish-Ukrainian Jewish family in such a drastic fashion? Why give up the hard-won advantages of a middle class home and the benefits of a British university education? Why go to live in a country that had been born in the midst of such a recent, bitter war with Britain, the country that had given my asylum-seeking grandparents shelter, a new home, a chance to make a life for themselves – not without encountering some harsh obstacles in the form of poverty and prejudice, but with the opportunities that are available in a free society to overcome such difficulties? Did I hate Britain? No. But this was an act of rejection, no question. And while I had long since found myself estranged from mainstream Jewish religious orthodoxy, having become an atheist in my mid-teens, I still had very warm feelings about my Jewish upbringing, the extended family of which I was a part and many Jewish cultural traditions.

Small numbers of young Jews had been making this choice since the British government in 1917 issued the letter that became the Balfour Declaration and was given the mandate to run Palestine by the League of Nations. Twists and turns in the policy on immigration into Palestine made this choice increasingly difficult to put into effect, but once Britain decided to give up the mandate and withdraw, ways of reaching Palestine expanded. And when military conflict broke out involving British soldiers and Arab and

Jewish military forces, Zionist organizations in Palestine developed a clandestine scheme, called *Machal*, to bring Jews from the UK specifically to fight both against the Arabs and the British.

So although I was not doing anything particularly extraordinary, the implications of this act of *aliya*, as it was called – literally 'going up' because it was regarded as a decision of high moral purpose – were far-reaching. I wasn't literally going to fight the British, but I was going to identify fully with a society and culture that still regarded Britain with great suspicion, a place where the exploits of some of the Jewish terrorist groups in the late 1940s, in which British soldiers were brutally murdered, were regarded as acts of heroism. (In recent years I have often wondered how far young Jews back then, and when I went to live in Israel, were motivated by feelings not altogether dissimilar from those of young radical Muslims who have chosen to leave their homes in Britain and become fighters in, as they see it, the cause of Islam and the struggle to defend the Muslim *umma*.)

A second factor was psychology. A secure home and loving parents did not protect me from developing academic and social diffidence in my teens. In the Zionist youth movement I found friendship, fun and a feeling of protection and confidence from formally belonging to a group with common ideals. I felt valued for aspects of my personality that had very little to do with school. It was my alternative or parallel home.

Presented with an idealistic picture of Israel from an early age, by the time we were becoming politically aware most of us in the youth movement had taken for granted the basic arguments for Zionism. Then the appeal of socialism kicked in, both as a necessity in Britain and as central to the utopian vision of Israel as a model state. As the younger and more rebellious of two brothers separated by only 18 months, I was drawn to the revolutionary temper and the endless discussion of how we could transform ourselves by practising socialism in our daily lives and within the movement. And how the pinnacle of socialist Zionist expression, the kibbutz, could be further perfected and Israel as a state become more like the kibbutz writ large. At the time, this was deadly serious stuff.

And hand in hand with socialism went rejection of bourgeois life. The semi-detached suburban house, the car in the garage, the steady job, the suit and tie – all seemed dreary and pointless when set against the excitement of building a new society, even if that meant personal and social privations.

But while my parents were not Zionists, they were the ones who introduced us to Zionist youth activity as we entered our teenage years, their motivation almost certainly being to give us the opportunity to continue mixing with other Jewish children and benefit from a more 'modern' form of Jewish education, just at the time when our formal, very rigid religious Jewish education, delivered four times a week at the synagogue Hebrew school (the *cheder*), had come to an end with the completion of our bar mitzvah ceremonies when we were 13. They no doubt hoped we would continue on the assimilatory path but not lose touch with Judaism and Jewishness. Whether or how much they regretted setting us on the Zionist path, I don't know.

And yet, within two years, I was back in England. I will not generalize from my experience – while many others who went from the youth movement came back, many stayed in Israel and made homes for themselves – but the exclusive belonging I expected to feel proved elusive.

For all of the state's privileging of belonging for Jews alone and my wish – dream even – to belong to the new state, the new Jewish nation, and to become a fully fledged Israeli, I constantly encountered obstacles. Put simply, I felt very little encouragement to belong, and the grounds for belonging I was offered seemed increasingly unpalatable.

I lived for a number of months in Jerusalem and found it difficult to get by without the magic dust of *protektsiya*, patronage: knowing someone in a position of relative power and influence who could get you a job, a telephone line, a better state-allocated apartment. This didn't look like the socialism I had lauded. Nonetheless, while in the city I tried to join the local Labour Party branch, but after being asked whether the routine leafleting and canvassing I would have to do was really worth my time, I had a sense that I was being made to feel that I would not fit in. On the kibbutz, I worked with young sabras – some born in the place, others from the *nachal*, groups of army conscripts who planned to settle on *kibbutzim* – who humoured me for my ideological commitment to Zionism and made me feel like an English intruder. It wasn't that they were in revolt against Jewish nationalism, rather that being born into the new state, they could take their patriotism for granted and were dismissive of anyone who insisted on verbalizing what for them came naturally. The older kibbutz members were instinctively distrustful. Could we hack it doing backbreaking agricultural work? (I had my own doubts about this from a year spent in Israel after I left school, but I suppressed them.) The default assumption seemed to be: probably not. Once again, desire and ideological commitment counted for very little.

Of most immediate significance was my three months basic training in the army. I was an enthusiastic if somewhat apprehensive conscript. When it became clear that we were all being treated like lazy, clueless recidivists I felt bitterly disappointed, I had no doubt been naive. But what truly disturbed and shocked me was something I had never encountered before: undisguised racist language about the Palestinian Arabs living in the area of the West Bank where our base camp was situated, used by our young commanding officer in a pep talk before we set out for a route march and live fire field training near Hebron. I envisaged the army's role as defending the country's borders from *Fedayeen*, 'terrorist' intruders, or from attacks by neighbouring states, not treating local inhabitants of the occupied territories as dehumanized 'others'.

Stripped of the illusions that accompany misplaced, youthful idealism, the questions I began to ask about the choice I had made, and which looked increasingly as if it were resulting in failure, became ever more searching. Denied the belonging I craved, I felt rejected. But then, in turn, what I had learned already about the flaws in the Zionist project led me to reject the belonging that was on offer. Back in England, I could not return to the belonging of my youth. Indoctrination is like a drug. The withdrawal symptoms are painful. For years I was lost, detached from myself. Like Kafka,

I felt 'I have hardly anything in common with myself.' Where did I belong? Around 1973 I read Thomas Wolfe's novel about the unfulfilled reliving of youthful memories and its title expressed for me an abyss of psychic loneliness I could never put into words: *You Can't Go Home Again.*

* * *

I can date the loosening of those early bonds of belonging from at least the end of my schooling. Between 1964 and 1973, when I restarted my university education at Sussex University, I had lived in 13 different places, including London, Manchester, Glasgow, Leeds, Jerusalem and two different *kibbutzim*. Divorce left me making regular 450-mile journeys from Sussex to Glasgow to see my young son, not what a student grant was designed to support. When I met Kathy in 1975, the woman who became my new partner, a fellow history student at Sussex, my sense of belonging was transformed in two fundamental ways.

As a German historian she brought me face to face with the reality of modern Germany, a place personified for me by my father's experience as a British prisoner of war – we were always denied West German toys and he vowed never to set foot in the country again – and by the figure of Adolf Eichmann, whose trial in Israel ended with his hanging in 1962, two years before I went to live there for a year, during which time its effect on Israeli society was still palpable. I went to visit Kathy in Koblenz and Munich while she was doing archival research for her PhD. When I first arrived I looked into the eyes of every old German man or woman and saw an Auschwitz guard. But once I met my partner's German friends, who were representative of a generation determined to continue driving Germany's quest to come to terms with its crimes and to make amends for them – as far as such a thing was possible – I found my self-understanding as a Jew changing radically. This was a country Jews needed to befriend and encourage since its choice of a moral, though difficult and complicated path was decisive for the continent as a whole.

The second transformation came from being exposed to Kathy's family: Scottish and Irish Presbyterians on her mother's side and English, somewhat unorthodox Christians, with many European connections, on her father's. Baptized into the Church of England, her mother's denomination, she soon lost any sense of Christian identity. Nevertheless, she could trace her lineage back to the seventeenth century. I could not go back further than the 1880s in what is now Poland. And yet I came to feel perfectly comfortable inhabiting and bringing together both of these worlds.

We were both pursuing doctorates, but I had not overcome my post-Israel sense of being lost, of feeling detached from myself. My academic career left me deeply unsatisfied, so in 1979 I abandoned lecturing and research for a PhD and went to work as a researcher at a contemporary affairs research body, the Institute of Jewish Affairs in London. Even at the time I knew this was in great part an attempt to recover the feeling of being immersed in a life-encompassing enterprise like the Zionist youth movement, but without the ideological baggage I had rejected and was rapidly jettisoning. Not perhaps a desperate grasp for a simple sense of belonging, but a conscious effort to find an anchor, to end the psychologically debilitating experience of being adrift.

That didn't happen, but instead I found something else. The place was staffed largely by European Jewish émigrés: Hungarian, Polish, Czech, German. Some were lucky to have reached Britain before the Nazis came. The director had spent three months in the hands of the Gestapo. One of the archivists was an Auschwitz survivor. Three researchers were forced out of Poland in the so-called government-initiated 'anti-Zionist' campaign in 1968. As a native-born Brit I was again one of a minority, but faced no rejection in this microcosm of Jewish diasporic diversity in which more than ten languages were spoken. Argumentative, learned, comic, conspiratorial, competitive, nostalgic, viscerally committed to exposing injustice, but never inclined to wallow in Holocaust victimhood – my colleagues were far more than just a colourful melange; they were the beginning of my education in what difference and pluralism meant.

It was like attending the university of life. I was able to question all the ideological baggage I had acquired and carried with me for more than a decade. I came to understand and appreciate that the Jewish diaspora was not doomed to die out; that in a globalizing world diasporas in general were becoming increasingly significant as transnational spaces of belonging. And that the crucible of the changing character and significance of the diaspora for Jewish life as a whole was in the continent of Europe. In time I came to reject Zionism and, especially after the collapse of communism in 1989, deeply distrust all nationalism. And although I did join, and help establish, a few groups and organizations reflecting my social and political concerns in the subsequent decades, I developed a fundamental resistance to any kind of formal belonging that demanded compromising my hard-won personal autonomy.

At the same time as I was being exposed to a Jewish diversity inextricably linked to a parallel European diversity, in 1980 Kathy took up a post lecturing in European history at what was then St David's University College in Lampeter, the heart of Welsh-speaking mid-Wales. We had been dividing our time between London and Brighton, although during this period Kathy lived more than a year in Germany; she had also lived a year in Munich as part of her undergraduate degree course. Neither of us felt rooted, attached to a physical location, and I had come to see my frequent changes of place as part of my dislocated existence, so neither of us baulked at the prospect of having two homes and driving the more than 200 miles backwards and forwards between them.

Nevertheless, Wales's green valleys and sheep-dotted hills, Llangeitho, the one-shop, one-pub village where we bought our first house, ambivalent attitudes towards us as intruding English, the strength of local Welsh nationalism and its extremist, fascist fringe, and the struggle to preserve the powerful traditions of Welsh culture and maintain the language – all impinged upon us deeply and, for me, posed new questions about belonging as we oscillated between remaining temporary residents and choosing to make Wales our home. We were 'others' – and there were many of us since the seemingly unspoilt rural location, its relative inaccessibility and the lure of self-sufficiency drew significant numbers of hippies, Greens, English retirees and arts and craft folk – and while most local people took us as they found us, an unavoidable element did not look kindly upon us and we didn't like it. This continued on and off for twelve years and was made more complicated by the fact that our first two children spent their preschool years at the kindergarten in the small university town, had Welsh accents and were in the process of becoming Welsh speakers.

For myself, I can now see how the Welsh episode, which came to an end when Kathy was appointed to a lectureship at a university in London in 1992, functioned as another expression of a wish to find a new, satisfying belonging and a project that would never be realized. It allowed me to keep floating, to avoid a commitment that might again end in rejection and disappointment. But what I am today reflects what I absorbed in the months and sometimes years I was a 'stranger' in Wales, Glasgow, Manchester, Israel and elsewhere.

In the last few years of English-Welsh ambivalence, during which I was appointed director of the research institute where I worked, a series of historic events occurred that brought Europe into focus for me in a way that dramatically altered my working life and shaped what, in retrospect, I now realize was the dynamic of my developing feelings about my sense of European belonging: the collapse of communism in 1989 and the revolutionary transition of former communist states to liberal democratic societies. My European consciousness was ignited. I saw that the European Jewish future had been transformed at a stroke and that it was linked to that of other minorities in an emerging multicultural Europe in which difference and diversity were valued. As events unfolded it also schooled me in the ugly and unacceptable face of nationalism, which in turn provided a wider context for my rejection of Zionism. I turned the institute I now headed into a policy think tank, the Institute for Jewish Policy Research, to pursue the path of 'working for an inclusive Europe where difference is cherished and common values prevail'. For me this was a concatenation of ideas, hopes and principles taking shape at different speeds in my head over the previous ten years. I wasn't suddenly converted to Europeanism, a federal super-state or a uniform European belonging. Far from it. I was focused on encouraging a thought-through and lived multiculturalism as the best future for all Europeans.

At least I no longer felt rudderless, lost or detached from myself. If there's such a thing as self-belonging, which implies neither solipsism nor narcissism, that's perhaps what I felt.

Although I then devoted 18 years to promoting the idea that Europe is good for Jews and Jews are good for Europe, and that this formula applied to all minorities, I don't ever remember feeling it necessary to define my connection to Europe, to 'formalize', as it were, the status of my sense of belonging to Europe, if that's what it was. It seemed to come naturally. Europe was amorphous, multifaceted, pick 'n' mix. To feel part of Europe did not require narrow commitment to some artificial European narrative. I was fully aware of the image many people had of Britain as semi-detached from the continent, its citizens reluctant Europeans at best, as the 2016 referendum vote to leave the EU confirmed, but I had no such hesitations about engagement with the continent. Project Europe was the crucible for a new social contract in which distinctions between majorities and minorities broke down, equality was fundamental and difference was valued. If push had come to shove I might have expressed some doubts about declaring myself as European, partly because I could see how easily Europeanism might become just another form of restrictive nationalism, writ large.

*   *   *

When the group feels threatened, or is told by its leaders to feel threatened, not to trust the outside world and circle the wagons, the guy in the middle telling everyone: 'Calm down, the threat is exaggerated, don't retreat into yourselves; it's more openness, engagement and connectivity that's needed, not less', doesn't stand much of a chance of securing attentive listeners. I was continuing to urge my fellow Jews to seize the historic opportunity of pluralist European belonging, playing a full part in the European narrative, and to avoid the narrow communalism driving some Jewish leaders to join the exclusionary anti-Muslim forces intent on viewing Islam as non-European. But I was also arguing that these same Jewish leaders were failing to recognize that the principles underlying full Jewish emancipation in Europe applied also to the Palestinians, and were thereby accommodating themselves to the wholesale denial of the human rights of the Palestinians, their history and their status as a nation entitled to self-determination by increasingly ethnocentric Israeli Jewish leaders. And that the unsustainable equation of virtually all criticism of Israel and Zionism with antisemitism was fundamentally a way of justifying the imposition of this restrictive and exclusionary politics of belonging on the Palestinians.

Because I was at odds with the Jewish establishment – and I wasn't the only one to find myself in this increasingly uncomfortable position from the turn of the century – it eventually led to my being ostracized from the Jewish community I had served for 30 years. When you are branded a 'self-hating Jew', you're being told in no uncertain terms that you don't belong.

It wasn't quite overnight, but the change in mood among many if not most European Jews, especially in the UK and France – from a celebration of multiculturalism as the facilitator of a more assertive, confident and thriving Jewish communal life, to damning it as one of the main factors in a perceived dangerous rise in antisemitism, the spread of Islamist terrorism and the deterioration in Israel's international position – was swift. I began the century still confident that Jews could be persuaded to feel that they belonged in Europe and that Europe belonged to them, but found myself more than ten years later vainly trying to push back the tide of opinion among Jewish leaders, most Israeli politicians and even 'sympathetic' non-Jewish media commentators declaring that we *don't* belong in Europe and asking whether it isn't time to leave. When doing the bidding of the antisemites is presented as a friendly act, history is truly being turned on its head. And yet the ground had been laid for seeing logic in this provocation since Jewish pro-Europe sentiment, very strong in the mid-1990s, was perceptibly weakening and Euroscepticism rapidly gained converts, reflecting wider trends in some European countries, but especially in Britain.

While the liberal and radical Jewish tradition of support for human rights, social justice and racial equality still exists, my experience clearly demonstrated that it's no longer the Jewish default position. I was being told that human rights was just another stick with which to beat the Jews, that the EU was conniving in excusing Muslim antisemitism and that pluralism was leading to the destruction of Jewish life.

*　　*　　*

Where I live now it's not difficult to imagine yourself as having reached, finally, a state of settled belonging, especially if, like me, you recently entered your eighth decade. But I cannot lay claim to such.

This is not because I am an immigrant, for example from Bangladesh, who has done everything to become British but who, after many decades, is still treated as a foreigner. Nor is it a matter of having chosen to remain mentally rootless even though the physical evidence of a settled life is in my case apparently so strong. Indeed, even to speak of an 'imagined' belonging might sound presumptuous or indulgent, given the hundreds of thousands still desperate to reach Europe, for whom belonging is not a choice over which they can exercise any control, since they are fleeing war, persecution and oppression and their fates are at the mercy of governments, which are free to determine whether they can belong or not.

In this essay, looking through the lens of belonging, I have described and reflected upon a journey during which I have inhabited different modes of belonging and non-belonging, experienced rejection and exclusion, and rejected some forms of belonging offered to me. I am a product of what I have retained as well as what I have jettisoned. I am not on a quest for a single, settled, all-encompassing place I could call home, so being rejected by leaders of a community whose legitimacy to exercise control and determine who belongs to it I do not recognize, feels like just one more stage on this continuing journey. And anyway, belonging is not a zero-sum game. One person's story of fleeing persecution does not invalidate another person's life journey during which they have passed through various phases of different belongings and non-belongings. Together they illustrate the irreducible complexity of belonging and, for me, make a powerful argument against forcing people into exclusionary, oversimplified, dehumanized categories as a manifestation of the power to slavishly and unfairly follow a false premise: that there is some definitive ordering of the norms of public recognition that ends the social contestations necessary for creating vibrant, living, flexible, diverse societies, once and for all. There is no living together in difference without accepting this reality.

Which is why for me, my chances of ever arriving at a place of settled psychological, emotional, existential and physical belonging are nil, and I'm more than happy with that. Not everyone would be and I would never wish to dictate or homogenize people's senses of belonging or non-belonging. But I would argue for a universal principle that every person should have the space to tell their own belonging story. And in Europe, more than anywhere, we should be listening, not telling. I confess that I say this partly for selfish motives. I'd feel like a sad case if all I had to wonder about is whether I've reached a settled belonging in my twilight years.

I began this essay anticipating that the exploration of my personal belonging would be like a journey without an end, not a quest for a destination. Now I see that the journey *is* the destination.

Bibliography

Antonsich, Marco, 'Searching for belonging: an analytical framework', *Geography Compass*, vol. 4, no. 6, 2010.
Beck, Ulrich, *Cosmopolitan Vision*, Cambridge, Polity Press, 2006.
Favell, Adrian and Geddes, Andrew, eds, *The Politics of Belonging: Migrants and Minorities in Contemporary Europe*, Aldershot, Ashgate, 1999.
Hall, Stuart, quoted in Yuval-Davis, Nira, 'Belonging and the politics of belonging', *Patterns of Prejudice*, vol. 40, no. 3, 2006.

Notes on Contributors

Rob Berkeley is an award-winning busybody, recovering academic and reformed social reformer. He currently advises the BBC on accountability. He volunteers on the boards of the Baring and Britdoc Foundations, has previously served on the boards of Stonewall and the Equality and Diversity Forum, and been Chair of Naz Project (NPL). He was Director of the Runnymede Trust (2009–14) and now leads the editorial team of community journalism platform BlackoutUK.com. Dr Berkeley was awarded an MBE in 2015 for services to equality.

Umut Bozkurt is an Assistant Professor in the Department of International Relations, Eastern Mediterranean University, Cyprus. She completed her PhD in politics at the University of York, UK. She is the co-editor of *Beyond a Divided Cyprus: A State and Society in Transformation* (Palgrave Macmillan 2012). Her latest work focuses on the political economy of the Justice and Development Party in Turkey and the nature of the economic relations between Turkey and North Cyprus.

Isolde Charim was born in Vienna, studied philosophy, taught in the Philosophy Faculty at the University of Vienna and was visiting Professor of Political Theory there. She is a columnist for the Berlin daily newspaper *taz* and the *Wiener Zeitung*. Since 2007 she has been curator of the programmes 'Democracy Reloaded' and 'Diaspora' at the Bruno Kreisky Forum. Her summer 2016 lecture 'I and the Others: Philosophical Reflections on Life in a Pluralist Society' was released as a CD by ORF.

Marion Demossier is Professor of French and European Studies and Head of the Department of Modern Languages at Southampton University. She previously taught French and European Politics and Society at the University of Bath. She holds a PhD in Social

Anthropology from the École des Hautes Études en Sciences Sociales in Paris. She has published more than 20 scholarly articles in leading academic journals in Britain, France and the United States, and is currently completing her third monograph on the anthropology of wine and terroir.

Lars Ebert studied theology in Heidelberg and lives in Amsterdam. He is programme coordinator for Castrum Peregrini and an independent advisor for policy and programme development in culture and higher arts education. He was deputy director of the European League of Institutes of the Arts. Driven by his belief in a united and inclusive Europe and the necessity for cultural leadership, Lars enjoys developing transnational and interdisciplinary cooperation projects. He is co-founder of EQ-Arts, the first international quality-assurance agency for higher arts education.

Şeyda Emek is a former administrative judge and an expert in constitutional law, European human rights law and administrative law with a wide range of practical experience in public service. She pursued law studies in Germany and the United Kingdom and holds a doctorate in law from Ludwigs-Maximilians-University Munich. Şeyda is a native of Göttingen and was born in Hildesheim, Germany, to Turkish parents who immigrated to Germany in 1973. She grew up bilingual.

Catherine Fieschi is the Director of Counterpoint, a London-based research and advisory group that provides public and private sector actors with strategic advice on how cultural and social dynamics affect politics and markets. She holds a PhD in Comparative Political Science from McGill University and is a leading authority on populist politics and mobilization. A regular contributor to press, radio and television debates, Catherine is the author of *In the Shadow of Democracy* (Manchester University Press 2008) and of numerous pamphlets and articles.

Montserrat Guibernau holds a PhD in Social and Political Theory from King's College, Cambridge. She was Professor of Politics at

Queen Mary University of London (2005–16), is affiliated to the Department of Sociology, University of Cambridge, and is visiting fellow in the Department of Politics and International Relations. She is the author of *Belonging: Solidarity and Division in Modern Societies* (Polity 2013), *The Identity of Nations* (Polity 2007) and *Catalan Nationalism* (Routledge 2004). From 2012 to 2014 she held a Leverhulme Research Fellowship in 'Identity, emotions and political mobilization'.

Brian Klug is Senior Research Fellow in Philosophy, St Benet's Hall, University of Oxford, and a member of the Faculty of Philosophy and Honorary Fellow of the Parkes Institute for the Study of Jewish/non-Jewish Relations, Southampton University. He has published extensively on Jewish identity, racism, antisemitism, Islamophobia and related subjects. His latest books are *Words of Fire: Selected Essays of Ahad Ha'am* (Notting Hill Editions 2015) and *Being Jewish and Doing Justice: Bringing Argument to Life* (Vallentine Mitchell 2011).

Antony Lerman is senior fellow at the Bruno Kreisky Forum, Honorary Fellow of the Parkes Institute for the Study of Jewish/non-Jewish Relations, Southampton University and associate editor of *Patterns of Prejudice*. He is author of *The Making and Unmaking of a Zionist: A Personal and Political Journey* (Pluto 2012) and many articles, op-eds and reviews in the *Guardian*, *Independent*, *New York Times*, *Haaretz*, *London Review of Books*, *Prospect*, *Jewish Chronicle* and other leading periodicals.

Hanno Loewy was born in Frankfurt in 1961. A scholar of literature and film, he was founding Director of the Fritz Bauer Institute for Holocaust Research (1995–2000). Since 2004 he has been Director of the Jewish Museum of Hohenems in Austria, and since 2011 President of the Association of European Jewish Museums. Dr Loewy is the author of various publications about film and photography, the Holocaust, Israel-Palestine and neglected subjects of Jewish history and culture such as *Jukebox, Jewkbox! A Jewish Century on Shellac and Vinyl* (Hohenems 2014).

Diana Pinto is an intellectual historian and writer living in Paris. She is the daughter of Italian Jewish parents, and grew up in the United States where she attended French and American (Protestant) schools and Harvard University. She has written about this multiple belonging in her intellectual autobiography, *Entre Deux Mondes* (Odile Jacob Paris 1991), while also writing professionally on pluralist democracy as a Consultant to the Council of Europe. Dr Pinto's most recent book is *Israel has Moved* (Harvard University Press 2013).

Doron Rabinovici, born in 1961 in Tel Aviv, is an award-winning novelist, essayist and historian living in Vienna since 1964. His novel, *Elsewhere* (Haus 2014), was shortlisted for the German Book Prize in 2010. He is the author of *Eichmann's Jews: The Jewish Administration of Holocaust Vienna, 1938–1945* (Polity 2011). From 2013 to 2015, Doron and Matthias Hartmann produced the performance, *The Last Witnesses*, first presented at the Viennese Burgtheater. Together with Natan Sznaider, he published *Herzl Relo@ded: No Fairytale* (Suhrkamp 2016).

Viola Raheb was born in Bethlehem, Palestine. She has a masters degree in Education and Evangelical Theology from the Ruprecht-Karls-University, Heidelberg. From 1998 until 2002 Viola headed the educational work of the Evangelical Lutheran Church in Jordan and Palestine. In 2002 she moved to Vienna where she works as an independent consultant on development cooperation and cross-cultural dialogue. Since April 2013 she has been a member of the Faculty of Protestant Theology, University of Vienna. She is a Senior Fellow at the Bruno Kriesky Forum.

Zia Haider Rahman is an author and Eric and Wendy Schmidt Fellow at the New America think tank. His first novel, *In the Light of What We Know* (Farrar, Straus and Giroux 2014), was published to international critical acclaim and won the James Tait Black Prize. In his varied career, Rahman has worked as an international human rights lawyer and anti-corruption activist, as a lawyer advising financial institutions on regulation, and briefly as a derivatives trader.

Göran Rosenberg is a Swedish writer and journalist and has been a reporter and foreign correspondent for Swedish radio and television. His book, *Det förlorade landet* (*Das verlorene Land*, Suhrkamp 1998, *L'utopie perdue*, Denoël 2002) was shortlisted for the Swedish August Prize. His most recent book, *A Brief Stop on the Road from Auschwitz* (Granta 2014), was awarded the 2012 August Prize. The French translation, *Une brève halte après Auschwitz* (Seuil 2014), was awarded the Prix du meilleur livre étranger.

Nora Sternfeld is professor for curating and mediating art at the Aalto University in Helsinki and co-director of /ecm, a masters programme in exhibition theory and practice at the University of Applied Arts, Vienna. She is co-founder of Büro trafo.K in Vienna, which does projects at the interface of education and critical knowledge production, and also of Freethought, a platform for research, education and production based in London. She publishes on contemporary art, exhibition theory, education, politics of history and anti-racism.

Nira Yuval-Davis is a diasporic Israeli Jew and Director of the Research Centre on Migration, Refugees and Belonging at the University of East London. Professor Yuval-Davis has been the President of the Research Committee on Racism, Nationalism and Ethnic Relations of the International Sociological Association and a founder member of Women Against Fundamentalism. Among her books are *Racialized Boundaries* (Routledge 1993), *Unsettling Settler Societies* (Sage 1995), *Gender and Nation* (Sage 1997), *The Politics of Belonging* (Sage 2011) and *Bordering* (Polity forthcoming).

Acknowledgements

The journey from idea to reality, from deciding to commission a book of original essays on belonging to publication of those essays by Pluto Press, took two years. It feels like a long time, but I know, from many years' experience of editing journals and yearbooks, that we have done rather well. Marshalling the work of such a diverse and very busy range of contributors was not easy, but all showed tremendous goodwill and cooperation, taking my reminders and queries in good heart and producing work of which I feel they can be justly proud.

Without the foresight, commitment and enthusiasm of the Secretary-General of the Bruno Kreisky Forum for International Dialogue, Gertraud Borea d'Olmo, who both initiated the original discussions on togetherness and belonging in Europe and promoted and backed – institutionally and financially – the plan to conclude the discussions by commissioning these essays, there would be no book. I am enormously grateful to Gertraud for her constant support, encouragement and friendship. And also to Patricia Kahane, one of the Kreisky Forum's greatest lay assets, for her personal support of the Vienna Conversations and the book and also for participating in some of the discussions.

The initial intellectual groundwork for the Conversations was undertaken by my old friend Diana Pinto, who also played a key role as one of a small editorial group which conceptualized the framework for the essays. The other members were Rob Berkeley, Lars Ebert, Şeyda Emek, Brian Klug, Hanno Loewy, Zia Haider Rahman and Göran Rosenberg. Their thoughts and ideas were incredibly helpful in giving shape and coherence to the project. More broadly, but too numerous to mention, all of the participants in the Vienna Conversations, by contributions they made to the discussions, played a part in making this book of essays what it is.

Six of the essays were written in German and translated by my partner Kathy. Working on the editing of these essays together at home proved to be remarkably amicable and stimulating, and the very positive feedback from the authors on the quality of the translations was enormously gratifying.

I knew from the beginning that a book of essays on the social and political challenges facing Europe would not automatically generate huge enthusiasm from publishers. But with all the essays submitted, I realized that the book had a very radical thrust, so I immediately turned to David Shulman, Pluto's commissioning editor, who had previously shepherded my own book through to publication in 2012 and with whom I had had some initial discussions about the collection when I started work on it. David responded with alacrity and after reading some of the essays moved incredibly quickly to get Pluto to offer the Kreisky Forum a contract to publish the book. I want to thank David and all his colleagues at Pluto very warmly for seeing the value of this collection and for setting all the production procedures in motion so efficiently. I'm also grateful to Dan Harding for his diligent copy-editing.

Finally, I want to thank all the authors, not just for being part of this collective endeavour, but also for the tremendous amount I have learned from reading and editing their work. For me it has enhanced my appreciation of the value of diversity and the great variety of feelings about belonging that characterize the reality of Europe today. Partly by virtue of geographical proximity and partly by dint of intellectual affinity, I owe a special thanks to my good friend and fellow north-Londoner Brian Klug. Over the occasional lunch and during intense conversation on flights to and from Vienna, Brian gave me sage advice and support, especially when bringing the project to fruition sometimes seemed beyond me and during the disastrous period when the majority of those who voted in the June 2016 UK referendum decided in favour of leaving the European Union.

Antony Lerman

Index